Pinkertons, Prostitutes and Spies

ALSO BY JOHN STEWART
AND FROM MCFARLAND

The Wreck of the San Francisco: *Disaster and Aftermath in the Great Hurricane of December 1853* (2018)

Jefferson Davis's Flight from Richmond: The Calm Morning, Lee's Telegrams, the Evacuation, the Train, the Passengers, the Trip, the Arrival in Danville and the Historians' Frauds (2015)

The Acrobat: Arthur Barnes and the Victorian Circus (2012)

Antarctica: An Encyclopedia, 2d ed. (2011)

Byron and the Websters: The Letters and Entangled Lives of the Poet, Sir James Webster and Lady Frances Webster (2008)

Confederate Spies at Large: The Lives of Lincoln Assassination Conspirator Tom Harbin and Charlie Russell (2007)

Broadway Musicals, 1943–2004 (2006; paperback 2014)

African States and Rulers, 3d ed. (2006; paperback 2014)

Italian Film: A Who's Who (1994; paperback 2012)

Moons of the Solar System: An Illustrated Encyclopedia (1991; paperback 2012)

Pinkertons, Prostitutes and Spies

*The Civil War Adventures
of Secret Agents
Timothy Webster and Hattie Lawton*

JOHN STEWART

McFarland & Company, Inc., Publishers
Jefferson, North Carolina

ISBN (print) 978-1-4766-7907-5
ISBN (ebook) 978-1-4766-3751-8

LIBRARY OF CONGRESS AND BRITISH LIBRARY
CATALOGUING DATA ARE AVAILABLE

Library of Congress Control Number 2019943099

© 2019 John Stewart. All rights reserved

No part of this book may be reproduced or transmitted in any form or by any means, electronic or mechanical, including photocopying or recording, or by any information storage and retrieval system, without permission in writing from the publisher.

On the front cover: Hattie Lawson with Timothy Webster before his execution (from *The Spy of the Rebellion* by Allan Pinkerton, 1883); background imagery © 2019 Shutterstock

Manufactured in the United States of America

*McFarland & Company, Inc., Publishers
Box 611, Jefferson, North Carolina 28640
www.mcfarlandpub.com*

For Gayle Winston, as always.
I've lost track of how many books I've dedicated to Gayle,
but I've never lost track of why.

Acknowledgments

Of course, without Gayle Winston the book couldn't have been done.

If it hadn't been for my friend Jane Singer, this book would have been a freight car looking for a locomotive. I wish her the best of all possible worlds with her latest book, *The War Criminal's Son*.

The ladies at Graceland Cemetery, in Chicago, were terrific.

It was my good fortune to deal with Elizabeth Riordan who, in December 2017, was a graduate research assistant in the Special Collections Department at the library in the University of Iowa, at Iowa City.

Angela Kindig was an archivist at the University of Notre Dame in January 2016 when she really went to bat for this book.

Paul Haggett, the archivist at St. Lawrence University, made my Adventure of the Pryce Lewis Memoirs more memorable and more fun than I deserved.

For Dan Gaddy, who let me play his piano whenever I couldn't get to mine.

Steve Wilson, my editor, had faith, as always.

Lisa Camp, at McFarland, for making it all so painless.

Tonya Hamby, at McFarland, waved a wand and made disappear all photo problems.

Table of Contents

Acknowledgments — vi
Prologue: The Trip of a Lifetime — 1
Introduction: The Trapping of Hattie Lawton — 5

1. One of Mother Fisher's Children — 13
2. The Taking On of Kate Warn — 16
3. The Brothers Warn — 22
4. My Name Is Timothy Webster — 24
5. Bridge Master with a Secret — 26
6. The Baltimore Plot — 32
7. The End of Mary Ellen Bailey — 39
8. Hattie and Tim Join the Secret Service — 45
9. The India-Rubber Doll — 46
10. The First Trip — 48
11. The Miller's Hotel Caper — 49
12. The Second Trip — 51
13. The Third Trip — 54
14. The Fourth Trip — 58
15. Lewis and Scully — 61
16. The Pryce Lewis "Memoirs" — 67
17. The Two Most Inept Spies in the World — 70
18. Things Go Horribly Wrong — 72

19. That Letter Has Sealed My Fate	76
20. Alone but for Specters	77
21. Mrs. Taylor	79
22. Scully's Trial	80
23. Pryce Lewis's Trial	81
24. The Priest, the Consul and a Deal	83
25. The Day They Came for Tim and Hattie	86
26. The Gag Order	90
27. The Trial of Tim	97
28. Post Trial	102
29. The Fatal Day Draws Nigh	104
30. The Morning of the Big Day	107
31. Tim Swings	110
32. Post Gibbet	113
33. The Languishing of Mrs. Timothy Webster	115
34. Hattie Gets Out	124
35. Notre Dame	129
36. Little Johnny and the Lost Cabin Mine	131
37. Post Pike's Peak Syndrome	133
38. The Death of Kate Warn	135
39. Kate Warn's Successor	137
40. The Portrait of Kate Warne	138
41. Carrie Lawton	140
42. Gambling Man	151
43. Warn Castle	155
44. The James Gang	156
45. Death by Poppy	156
46. Out on the Old Bozeman Trail	160
47. Three Girls Bonded for Eternity	162

Appendix A: The Warn Family	169
Appendix B: George Warn at Notre Dame	171
Appendix C: H.H.L.	173
Appendix D: Online	176
Chapter Notes	181
Bibliography	220
Index	227

Prologue: The Trip of a Lifetime

She was a lady. A real lady. You could tell that from the moment she took the telegram from the boy and opened it; by the way she faced the fear. These things were never good news, but this was as bad as it gets. Her husband had just blown his brains out. He was still breathing but she would have to hurry. She was on the next train out of St. Louis.

That very Wednesday morning, two hundred miles to the north, in Dixon, Illinois, town barber Wallace Shelton was shaving the dying man. He wanted to make the old fellow look good for when he passed over. First impressions are everything, for the quick and the dead both. But, then again, so are last impressions, at least when one is being held up close to the mirror of an earthly life spent. Everyone in town was talking about it. Some were saying it just wasn't right for a man to shoot himself like that on a downtown street. Those few farmers and hermits out in the more remote parts of the county who hadn't yet heard would be reading about it soon enough on the front page of today's *Evening Telegraph*, June 10, 1891.

The not-quite-yet deceased had lived at his wife's Palmyra, Illinois, family farm for five years or so, and in all that time he'd hardly ever gotten into the old buggy to make that short trip up the river road to town. Well, why would you want to go out when you live with a bunch of young half sisters-in-law? While it lasts, while your every dwindling need is taken care of, why bother to seek new landscapes when for a decade now you've been careening down that icy north face of Locomotor Ataxia, arms and legs flailing because you can't control your body parts, and every time you come to a turn, all crouched over, there's the same skull and crossbones sign screaming "Dead Man's Currrrrve." And besides, what interest could the city possibly hold for a blind man? What the hell's the point of it all? But this morning Smith was more interested in town than he'd ever been, certainly more than he would ever be again. Everyone who was acquainted with him knew what he was like; there was no telling what he'd get in his head next…

As Ella helped him up into the passenger seat, he turned and handed her his gold watch. He would never wear it again, he said. She laughed gaily at the jest. No, no, seriously, it was hers now; a gift, an heirloom, something beautiful to remember him by. He wished, for her sake, that it had been a lady's model, so she could sport it out in the open, as her very own. She laughed again. They said later that never once did Laughing Ella guess what was on the old boy's mind. But despite what she told the reporters, they couldn't have known what she was really thinking. She may not have been married yet, but she was, after all, twenty-six years old. Perhaps she did know a thing or two. In which case, it was better to laugh.

Ella's sister, Libby, on the other hand, didn't laugh so much these days, what with her instincts having been somewhat blunted by the unceasing drill-bit of marital torpor on Second Street. Living in the first house west of the Baptist Church didn't help matters, but she faced east and prayed and, like everyone else, did the best she could, and then prayed some more. It was almost half past four when Smith pulled up in the buggy, looking for Frank. Libby asked him if he would like to come into the house and wait. But he wasn't going to be eating with them this time, and he told her to go in and get Frank's supper ready. As for the buggy boy, Smith sent him down the street to do some shopping.

When Benjamin Franklin Miller came home from work a few minutes later, as regular and faithful as his red, white, and blue name, he lifted his two-year-old, Edna, into the carriage. Old Smith played with her for some time, then kissed her and remarked, "Take her out. She's getting to be a nuisance, pulling my whiskers." He asked for a drink of water, and after handing the glass back to Frank, he got him to hold on to the horse, in case the animal became frightened at something. Frank had become accustomed to the blind man's whims and didn't even think to ask what that "something" might possibly be. He slipped his arm through the lines and leaned against the carriage, holding the glass in his other hand, the unidentified man in the unidentified town, trapped for eternity in the sepia photograph, looking at the house. While Frank had his head turned for that moment, T.J. Smith, former eminent sportsman and gambling man, took a pistol from his coat…

At the sound of the gunshot Frank spun around in time to watch, horrified, as Smith straightened bolt upright in his seat and then toppled over against the side of the carriage. He grabbed him immediately to prevent him from falling out onto the ground. At that moment Billy Coffey rushed to the scene. He and Frank carefully lifted the dying man from the vehicle.

They took him to Bert Ayres' harness shop and laid him down there. It wasn't long before Dr. H.E. Paine and Dr. G.W.I. Brown were at his side. In a comatose state, Smith was moved to the Central Hotel on Hennepin Avenue and at nine o'clock taken from there back to the Miller house where a bed had been prepared for him. The doctors found that the ball had entered the right side of his head a little above the ear, had then passed through the brain, and was now lodged on the left side. In order to extract it an incision would have to be made there through the skull. But an operation seemed pointless.

At three o'clock the following morning, they asked Smith a question, a basic question, nothing to tax his brain. "Yes" was all he could manage. It was the last word he would ever utter. Judging by the occasional slight hand pressures he was giving, friends felt that he might be conscious, but they didn't know for sure. It might have been the long drawn-out death twitch. The physicians considered the wound fatal, although they added, with the indecisiveness of all professional prognosticators, that he could possibly live several more days. Mrs. Smith arrived that afternoon.

The next day Smith was very low. The new medical consensus was that he wouldn't see nightfall. His wife stayed at his side, hour after hour, as his life hung by a thread that with the passing of each minute could only get more and more slender until finally, and mercifully, it would snap under what remained of his weight, and his soul would ease over into that world from which there is no expected return.

The doctors were wrong when they predicted he wouldn't last out the day, but it truly was just a matter of time; two mornings later Smith lay dead in his open casket at the B.F. Miller house, "a profusion of beautiful flowers about him," while friends and relatives filed by, gazing at this "most handsome specimen of manhood." Then the cortege set out for Oakwood Cemetery.

Two days after the funeral the widow headed home, alone. For some of the time, as the cars thundered south over the Illinois rails, she must have turned over and over in her mind those last few sad days in that dark little room, just sitting there with her husband. Nothing she could do. But then gradually and inevitably, the way one thing leads to another, and with the motion of the train to help jog things along, we may imagine that her mind slipped away from the present. The fog, the barrier of memory, lasted only a few seconds and then she had passed through it, to a time long ago, to a place far away, into a world that no longer existed. And there she was, once more, day after day, night after night, maintaining a lonely bedside vigil beside her husband as his life ebbed away in front of her very eyes. A different husband, but this time the terrifying thing was that she knew precisely when he was going to die. Down to the very hour. He knew too. So did everyone in the country. 11 a.m., April 29, 1862, was Timothy Webster's date with the Confederate hangman.[1]

Introduction: The Trapping of Hattie Lawton

Hattie Lawton was a Pinkerton detective in her late twenties who, with her partner, Timothy Webster, became famous as a spy for the U.S. Secret Service during the Civil War. Living deep under cover in Richmond, the very heart of enemy territory, the two agents posed as man and wife, living together, eating together, sleeping together, whatever it took to get the job done. A dazzling New York blonde with blue eyes and a lurid past; a tall, handsome Englishman with just as much to hide—they were evenly matched in charm, cunning, and duplicity, and bold to the point of recklessness. Fully aware that the slightest slip meant death, they survived the greatest perils by running on an ice-cold nerve, a hot passion, and a wonderful knowledge of the human mind. They were a good team until quite suddenly, from out of nowhere, it came to a terrifying and tragic end. Betrayed by their own spymaster, Allan Pinkerton, they fell into the hands of the dictator of Richmond, the notorious General John H. "Hog" Winder.

Just because the Confederates gave Tim a court-martial doesn't mean they were doing him a favor. Far from it. They hanged him. The first spy to be executed in the Civil War. Hattie, without benefit of trial, was thrown into prison, not knowing from one day to the next what lay in store for her. The good thing was, they didn't execute women; well, they hadn't yet. Now, though, with the press whipping the people of Richmond up into a daily frenzy over the danger of Yankee spies, there was no telling what the mob might cry for. So, if the rats didn't nibble Hattie to death in her cell, the hangman was always prowling about out there, just waiting to have his next victim tossed to him by the slavering crowd.

It wasn't until the second week of December 1862, after having suffered eight months and eight days of durance vile, that Hattie got out of Dixie on a flag of truce boat, at which point, as all the scholars will tell you, she disappears from history.

It's not only what happened to Hattie Lawton afterwards that has puzzled historians, it's who she was, where she came from, what her real name was.

In real life she was never Mrs. Hattie Lawton. That was a name invented for her by Allan Pinkerton in his semi-fictional biography of Timothy Webster, *The Spy of the Rebellion*, which was published in January 1883, two decades after the events. In spite of the red herring, it was the first time Hattie was ever given a name. She was no longer just the "Mrs. Timothy Webster" of the 1860s newspapers, not merely the distaff adjunct of Pinkerton's great Civil War spy and patriot; she was now a person in her own right.

We've never had anything, not even a hint of anything, biographical. All we've ever known of Hattie is a few of her adventures in 1861 and 1862. Researchers have tried over the years to trap her, but no luck. Pinkerton is mostly responsible for that. It has been said of the old man that he would go to any lengths to protect the identity of his living agents. If that's true, then he certainly did a good job on Hattie. On the one hand, he did give us a name: Hattie Lawton. And because the name is so obviously false, we can, on the other hand, assume that she was still alive in 1883, when Pinkerton's book came out. That's a lead in itself. Not much, but it's something. It may not shine even a dim light on the needle, but it considerably reduces the size of the haystack.

Every fifty years or so a little scrap of new information has come our way, but it has always been so picayune, almost miserly, that the history books are no closer to the truth than they ever were. Hattie Lawton has remained as impenetrable a mystery as ever. But things always change…

In order to research something successfully, especially something with as little to go on as we've always had in this case, one needs interest. For the first several decades after Pinkerton's book came out there was no published interest in trapping Hattie Lawton. That lack of interest just might have been fueled, to some degree, by the confusion caused by a character in *The Spy of the Rebellion* named Mrs. Carrie Lawton.

Mrs. Carrie Lawton? In *The Spy of the Rebellion*, two major Pinkerton agents based in Richmond at the same time, both named Mrs. Lawton? That is simply one too many Mrs. Lawtons, in anyone's book. Completely unacceptable. The most logical answer is that the house that published Pinkerton's book had no or next to no editor, which, independent of this Lawton issue, certainly does seem to have been the case. Therefore, due to sloppy editing, Carrie equals Hattie. It's just one woman; it must be. And that's the way it has gone down in history, with historians all the way from Carl Sandburg to the present day simply picking which name they prefer to go with, Hattie or Carrie, or both. Eeenie, Meenie, Minie, or Mo.[1]

But Hattie and Carrie are not one and the same woman. They can't possibly be, not given an even halfway intelligent read-through of Pinkerton's book. By trying to conflate two unconflatable ladies, historians have made a bad situation almost impossibly confusing, not only for their readers but for themselves as well. They have painted themselves into such a corner of nonsense that their readers tend to shy away, taking their interest with them.

So why don't we start again, from the beginning? Go back to *The Spy of the Rebellion*? It is very clear, despite the lack of an editor, that Pinkerton wanted his readers to understand that Mrs. Carrie Lawton was a woman quite distinct from Mrs. Hattie Lawton. Two women. So, why did he use the same last name for both?

As much as this confusion might have deterred some scholars from pursuing Hattie, there was another overwhelming reason why the hunt for her wasn't joined. It simply never occurred to anyone to try. But if it had, a significant breakthrough in the identification of the lady would have come in 1897 and 1898, during two completely separate Billy Pinkerton interviews in which he named his father's spy as Hattie Lewis—not Hattie Lawton at all, but Hattie Lewis. This name was reinforced in 1910, once more by Billy when he granted an interview to William Gilmore Beymer, for an article on Timothy Webster that Beymer was writing for *Harper's Magazine*. This article was reproduced, word for word, as a chapter in Beymer's 1912 book, *On Hazardous Service*. Pryce Lewis, another Pinkerton agent and Civil War spy, was a key player in the events of 1862. His belly flop from the top of the World Building in 1911 sparked a long *New York Times* article in which the lady in question is called "Hattie Lewis, the girl who loved Webster."[2]

All of this, the Billy Pinkerton interviews, the Beymer book, the *Times* article, was widely disseminated, reproduced in one form or another, all over the country, for decades. It was hard to miss. Pretty much all you ever saw, when reading on this subject, was the name Hattie Lewis. In other words, you rarely saw Hattie Lawton, and only then in articles derived exclusively from Pinkerton's old book, *The Spy of the Rebellion*. But then came the era of the 1930s and along with it a new breed of historian, the Pinkerton biographer, and everything to do with this Lewis/Lawton issue took a step back into the Pinkertonian dark ages. From that time on, from Richard Wilmer Rowan through Jim Horan, James McKay, and all the others, the name Hattie Lewis was expunged from history, not as the result of any deliberate design, but merely due to the sad fact that no modern researcher has ever seen those Billy Pinkerton interviews. Whenever the name Hattie Lewis has appeared from long ago, for example in Beymer's book, or in the Pryce Lewis "memoirs" or in newspaper articles about his suicide, it has simply been dismissed as a mistake. Hattie Lawton rules, okay?

In 1949 Norma Cuthbert published her book *Lincoln and the Baltimore Plot*, referring to a plot, thwarted by Pinkerton and his operatives, to kill the president-elect as he passed through the city of Baltimore in February 1861. Miss Cuthbert had access to Pinkerton material that had previously been unavailable. This material included field reports from Timothy Webster. Not only does Webster name a female operative he is working with as H.H.L., but there is a separate report sent in to Allan Pinkerton by that very lady, H.H.L. Post-Cuthbert historians have assumed this to be the agent Pinkerton names in *The Spy of the Rebellion* as Hattie Lawton, and they're right, even though no one was ever able to prove this beyond the shadow of a doubt until the recent release of the Thomas Eckert papers. There it was, in a telegram, all along, spelled out. And no one ever knew it was there.

In or around the year 1997, St. Lawrence University, in New York, acquired the Pryce Lewis "memoirs." In what the author intended to be a book, but which has remained to this day an unpublished work, the "Mrs. Timothy Webster" of the Civil War is called Hattie Lewis in the one mention that is given to her.

Corey Recko, author of the 2013 book *A Spy for the Union*, the first ever real biography of Timothy Webster, found a letter, written by Pinkerton from New York on October 26, 1882, to his good friend Joseph Boggs Beale, the famous Philadelphia magic lantern slide artist and, more to the point, illustrator of *The Spy of the Rebellion*. The letter, sent during the preparation of Pinkerton's book, names his wartime operative as Hattie Lewis. Recko's find, more than anything, finally shook up the stodgy mind of modern, post–1930 history and shifted Hattie away from Lawton to Lewis. We've now done a full circle, back to where we were a century ago, back to when we had it right.[3]

Despite all this, our biographical knowledge of Hattie has still not increased; intensive pursuit of both names, Lawton and Lewis, has revealed nothing. So, this is the situation as it has stood until now: Her name was either Hattie Lawton or Hattie Lewis, both, or neither one. She was the Pinkerton agent H.H.L. who worked with Timothy Webster in 1861, posing as his wife. She was the "Mrs. Timothy Webster" who was imprisoned in Richmond, and who was finally set free in December 1862. And all that is pretty much what we've always known. As for who she was, where she came from, what happened to her after the end of 1862, all this has remained not just uncertain but totally unknown. However, things change…

It was while I was going through the probate papers of an ex–Notre Dame student that I discovered something startling, so startling that I dropped the project I was working on and immediately began to write another book instead: this one. What was so shocking was not that young George, my original subject, overdosed on morphine in St. Louis in 1875, or that by omitting to leave a will he left a testamentary mess of his modest estate in rural Illinois. No, it was that the prime mover in getting these probate matters settled was his sister, Mrs. Hattie L. Smith. As soon as I saw that name I knew I was on the verge of a significant discovery. George never had a sister named Hattie.

The reason I was into George's probate papers in the first place was that I was strongly considering writing the life story of the eldest of his siblings, Angie, who, although quite well known to American history, has never been the subject of anything remotely resembling a biography. That's certainly not due to any lack of interest; it's just that nobody has ever been able to find out anything about her, really. Some would call Angie a footnote, others a legend; either way, with a fast-expanding canon of romantic novels revolving around her, big-budget TV shows with her as a central character, she has undeniably become a very attractive cult figure over the last few decades. After having done considerable research on the family, I knew it well. Then from out of the blue, a sister I'd never heard of? By name Hattie? One of George's sisters? One of Angie's sisters? This couldn't be. And, of course, because it couldn't be, it wasn't. Nevertheless, it was…

By the time the courts began the process of probating George's estate, it had been over seven years since Angie had died. In fact, it was the very piece of land she had left to George that was now under the legal microscope. Her two notorious sisters, Kitty and Belle, both queens of the St. Louis tenderloin, had been dead almost as long as Angie had. That left only one full sister, a bit of a mystery. A big mystery, in fact. I had completely lost track of Lucy Ann just before the Civil War broke out. She was 27 then. It was as if she'd just up and vanished in 1860, as if she'd become part of some 19th-century witness protection program. I was beginning to wonder if I would ever find Lucy Ann when all of a sudden, and just at the right moment, Hattie L. Smith appeared in George's probate papers.

The intuitive part of the human brain works a lot quicker than the conscious planning part, and I already knew I'd inadvertently trapped a Pinkerton agent. A spy was coming in from the cold. I could feel it. I could see her more and more clearly with each passing second as she emerged from the mist of obscurity. Welcome home, Lucy Ann.

The idea that Lucy Ann, Hattie L. Smith, Hattie Lewis, and Hattie Lawton were all one and the same person came as a shock, but the voltage produced recognition and clarity, not disbelief. It was immediately obvious, given who her older sister, Angie, was. Hattie Lawton's identity had been staring us in the face all this time. The pieces had all been there, waiting to be fitted into place, like a jigsaw puzzle. Each piece had been right next to the one it was meant to fit into, not across the other side of the table, and that's why we'd been missing it every single time. Hattie Lawton, the Civil War's most mysterious spy, had been hiding, yes indeed, but she'd been hiding in plain sight.

The only thing needed now was proof, proof that Mrs. Hattie L. Smith was Hattie Lawton. And that proof came in the most dramatic of ways. During the time "Mrs. Timothy Webster" had been a prisoner in Castle Godwin, in Richmond, back in those dark, depressing days of '62, she had written to Jefferson Davis, the President of the Confederate States of America, pleading to be set free. We have that letter and it is in her own very distinctive handwriting. All we needed now was…

It wasn't much of a sample, just her signature on her brother George's probate papers, written years and years after Castle Godwin, and under tremendously different circumstances. Nevertheless, the two individual handwritings were identical, and established beyond reasonable doubt that Mrs. Hattie L. Smith, of St. Louis, had once been Mrs. Timothy Webster, the Civil War's most mysterious spy, the remarkable woman Pinkerton had named Hattie Lawton. But "beyond reasonable doubt" is not "beyond the shadow of a doubt," and just might be interpreted by some as an educated guess, which really means no proof at all. What was needed was something irrefutable, geometrical, something that actually comes flat out and tells us that this particular Hattie Smith was a Pinkerton agent. Something you could take to court. At that point I came across a letter written in 1875 by a man named George McQueen. If it please Your Honor, I would like to bring to the stand Mrs. Hattie Lawton.

1. One of Mother Fisher's Children

Some things just happen in a girl's life. That nice Fred Barrett, for example. He's just everyone's idea of a first husband, 66 inches of Rock County man. Out of the 543 males in Magnolia, Wisconsin, 542 were white, and Lucy Ann had to go and pick Fred, who, needless to say, did not number himself among the contingent with African ancestry. After two and a half long years of marriage, Lucy Ann broke up the snug family hearth, that warm Christmassy picture of utter human contentment portrayed so phonily by mid–1850s lithographers.[1]

Lucy Hansen. Sarah Simmons. Harriet Lewis. Hattie Lewis. A lady of the evening needs good aliases, especially in a whore-heavy town like Chicago, where this particular demoiselle arrived from the sticks of Wisconsin in or around March of 1856, a fairly typical refugee from domestic bliss. Untypically, though, she had support if she ran into trouble; her sister Angie was already well-established in town, working in a very responsible position.[2]

Chicago. Formed as such in 1833, with a quorum of 200 persons, a suitable number of whom, according to nature's inevitable proportions, you can bet were somewhat dubious characters, male and female. A quarter of a century later, with the general population of the city now at around 80,000, and exploding, exploding, and because nothing much changes in the human story, a sturdy number of these souls were Cyprians, denizens of the demimonde if you desired things Frenchified, ladies of infinite pleasure perhaps, if you wanted the words to roll off your tongue like a drooling European linguist. Your choice of euphemism was drawn from an argot pool that, while not endless, was certainly as tumescent and throbbing as the Sands, that particular district that swelled with the constant coming of young things fresh from rapid train rides from the port of New York. Boys or girls.

It didn't matter what your preference of gender or race was. Take your pick, make your choice, effect your selection from the over-abundance of houses of ill fame, of dens of iniquity, of stews.

By the late 1840s projectors were putting out a Chicago city directory every year, a worthy publication supported by advertising. The annual immediately became a Yellow Pages for jacks and jills of all trades: Name, address, and sometimes an occupation. You just had to be a trifle careful when you took an article of clothing over to be stitched by a dressmaker or a seamstress. Chances are you'd get a lot more than you bargained for. A well-bred lady who sashayed into a milliner's storefront looking for a fancy hat might just have a new interest in life thrust upon her and never come out, except, of course, to take the air on her way to Police Court.[3]

Or, for the man who has everything, perhaps you'd like to partake of something a little less genteel, Sir, a certain something where there's more than a girl's ninety-ninth hymen at stake. Howzabout an eye-popping, fly-popping show featuring inmates of two rival dens? Howzabout a prize fight at the Sands between Big Lib Wood and Roxana Brooks? Ding dong. Round one. Not a policeman in sight. Twenty minutes later, by the end of the bloody and desperate battle Lib had an eye gouged out and her face was so badly pulped it had to be taken away in a bucket. Didn't stop her business though. Some gents prefer the imperfect face: One eye, pock marks, a busted nose.[4]

The mesdames and their "children" were so used to swatting off the coppers with a ball bat that it was no more serious an activity than lancing the occasional pubic boil with a pen knife. An irritant, nothing more. Get it out of the way and move on. Police corruption was so bad, a "descent" was always being made on some cat-house somewhere in town in order to maintain the facade of law and order and to keep the grimy wheels of commerce greased from top to bottom in the dung heap of elected politicians. Every day's Police Court had a roster of the usual bawdy-house suspects who had to fight their way through the teeming crowd of exhibitionist perverts to get to the dock so they could make their regular contribution to the city's coffers. Fines for both types of case, whoring and "exposing one's person on the street," ranged from three to thirty dollars, and that's only the cases that made their way to court. To the great relief of the honest and hard-working taxpayer, there was always a steady and guaranteed flow of private parts coming under scrutiny one way or another in the Windy City in those days.

Sometimes real justice prevailed, for example in the so-called "Conspiracy Case," which made its way to the Recorder's Court in late May of 1857. The case, involving the shakedown of madams and their inmates, made minor celebrities of such brothel keepers as Kate Howard, of 118 Wells Street, and Mary Fisher, of 287 South Clark. (Just in case you missed the addresses, Gentlemen!) As a result of this exposure, some of the prostitutes found that their cheeks had taken on that rosy hue of fame for just that brief spasm of time. Hattie Lewis testified that she resided at Mrs. Fisher's, and that the previous summer Mrs. Fisher and all the inmates had been taken to the Police Court on warrants, and that they had all been fined by Justice Prendergast. It was in the wake of that, with the irritatingly persistent pimp Michael Ford shaking Hattie down for $7.50, that the original seeds of the conspiracy were sown. There was no conspiracy as such, despite the name of the case, but it was Hattie's big day in court.[5]

Mary Fisher, "the notorious woman who keeps a brothel on Clark street," was brought before the Police Court on Saturday, August 22, 1857. Notwithstanding the ingenious defense by able counsel that his client did not "keep" the house, but rented the rooms furnished, and that one of her damsels, for example, was an "artist" by profession, and another a "milliner," Madam Fisher was fined $50. Her lawyer entered an appeal. The girls were also brought up on the charge of being inmates, but their trial was continued until the following Monday. "The police are determined to suppress these dens (or make money out of them) if possible."[6]

The following day's *Tribune* reported: "Police court was quite an object of attraction among certain characters yesterday afternoon on the occasion of the trial of three of Mother Fisher's 'children,' Ellen Miles, Emma Hoyt, and Lucy Hansen. Peter Snyder was the witness and testified that he had seen them at Mrs. Fisher's house of ill-fame. They were each fined $6, and entered an appeal. A warrant was immediately sworn out by one of them against Peter, on the same charge. He was arrested and fined $6."[7]

The following spring, Melodeon Hall was packed to the gills with pimps, thieves, prostitutes, and gamblers. A fancy dress ball was in progress, a do of the worst character, it was reported. Nothing unusual there. This sort of thing went on all the time at the hall, but this Monday night, March 29, 1858, several fights erupted and the local citizenry, the residents of Dearborn Street, finally pressured the Chicago police into descending upon this den of nastiness. Although a number of persons in very interesting outfits escaped by leaping from second story windows, many arrests were made, including Minnie Waters, alias Ann Brown; Sarah Simmons, alias Hattie Lewis; Emma Glenwood, alias Canada Maria; Mary Taylor, alias Rocky Rhodes; and Eliza Williams, alias Eliza Roe. They each made a contribution of $5 to the cash-box of a grateful city.[8]

On the morning of April 9, 1859, the police made a wholesale descent upon the lewd houses of Chicago, arresting the keepers thereof. Taken into custody were such well known madams as Kate Howard, Kentucky Joe alias Josephine Davis, Caroline Duffy, Mrs. Dingman, Jenny Perry, Minnie Clayton, Gentle Annie Stafford, Eliza Williams alias Eliza Roe, Jenny Cordell, and Hattie Lewis. It is clear from this that Hattie had graduated from being a mere inmate to being a madam; her position had been significantly and noticeably elevated. Nevertheless, promotion or not, there is no more mention in the press or in the city directories of this lady. That's because she had changed professions as well. Quit while you're on top. After a friendly chat with her sister Angie, who knew how to arrange things, she had metamorphosed from Hattie Lewis, queen of the Tenderloin, into Hattie Lewis, Pinkerton detective.[9]

---

2. The Taking On of Kate Warn

Allan Pinkerton, the great detective and spymaster, once wrote: "Previous to the early part of 1855, I had never regularly employed any female detectives. Nor were women engaged in that capacity in any part of the Union. My first experience with them was due to Mrs. Kate Warne, an intelligent, brilliant, and accomplished lady. She offered her services to me in the early spring of that year." Aside from Pinkerton, there is no other primary source for the taking on of Kate Warn, and Pinkerton is a notorious liar. Therefore, we're always in a bit of a quandary. Is Pinkerton fabricating or isn't he?[1]

So, we really don't know, with any confidence, how Kate Warn came to work as a detective for Allan Pinkerton. We have only Pinkerton's word for how, when, and where he first met his future star female operative, and knowing that Pinkerton couldn't lie straight in bed, either with or without

2. The Taking On of Kate Warn

Allan Pinkerton and his wife, Joan Carfrae (date and photographer unknown; Records of Pinkerton's National Detective Agency, Box 4, Folder 6, Library of Congress).

Kate, it would be foolish to accept his word without great reservation. But, of course, he did meet her somewhere, under one set of circumstances or another. It might even have been in a house of ill repute, for all we know. It's highly unlikely that we'll ever come up with an authentic alternative to his story, so we're forced to go with what he says. Who knows? It may be true.[2]

Many is the historian who will tell us that as Kate was progressing along the sidewalk one day she saw an advertisement in Pinkerton's office window. Some even say the window was on the ground floor, and it's always a relief to hear something like that. However, most books, magazines, websites, and so forth hold that she simply happened to be glancing through the want ads in the *Chicago Tribune* or some other local paper when her eye was caught by the famous "We Never Sleep" logo.

The truth is, till the day she died Mrs. Warn never saw that logo. It was not created until 1874, six years after her death, and then only for the cover of one of Pinkerton's books, *The Expressman and the Detective*. It wasn't adopted as the company's logo until a couple of years after that, but by 1876 one starts seeing it regularly in their Chicago newspaper ads. As a matter of interest, Pinkerton's, as a company, only registered the eye logo and motto in 1950, claiming that they had been using the image since 1884.

But it doesn't really matter. This whole advertisement business, with or without the eye logo, is an invention of latter-day historians; i.e., fiction writers. Pinkerton never mentions an advertisement. However, it does have the ring of truth to it. Kate Warn might well have seen something as she glanced through the Chicago journals. And there were things to be seen, relevant things. Not just filler to pad out a page.

How about this in the *Chicago Daily Times* of March 2, 1855? It's not a want ad, it's Pinkerton introducing his brand new business to the public: "North-Western Police Agency. No. 89 Washington st., cor. Dearborn. Chicago, Illinois. Pinkerton & Co. Devote their attention to the transaction of a general detective police business in Illinois, Wisconsin, Michigan and Indiana. Allan Pinkerton." A couple of weeks later an item appeared in the Milwaukee paper about Pinkerton and Edward A. Rucker, a Chicago attorney, analyst, and systems man who had, back in 1847, founded the famous company Chicago Title: "Messrs. Allan Pinkerton and E.A. Rucker have formed a detective police agency in Chicago. Mr. Rucker has been for years much engaged in this kind of business, and Pinkerton is well known throughout the west and north as one of the most vigilant, shrewd, energetic and successful police officers in the land." Kate Warn must have been one of the very first operatives the old man ever took on.[3]

In *The Expressman and the Detective* (1874), Pinkerton gives us what purports to be his first impressions of "Mrs. Warne": Above medium height, slender, graceful in her movements, and perfectly self-possessed. He goes on to tell us that her features, "although not what would be called handsome," were of a decidedly intellectual cast. "Her eyes were very attractive, being dark blue, and filled with fire. She had a broad, honest face which would cause one in distress instinctively to select her as a confidante, in whom to confide in time of sorrow, or from whom to seek consolation. She seemed possessed of the masculine attributes of firmness and decision, but to have brought all her faculties under complete control."[4]

And this, nine years later, from *The Spy of the Rebellion*: "Mrs Warne was ... of rather a commanding person, with clear-cut, expressive features, and with an ease of manner that was quite captivating at times." Pinkerton says that "she was calculated to make a favorable impression at once," and that she "was a brilliant conversationalist when so disposed, and could be quite vivacious, but she also understood that rarer quality in womankind, the art of being silent." He also tells us that she was of Northern birth.[5]

"In a very pleasant tone she introduced herself as Mrs. Kate Warne, stating that she was a widow, and that she had come to inquire whether I would not employ her as a detective."[6]

Was she really a widow? We don't know. To tell the truth, we don't know if she was ever married. But it seems a fair bet that she had been. Either way, she was now fancy free, and perhaps footloose, a happy condition that could be made available to a married woman via one of two well-beaten paths: Death or divorce. That is, if she had an obliging husband. Not to mention a bit of luck.

When Kate Warn pops into one's head, for whatever reason, the image is probably going to be the one set in stone for us by Allan Pinkerton, and so it may be rather shocking to consider that this iconic lady might have been divorced. But why not? All her sisters were, or soon would be, after very short marriages, so why not Kate? You can almost put money on it. Despite the fact that divorce was rampant in the Midwest in those days, it still carried a stigma, and most divorced women, and men too, for that matter, claimed to be widowed, at least on paper. It was easier that way. A convenient fiction. Mrs. Kate Warn, widow. Just as it says in the city directories.[7]

And what sort of occupation did divorced women go into in the early to mid–1850s, especially in big towns such as Chicago? Not engineering, that's for sure. Teacher, maybe. There were a lot of teachers, music and otherwise, some of whom actually taught music, and some who taught otherwise, couldn't tell a flat from a sharp. And there were some traveling salesladies, and plenty of servants. Actresses didn't exactly abound, except on the stage, and we all know about actresses, don't we, Mrs. Worthington. But by far the most common way for a divorced woman of the lower classes to make her way was by setting up as a milliner or as a dressmaker. These were both tricky businesses, though, that could get pretty physical at times, violent even, and there were the regular police shakedowns to worry about if not to shuck off as part of the job. But what's a girl to do, alone in a great city? Start your own business, maybe, after a while, if you had the get up and go: rent a good, sizeable house, hire other girls to do the basic work while you rake in the profits and improve your social status. Lessens the risk of a pubic abscess, increases your chances of living beyond the age of thirty. Three out of three of Mrs. Warn's sisters were manually dexterous enough to follow the occupation of seamstress. So why not Kate herself? If you find the possibility of Kate Warn, divorcee, startling, then Kate Warn, milliner, is enough to make your head throb. Possible? Certainly. Probable? No. Worth thinking about, all things considered? Definitely.

Up until the time he hired Mrs. Warn, Pinkerton had never dreamed of employing females as detectives, and even then he couldn't understand quite how they could be employed "consistent with a strict regard for the prejudices of community." This is what he says in *The Expressman and the Detective*: "At this time female detectives were unheard of. I told her that it was not the custom to employ women as detectives, but asked her what she thought she could do. She replied that she could go and worm out secrets in many places to which it was impossible for male detectives to gain access. She had evidently given the matter much study, and gave many excellent reasons why she could be of service."[8]

"After several interviews, however, Mrs. Warn succeeded in convincing Mr. Pinkerton that the innovation could be realized, and she entered his service."[9]

Was it really several interviews? Not that it matters much, but it's nice to get it right. In *The Expressman and the Detective*, Pinkerton tells us that after hearing her out, he needed time to think about it. After all, what she was proposing would be "the first experiment of the sort that had ever been tried." If she would be good enough to call again the following day, he would give her his answer. Good-day, Mrs. Warn. Pinkerton went out of his way to assure his readers that because he was living in a progressive age and a progressive country, "I finally became convinced that it would be a good idea to employ her." In fact, it was quite clear that fate had placed her in Pinkerton's office because "Mrs. Warne was a splendid subject with whom to begin" this new and noble social experiment. "At the time appointed she called. I entered into an agreement with her, and soon after gave a case into her charge. She succeeded far beyond my utmost expectations, and I soon found her an invaluable acquisition to my force."[10]

But why is she known as Kate Warn when that wasn't her name? It's not just a case of Warn without the "e." You'll see Warne everywhere. That was even the spelling used by Pinkerton later in his life, after he had been bombarded and indoctrinated with the human virus of incorrectitude. In fact, one hasn't seen the correct spelling of Kate's last name in a history book in decades. No, it's the name Kate. Her name wasn't Kate at all. It was Mahala. Mahala Ann Warn. She was born in October 1829, in the village of Erin, in the lower tier of western New York state. It was one of her younger sisters who was Kate. So, why take her sister's name? Why not stick with Mahala? Well, the answer to the last question is pretty obvious, especially to anyone whose name is Mahala. But why couldn't she have used Ann, or Annie? Both perfectly good names, nice names. We can only guess at the answer. The fact is, she did take her sister's name, which was a pretty safe thing to do because, at that moment, in the spring of 1855, the real Kate was a teenage bride living in Rockford, Illinois, and by October of that year she would be even farther away, in St. Charles, Iowa. But it wasn't long before nomenclature became an issue. The real Kate left her husband Oscar to root for himself among the corn and pigs, and made her way, like her sister who had taken her name, to the big city of Chicago. She was still in her early twenties and would be needing a job, and a name or two.[11]

Sometime within five years of "Kate" Warn being taken on as the world's first woman detective, it became clear to her and Pinkerton that it would be smart to create a female department within the organization, with Kate as the superintendent. So now she was in a position to hire female detectives, and who better than women she already knew very well indeed? As Pinkerton wrote in her obituary: "she exhibited great kindness, strength of will and force of character, embruing all who surrounded her with the strict rule of moral probity and right she had made her own."[12]

Pinkerton would go out of his way, and with a straight face, to assure the public that "female detective" was, although not exactly the oldest profession in the world, still an honorable one. He was always up against it from the temperance-minded hypocrites: The moralizers who never had an indecent thought they could brag about, except to themselves, and only then in the privacy of their own closet; the do-gooding gentlemen who, night after night, and all dressed up, stalked the streets of their big city, looking for fallen women to save, guardians of public purity only too familiar with the well-beaten path to hell, littered as that track was with the skeletons of their own conscience.[13]

3. The Brothers Warn

Passing counterfeit money can be exciting, a real thrill for a young man, especially one fresh down from Rock County, Wisconsin; but it's also a serious crime. Get caught "shoving the queer" in the mid–19th century and you'd be standing in the dock looking up at the judge with tears in your eyes, and staring down the barrel at a good stretch in a state penitentiary. And you'd be lucky. There have been times in American history when they would have put your neck in a noose for such a crime.

"But Magnolia's a mighty boring place for a young fellow of twenty-two, Judge" was not going to cut any ice in a Recorder's Court in Chicago as an excuse for passing altered bills on the Racine Bank, or being in the business of pushing counterfeit money generally.

At 6 o'clock in the evening of January 26, 1854, Allen B. Warn's twelve good men and true retired to the back room, and the following morning tendered their solemnly considered verdict: Not guilty.[1]

Among whatever small crowd may have rooted for Allen Warn in that courtroom, there must have been some hopes riding on Emma Moore. After all, she was reputed to be the daughter of a Pennsylvania physician. No one had ever heard of Dr. S.P. Moore, at least not in Chicago, but it all sounded hopeful, in a vague sort of way. Maybe Emma would bring to the marriage something more than mere prestige, something that might actually help Allen in his rather heavy-footed waltz through life. Of course, it didn't work out that way. The two of them would eventually learn how to do what even stick insects can do without any trouble. But that was the climax of their achievement together, their acme. At least they had an acme. The son, Frank, would never even have an acme. Never had the chance of an apex even, not given the father he had. Franklin B. Warn would survive, by default, into the 20th century; he never married, he lived in Iowa, and despite his grandiloquent name, never did anything, anything at all, and when he died, he did so in silence, and no one ever knew.

In the late 1850s, just before the outbreak of the Civil War, the two words Pike's Peak began to prick the consciousness of that set composed principally of delusionals for whom the quick buck represented the American Dream. It was the 49ers all over again, but on a much smaller scale, with the alluring yellow mineral not quite so brilliant this time. The Pike's Peakers themselves just didn't seem to have that optimistic glint in the eye that had driven so many to their doom in California a decade before in the greatest mass movement of humanity since the Crusades. Ah, those golden days of yesteryear, those brazen years of '49 and '50 and '51; there will never be anything like that again. Among some 100,000 who went to Pike's Peak in search of gold, Allen B. Warn would fit right in. He handed his wife and infant over to the family in Lee County, Illinois, waved bye-bye, yelled out "Pike's Peak or Bust!" and took the train for Chicago, whence, on April 7, 1859, a large party left the Burlington depot bound for the Rocky Mountains, for Kansas Territory, the place that offered the stuff, taking with them pots and pans, knives—and forks if they were really sophisticated. Those who weren't took wives, children, and cradles. The latest American Nightmare was under way.[2]

And then it was all over. A long year-and-a-half digging yielded nothing except calloused hands, a big testicle, and a hunched back for most. Not a damned thing to offer a future employer, not even a reference.

The small but important town of Brownville had come into being only a few years before the Pike's Peakers started going through. Nebraska was still a territory then, and Brownville was a part of it, lying right on the Missouri line and right on the road to the gold mines. There was never an overabundance of people in Brownville, but, or perhaps because of that, it was home to the *Nebraska Advertiser*, a worthy newspaper. On the night of Saturday, October 20, 1860, a party of Pike's Peakers arrived in town, returning Pike's Peakers, you could tell by the long no-luck faces. "One of them, named Allen B. Warren," was charged by another of the party, George Miltimore, a youth, of robbing him of $268 in gold, which was all the poor bloke had to show for eighteen months' labor at the Peak. The theft, which was attended by aggravated circumstances, had taken place on the plains, near the Blue, between Pawnee Ranch and Brownville. It was Allen who was doing the stealing, of course. He himself wasn't being robbed. Which means his career as a Pike's Peaker had been a washout, like most of them. Those who knew Allen would have been shocked if the financial return on his effort had been anything else. A committee of citizens was appointed in Brownville, investigated the matter, and searched the accused, upon whom the stolen money was found. A trial took place before Justice J.D.N. Thompson, and ample testimony was produced to warrant binding over, which was done. The prisoner, however, was afterwards released on a writ of habeas corpus. "Warren was on his way to Janesville, where he has friends."[3]

While Allen was away prospecting for fool's gold in the Rockies, Little Johnny, his younger brother, married Alice Andrews in Dixon, in January 1860. Earlier that month, Alice had turned fourteen, but she still cried, not so much because she had to put her doll away but because she realized, through the tears, that she had parlayed herself into a hackneyed phrase. The newlyweds went out to Lyons City, Iowa, where John manfully attempted to embrace the occupation of day laborer, not as glamorous as being a Pike's Peaker, perhaps, but a lot more rewarding financially.[4]

Johnny's sojourn in Iowa didn't last long; in fact, it turned out to be an utter waste of time and effort. He and Alice were soon back in Dixon where, on April 12, 1861, a nine-month-old memory surfaced in the form of a blessed event, whom Johnny named E.T., Edward Thompson Warn. The same day in Charleston Harbor, South Carolina, the Confederates fired on Fort Sumter and the Civil War began.

4. My Name Is Timothy Webster

"My name is Timothy Webster, Jr.; I am thirty-five years of age; I reside in Chicago, Illinois; I am a detective policeman by occupation; I suppose it would be more proper to say private detective policeman; I am in the employ of Allan Pinkerton, formerly called Pinkerton & Co.; I am employed by the year—engaged by the year; I receive $900 per year, disregarding my success in my undertakings."[1]

Q: How long have you resided in Chicago?[2]
A: Since January 1856.

Q: What was your last place of residence before coming to Chicago?
A: New York City.

Q: How long had you resided in New York City?
A: A number of years; I could not tell without figuring it, but I think since 1835; but I have lived in New Jersey some of the time since my first going to New York to learn my trade, in 1835 or 1836.

Q: In what place in New Jersey did you reside?
A: Princeton, then a town, now a city.

Q: How long did you reside in Princeton?
A: I cannot say positive, without referring to my father's books, that being the only way that I can give the exact time, he being in business there.[3]

[Being asked about his detective's salary:]

Q: Do you consider yourself amply compensated for such services by that price?
A: I do not, but I have agreed to work for that price, and I intend to fulfill my agreement.

Q: How much would you consider an adequate compensation?
[They toss a few figures around.]

Q: Do you consider fifteen hundred dollars a year a fair and reasonable compensation for a man of your physical and intellectual capacity to sell himself as a common imposter; and to devote himself to the business of misrepresentation and falsehood as a profession?
A: I do, where they do it to further the ends of justice.[4]

[Tim allows that he engaged with Mr. Pinkerton more on account of moving out West than anything else.]

[As for Tim's feelings about his work:]

Q: Have you been conscious of experiencing any sentiment of remorseful regret or self-degradation while reflecting upon the nature of your transactions and the complication of misrepresentations, falsehood and deceit in which it involved you?
A: I have not.

5. Bridge Master with a Secret

The Rock Island Line ran across Illinois from Chicago to Rock Island, a town situated on the east bank of the Mississippi River. It was owned by the C&RI RR Co. On the other side of the river the Mississippi & Missouri Railroad Company stretched a track out west across Iowa, to Council Bluffs. All that was needed now was a bridge across the Mississippi, and the first stage of a transcontinental railroad would be in place. A dream in the making. So the two railroad companies got together around a table and formed a third company, the Rock Island Bridge Company. This new company, along with the M & M per se, began to build the bridge. The Chicago & Rock Island came into the venture a year later, and the job was finished in April 1856. For the first time ever, passengers and freight were able to cross the country's greatest river without having to pay the ferryman. From Rock Island they poured over to Davenport, on the Iowa side, and then back again. A constant stream, they came and went on foot, by horse and by carriage, and, most significantly, in trains belonging to the two railroad companies.

The Father of Waters had spoken, and the word that was jumping out most pipingly from the more baritone rumble of the excited crowd was progress. But not everybody wanted progress. It wasn't just the unemployed boatmen who were scowling into their bad whiskey in saloons up and down the Mississippi River these days, it was all the townsfolk whose way of life had been built upon the old ways. There wasn't a great deal of whooping and yelling for joy in those places. But there was much mumbling, sinister discontent growing like stinkweed, until they came flat out and declared war. The most vociferous and violent opponent of the bridge was the St. Louis Chamber of Commerce. They sent men upriver with bad intentions.

The bridge was 1581 feet long, made principally of wood, and constructed in six spans, one of which was moveable. This was the draw span, roughly in the middle of the bridge and flanked by two fixed spans on the Illinois side and three on the Iowa side. The draw's normal position was open, to allow unimpeded passage for river-going vessels, but, supported by the huge center pier, it could be rotated horizontally back to its closed position whenever a train was approaching on the single line of track. The

5. Bridge Master with a Secret

The Rock Island Bridge, about 1860 (from *Rock Island Arsenal: In Peace and in War*, by B.F. Tillinghast, 1898).

draw span, in action, could be quite exciting to watch, especially if a train was approaching at the same time as a ship. There was a certain amount of signaling, or flagging, involved, and that had to be done properly or there would be a nasty scene. It was not a particularly complex operation but it was a responsible, full-time job for a bridge master, one that required alertness and intelligence. Seth Gurney, a millwright from Maine, was the first to occupy this position. He and his assistants soon had the job down pat, and it wasn't long before they could pass a train over the bridge and then, in two minutes flat, have that draw back open. Mr. G. bought a log book, which was ruled off to keep an accurate record of all the boats and barges, and the number of passengers crossing the bridge; the temperature at 6 a.m., noon, and 6 p.m., as well as the temperature in the sun; the stage of water in the river; wind speed and direction; and all the other data necessary to the keeping of a bridge for each day and for every week, ending Saturday. As bridge tender, Seth was expected to hand in his weekly report to the company, and, as a good will gesture, an abbreviated version was mailed to the local newspaper, where it was invariably printed on Tuesday's front page.

The bully boys from St. Louis pulled one stunt after another until, by the summer of 1859, more than rumors were reaching the ear of John F. Tracy, the all-powerful superintendent of the Chicago & Rock Island RR.

There was a plot afoot to burn the bridge down. At three o'clock in the morning on Sunday, June 5, the bridge watchman patrolling the Iowa end as he made his way toward the draw span trod on something that smelled offensive. After painstaking examination up close to his nose he determined that it was brimstone, and there was a lot of it. Brimstone, as in "fire and brimstone." There was a whole heap of other stuff too, dangerous materials, components already set in place. All that was needed was a torch and the whole bridge would go up. Suddenly the watchman saw movement below, in the water. A skiff was rapidly moving away from the bridge, and there were men in it. Word soon got to Mr. Tracy, and he called in the Pinkertons.[1]

Seth Gurney went to bed as usual on the last Saturday night of July 1859, in the fairly substantial two-story house the Bridge Company had provided for him on the turntable pier immediately beneath the draw span. His draw, his bridge. He had no idea, not so much as an inkling, that come the morrow he would be out of a job, and out of a home. Not only that, his replacement had already been hurriedly brought into town under cover of dark, so that no one would see, no one would ask awkward questions. Some relative of Mr. Tracy's from Pennsylvania, perhaps. Old Seth was 53, and that was too old for a new career yet at the same time too young to be given a golden handshake and told to keep his mouth shut. It was the Sabbath, after all, a day on which everyone in this e pluribus unum country took a break from their unceasing labor to reflect on the greatness of that greatest of all American deities, Mammon. Seth, like every other church-going member of the animal kingdom along the Mississippi River, knew that Gold moves in mysterious ways. The railroad sent a man in to the bridge house to remove the company log-book and other records. As for the furnishings, the company didn't bother too much. The incoming bridge master wasn't going to be spending a great deal of time in the prescribed accommodations anyway; for a dollar a day he was going to be staying at the New Pennsylvania House, on the corner of Fourth and Iowa, in downtown Davenport. Here, on a nightly basis, the kitchen offered a choice dish. With the eye of an experienced food critic, he had already spotted her.[2]

It was all done so fast, it took several days for the community just to realize old Seth was gone and that a new man had come to town. As for what had really happened, and why, it would be a long while before any of that ever came out, and by that time no one was alive any longer either to care much or to provide the details.[3]

Monday, August 1, 1859, the morning after the night he arrived in Davenport, was J.R. Reed's first day on the job as tender of the Rock Island Bridge. He had no log book in which to make his reports, since the Bridge Company's man who had carried off Seth Gurney's book had failed to return it. So Reed went out and purchased his own and began it that day. Just like Mr. G's had been, the contents were very technical. Nothing of the remotest biographical interest. Nothing human. Except on the inside front cover where the new bridge master practiced his new signature over and over, to get the hang of the name: "John R. Reed, Richmond, Virginia." Why Richmond? Up to that time, "Mr. Reed" had had no special connection to the capital city of the Old Dominion. It's almost as if he could see into the future, that he somehow knew that within three years Richmond would be the last city on earth he would ever dance in.[4]

Seth Gurney's summary dismissal as bridge master was covered by the Davenport press, as it really had to be: "Mr. Gurney, we regret to learn, has been removed from his office as Bridge Master, and a Mr. Reed, of Chicago, appointed his successor. We know nothing of Mr. Gurney's successor, but we do know that Mr. G. was a faithful and accommodating officer."[5]

But soon enough the city would learn first-hand what they needed to know about the new bridge tender, and they would generally like what they saw. But there would be some who didn't.

One of the first things Reed did on assuming his new position was hire as one of the watchmen a man he had met very soon after his arrival in Davenport, a cooper named Joseph Burgess. It was an act of generosity that would backfire on him one day and bring him to within an ace of getting his head blown off.[6]

As 1859 became 1860, following the American tradition, an election year began—the most important election year the nation ever had. August 9 of that year was the day the *Chicago Tribune* blew J.R. Reed's cover. The headline was innocuous enough: "Important Arrest of Conspirators. A Plot to Burn the Rock Island Railroad Bridge." It was the words in the actual text that were damaging: "Special Deputy Tim. Webster, Bridge Master of the R.R. Company at Rock Island, served the papers...." Well, thanks to the long arm of the *Tribune*, the cat was certainly out of the bag now, wasn't it? Later that day, a few days at the very most, everyone in Davenport and Rock Island would know that J.R. Reed, bridge master, was, in fact, Special Deputy Timothy Webster. They would, wouldn't they? But no. They never got to know the truth, thanks to an unusual set of circumstances, one that only a friendly fate could have arranged.[7]

The Rock Island paper of the following day was so busy pontificating, as was their wont, and so preoccupied with getting the wording right for their sonorous opinion on the case, that they never fully digested what was in the *Tribune*. They opened their article with "Our citizens will be somewhat surprised when they read the exploits of Pinkerton & Co., in regard to the arrest of Messrs. Bissell and Chadwick." The paper admitted that they knew nothing of the evidence, but they ventured the belief that the whole thing was "a vile conspiracy on the part of the defenders of the bridge nuisance." Anyone who knew anything about how "secret spies and policemen" manufactured evidence would surely wait for the proof before they believed the men guilty. The paper tells us that the telegraph spoke of the arrest of Mr. Chadwick by "Officer Webster," and then asks "Who is he? We hear that it is Tim Webster, the bridge tender! We shouldn't wonder if it turned out that the 'conspiracy' was on the other side."[8]

The bridge crossed the Mississippi between Rock Island and Davenport, and changed the lives of the citizens of both towns totally and forever. The bridge, therefore, was of monumental importance to everyone on both sides of the river. To a certain degree, therefore, the bridge master must have been too, and, indeed, he is fairly covered in the Davenport press. As for the *Rock Island Argus*, for example, his name is never mentioned, from July 1859, when he arrived, until May 1861, when he left. Even under the extreme provocation of a great potential story such as Bridge Master Reed being, in reality, Officer Tim Webster of the Pinkertons, not a squeak. Didn't the paper know that J.R. Reed was the bridge master? Of their own bridge? They don't seem to have had a clue. On the other hand, T.D. Barnes, the bridge tender of the Rock River Bridge, a much smaller toll bridge over the Rock River in the town of Rock Island itself, gets quite a lot of press in that same time frame.

Timothy Webster, 1860 (from *Timothy Webster: Spy of the Rebellion*, the very brief biography published by the Pinkertons in 1906).

It was a different story when the editors of the *Davenport Democrat* got their hands on the *Chicago Tribune*. They read

5. Bridge Master with a Secret

it with enormous interest, noting that the Chicagoans had confused this Special Deputy "Tim. Webster" with J.R. Reed, who everyone in Davenport knew was their bridge master, one of Davenport's own, so to speak. The Chicago paper had obviously conflated the two men. So, when it came time to regurgitate the story for their local readership, the *Democrat* doctored that part of the long article, and only that part, by unconflating the two men, so that in Davenport, and only in Davenport, the section read thus: "Special Deputy Tim. Webster and Mr. J.R. Reed, Bridge Master of the Railroad Company at Rock Island, served the papers...." It's the inserted words "and Mr. J.R. Reed," that are all-important. Just four little words.[9]

Phew! Saved again. Mind you, it is somewhat difficult to imagine in what way Tim could possibly have suffered if his true identity had been exposed. After all, he had brought the case in, the villains had been bagged, and he was free and ready to leave Davenport, surely. In fact, he should have left Davenport immediately, job done, mission accomplished. But it didn't happen that way. For some reason he would remain in Davenport, as bridge master what's more, for another eight months. That's a long time. What's going on?

Could it be that Mr. Tracy, the railroad superintendent, wanted Reed to stay on beyond the actual trial of the plotters, to try to uncover other villains who might be threatening to destroy the bridge? We hear nothing about this at all, or of any other dastardly schemes requiring the attention of the firm of Chicago detectives, but if that was, indeed, the case then Tracy would have had to clear it with Pinkerton first. But surely Pinkerton would have had great need of Tim's services back in Chicago. However, suppose Pinkerton was out of the picture. Suppose Tim had quit the detective business, and was now, as he indicates in his two 1860 census entries, a genuine railroad employee. After all, we remember how unhappy he was with the miserable wages Pinkerton was paying him. And then there was the girl. Always the girl. That back burner, turned on, hot, on the boil. Could it be? A new life in Iowa with a young woman half his age? Are we saying Mary Ellen Bailey or Mary Ellen Webster?[10]

Was it politics? In 1868, almost six years after Timothy Webster was hanged in Richmond, and three and a half years after the Civil War had ended, the Davenport *Democrat* would write a little reminiscing piece about their former bridge master, J.R. Reed, which included this: "Politically he was a Democrat of the strictest sect, a great admirer of Senator Douglas, and in the presidential campaign of 1860 was one of the most earnest and most hopeful of the campaigners." Reed's man, Douglas, may have lost in the general election in November, but that wasn't the end of J.R. Reed's own political career in Davenport.[11]

We mustn't belabor this point of Webster staying on in Davenport, for whatever reason, because the ice under our feet is so thin, especially at this time of year, and there's not enough substance to reinforce it, but what was he doing still working as bridge master for another eight months after he had solved the case he was sent out there to solve? What was he doing pursuing his relationship so vigorously with a young girl when he knew it was all going to come to an abrupt end any day? Why was he getting so involved with local politics when all the while he was a Pinkerton man liable at any moment to be relocated? One understands that this was a trend with Tim, this going a little too far in his undercover roles, this tendency to overact, but this was something else.[12]

On Thursday, the last day of January 1861, with the weather moderating beautifully and the roads now almost totally clear, Timothy Webster walked alone to the depot in Davenport and boarded a train bound for Chicago. He was in a hurry.[13]

6. The Baltimore Plot

It was early January 1861, and within a few all-too-short weeks Abraham Lincoln would be leaving his home in Springfield, Illinois, bound for Washington, D.C., in order to take up his new post as president of the United States. Traveling 1,904 miles by train, on 18 separate railroads, in the most glaring of public spotlights, he would be passing through many cities, one of which was Baltimore, a notorious hotbed of secessionism. It had been put about, true or not, that a disproportionate number of Baltimoreans did not want to see this man in the Executive Mansion, and some, it was said, were determined to make sure he didn't get there. Since before Lincoln's recent November victory even, plots to kill him had abounded, or so it was rumored, and the subject had been much and constantly discussed throughout the country for months. Bookies were giving odds; will

6. The Baltimore Plot

Honest Abe make it to Washington for his inauguration or won't he? Specifically, will he get through Baltimore alive? By the middle of January, Samuel Morse Felton, president of the Philadelphia, Wilmington and Baltimore Railroad, had been hearing disturbing rumors that these firebrands were planning to wreck his railroad in order to stop the president-elect dead in his tracks. Felton contacted the authorities, who dismissed the notion as preposterous. So he wrote a letter to Allan Pinkerton in Chicago. The famous detective promptly got on a train and went to see the railroad magnate in Philadelphia. Could Pinkerton ascertain if there was truly a plot to seize the large steamer that the PW&BRR used in ferrying their trains across the Susquehanna River at Havre de Grace? Could he discover if there were villains actively planning to burn the company's bridges between Havre de Grace and Baltimore?[1]

Pinkerton studied the situation, but, like the official police, found no cause for alarm, and returned to Chicago. After receiving another panicky letter from Felton, Pinkerton replied, on January 27: "Sir, Should the suspicions of danger still exist, as was the case at our interview on the 19th inst., I would suggest in view of the brief time we now have to operate in— that I should myself, with from four to six operatives, immediately repair to the seat of danger...."[2]

On the 30th, Felton sent Pinkerton a desperate telegram, and so, at last, the great detective accepted the case, not because he believed in it, per se, but in order to get Felton off his back and to make a bit of money in the bargain. And there might have been one other reason, much more important than the others. It would be fair to suggest that a light bulb had gone on in Pinkerton's head but for the fact that light bulbs had not yet been invented.

So, despite not having artificial light to guide the small but intrepid band of detectives, the adventure of the Baltimore plot had begun, and with it the woman who would become known as Hattie Lawton is introduced to history.[3]

At this very period of time, Pinkerton's firm numbered about fifty personnel, "a few of whom are females." Half a dozen of this staff were located in Chicago permanently, as managers and clerks, and 45 were immediately connected with the detective business in "all parts of this country." One of the rules for Pinkerton operatives was that they had to make a complete record of each day's work, accounting for every hour on the job. The report had to be sent immediately to headquarters, and there entered upon the record.[4]

It was an intensely cold day upon which Pinkerton, accompanied by several of his detectives, left Chicago, bound for Baltimore. Precisely how many of his operatives went with him, and who they were exactly, still remains a subject for deduction, if not debate or fruitful research. As Pinkerton had mentioned in his reply to Felton four days earlier, he planned to take between four and six, but obviously that was a spur of the moment thought, and so we really don't know how many he did take. According to the article Cleveland Moffett wrote for *McClure's* magazine in 1894, eight agents, besides Allan Pinkerton himself, left Chicago on February 1, 1861: George H. Bangs, Hiram B. Jones, William Norris, Paul H. Dennis, John Kinsella, Francis Warner, William H. Scott, and Timothy Webster. However, some later historians, ones who perhaps never saw the *McClure's* article, have maintained that there were only five agents; some name six. These modern day lists usually include real and imaginary operatives such as Harry W. Davies, John Seaford, Charles D.C. Williams, as well as Kate Warn and Hattie Lawton. There can be no doubt that the two ladies were part of the group while it was actively counterplotting in the east, so, if they were not part of the company that left Chicago on the first of the month, then perhaps they followed on a day or two later.[5]

One good thing about 44 South Street in Baltimore was that if you were afraid of someone seeing you go in through the front entrance, you could always go down the alley and in the side door. James H. Luckett was a stockbroker who rented office space in the building. His clients tended to use the main door. In early February 1861 another stockbroker, this one from Charleston and wishing to establish his Baltimore headquarters, moved into offices on the same floor as Luckett. The two men immediately became acquaintances. John H. Hutchinson's clients tended to use

George H. Bangs (photograph by F. Gutekunst in Philadelphia, date unknown; Records of Pinkerton's National Detective Agency, Box 27, Folder 5, Library of Congress).

the alleyway. They weren't really clients, of course, but operatives, and Hutchinson wasn't really a stockbroker, and he wasn't from South Carolina. He was that famous chief of detectives from Chicago, Allan Pinkerton.[6]

In his 1883 book, *The Spy of the Rebellion*, Pinkerton doesn't even allude to Hattie Lawton in connection with the Baltimore plot, let alone discuss her major role in it as the agent posing as Timothy Webster's wife, the woman spending nights on end sharing hotel rooms with a man who had a wife and children in Illinois. That's because, with that wife and one of the children still alive in January 1883 when the great detective's book was published, Pinkerton was being delicate. What's he going to say? How's he going to handle the Tim and Hattie situation in print? Best thing is to pretend Hattie never existed, as a part of the Baltimore plot, anyway. But there would come a time in his book, and it would come soon, when he would no longer be able to put off revealing the truth.

He does, however, mention the lady—Hattie, that is—in the letter he wrote to his old law partner, William Herndon, on August 23, 1866. In this letter he tells how, upon arriving at Baltimore, he distributed his operatives around town. "One of those Detectives, named Timothy Webster, accompanied by a Lady, was stationed by me at Perrymansville, a Station about nine miles South of Havre de Grace, on the P.W.&B.R.R., where a Rebel Company of Cavalry were organizing. Webster, as you will find from his Reports under the Heading of T.W., and those of the Lady who accompanied him, under the Heading of H.H.L., succeeded admirably well in cultivating an acquaintance with the Secessionists."[7]

This letter to Herndon first saw the light of day in 1913, in *The American Magazine*. But for a curious quirk of fate the code name H.H.L. would have entered mainstream history with the publication of that letter, rather than having to wait until 1949, when Miss Cuthbert's book on the Baltimore plot came out. But in 1913 someone doctored the letter, almost certainly the magazine's editors after they had received a copy of it from Jesse Weik, Herndon's old writing partner. This is what appeared in the magazine: "One of these detectives, named Timothy Webster, accompanied by a lady, was stationed by me at Perrymansville, a station about nine miles south of Havre de Grace, on the Philadelphia, Wilmington and Baltimore Railroad, where a rebel company of cavalry was being organized. Webster, as well as the lady who accompanied him, succeeded admirably in cultivating the acquaintance of the Secessionists in that region."[8]

"Mr. Pinkerton had also a lady who represented herself as being from

Montgomery, Alabama, where she had actually lived, and she moved in Society in Baltimore to learn what the ladies had to say on the subject." This lady was Kate Warn, alias Mrs. Barley, alias Mrs. Cherry, alias Raisins, and the quote is from Leonard Swett's article, "The Conspiracies of the Rebellion."[9]

"The reports of my operatives, A.T.C., C.D.C.W., and M.B., clearly indicated to me the state of feeling in Maryland at that time, and how embittered and poisoned it was, showing that the Secessionists were prepared to do anything which they deemed necessary in order to break up the Union."[10]

In Baltimore, within a few days of his arrival, Pinkerton discovered a plot to assassinate Lincoln as the president-elect passed through that city on his way to his inaugural. This was a real plot, he claimed, not just one of the hundreds of rumors going around. It was real, wasn't it? Or did the celebrity sleuth make it all up, to burnish his reputation and to put Lincoln in his debt? There are two schools of thought today, as there were then.

Pinkerton consequently sent a warning to Chicago lawyer and politician N. B. Judd, who was perhaps Mr. Lincoln's greatest supporter. On February 11, Judd would be leaving Springfield with the Lincoln party. After passing through Indianapolis, the presidential party were, at close of day on the 12th, in Cincinnati, and here Judd received Pinkerton's written note which concluded with the comforting information that the great detective would communicate further as they progressed eastward. Judd kept the bad news from Lincoln. Bad news about the plot, or bad news about Pinkerton being on the job? Again, two schools of thought. One can always smell an office seeker; the trouble is, they don't all smell the same. Happy birthday, Mr. New President. From Cincinnati it was on to Columbus, Pittsburgh, Cleveland, and Buffalo, where, on the 17th, the busy celebrity had a Sunday of rest. It was less relaxed for Judd, who received a second letter from Pinkerton, saying that the evidence of the plot was accumulating. Was it, or wasn't it?[11]

Abraham Lincoln (Library of Congress).

6. The Baltimore Plot

On Monday, February 18, 1861, M.B. wrote her report, from which one can see that she was just as cloak and dagger as her boss. She just loved this sort of stuff: "I got up at 7.30 a.m. and breakfasted at 8.30 a.m.—During the forenoon Mr P.—called and said I must get ready to go to New York on the 5.16 p.m. train. He also gave me my instructions and some letters for N.B. Judd, and E.S. Sandford [sic], and then left. After dinner I made arrangements to leave, paying my bill &c—and told them I wanted to take the train for Philadelphia. At about 4.00 p.m. I left for the Depot, where I saw Mr. P.-, and at 5.16 p.m. I started for New York."[12]

M.B. reported, on the 19th, that she arrived in New York at 4.00 a.m., took a carriage, drove to the Astor House, where she got a room after much trouble, and finally went to bed. But, being an eye, she didn't sleep, and got up at 7.30 a.m. After breakfast she sent a note to E.S. Sanford at the Adams Express Office.[13]

And so the plot developed as Lincoln made his inexorable way through Albany to New York City, and from there to Philadelphia, with Kate Warn traveling here, there and everywhere, watching events closely, keeping Allan Pinkerton abreast of the situation, until she, Pinkerton, and Lincoln all met up in the City of Brotherly Love.[14]

While Mrs. Barley was orchestrating events on a national scale, her sister agent, Hattie Lawton, using the code name H.H.L., was operating in Baltimore on a more local level. "Some of the women employed by the detective went to serve as waiters, seamstresses, &c., in the families of the conspirators, and a record was regularly kept of what was said and done to further their enterprise."[15]

After a night's sleep at the Continental, Lincoln left Philadelphia at nine o'clock on the morning of the 22nd, and at around 1.30 p.m. arrived at the Vine and Second Street Railroad Station, in Harrisburg. That night, while the inaugural train and most of its passengers remained in that town, silent forces snuck Lincoln and his friend, the imposingly huge Ward Hill Lamon, onto another train, a special train, a secret train, which took the two men on the Pennsylvania Central Railroad back to Philadelphia where Pinkerton and Kate Warn had reserved three of the four sections of the sleeping car at the rear end of an ordinary, regularly scheduled train of cars leaving for Baltimore. Curiously, the fourth section of the sleeping car was occupied by the superintendent of the New York Police, who had no inkling of who was just down the corridor. As Pinkerton wrote, years later, in his October 31, 1867, letter to Ward Lamon: "You accompanied me on that important trip. You were my only companion with the exception of Mrs. Warn. You know that John A. Kennedy was a Passenger on that train, and occupied a berth in the same sleeping Coach in which we took passage, yet knew not that he was traveling in Such excellent Company." The train pulled into Baltimore, into the PW & B's President Street Station, at the corner of Canton Avenue. From there the president's secret car was drawn by horses through town along Pratt Street and down Howard, to the Camden Station belonging to the Baltimore and Ohio Railroad. From there it was hooked up to its new locomotive and was soon on its way to Washington City. Not one of the four secret passengers—Lamon, Kate, Pinkerton, and Lincoln—slept a wink from the time they left Philadelphia about midnight until their train pulled into the nation's capital at about six in the morning, and, alas for them, not even then.[16]

Meanwhile, later that day, the real inaugural train, i.e., the one without Lincoln on it, left Harrisburg as a decoy, went through the Pennsylvania town of York, and finally, in its turn, arrived at Baltimore. If anything was going to happen, it was going to be here, in this most explosive city, and since the much-talked-about desperate assassins assumed this train to be the one Lincoln was on, this was precisely the moment something was going to happen. But, as with the secret train earlier that morning, there was not even a hint of trouble, and it wasn't long before the passengers were on their way to the capital of a nation rapidly tearing itself in two. Taking both trains into account, it was a star-studded group that checked into the Willard that day: Hon. A. Lincoln, Ill.; Mrs. Lincoln and 2 children, Ill.; R.T. Lincoln, ditto; W.H. Lamon, ditto; Hon. N.B. Judd; E.J. Allen, of New York; and T. Webster, of Pennsylvania.[17]

That second train, the one with Mrs. Lincoln and her family aboard, was also carrying four Army officers, who had been selected as the official bodyguard, the Scott Guard. One of the quartet, a Kentuckian not yet 39, would, just over a year later, become the plaything of a fickle fate when he found himself in command of all the Union forces in Virginia. In the meantime, on arriving at Washington, and while he awaited the command of history, young Captain John Pope checked into the Willard with the rest of the presidential party.[18]

The press were all over Lincoln's arrival, naturally. The *Chicago Tribune*'s very own correspondent in Washington was among those who composed their articles that day, and four mornings later his readers awoke to discover the reason for the president-elect's premature arrival in the capital:

"Pinkerton, the famous Chicago detective, has been in Baltimore for some time past, and taking notes and penetrating the secrets of the Secessionists of that city. He satisfied himself that a plot was matured to make the attempt to assassinate both Lincoln and Hamlin while passing through that city." It goes on to tell us that Hamlin passed through the city a day earlier than scheduled, and then it proceeds to give a pretty accurate precis of what happened to Lincoln the night of his secret ride. This was all great publicity for Pinkerton.[19]

On Tuesday, February 26, 1861, T.W. reported: "I then went to the Office, and reported to Mr. P.-, after which I left for the Howard House, where I met H.H.L.-, and went with her to Mr. Springers Store. He told us he would be in Perrymansville in the morning."[20]

After all the excitement had died down, Pinkerton took his operatives back to Chicago. Hattie Lawton continued actively working as one of his detectives, but since that select group of people, as individuals, didn't ordinarily make the newspapers, we have no way of knowing where she was stationed or what she was involved in. We do know that Pinkerton and "a large corps of detectives" were in and around Pittsburgh in the second half of March 1861, running down a gang of potential train robbers "as noiselessly as snow-flakes fall upon the sod," but whether Hattie was part of that operation or not we don't know. One thing we can be sure of is that she was not traveling with Timothy Webster during this period. Webster had things to do that he could only do alone.[21]

---

7. The End of Mary Ellen Bailey

J.R. Reed, well-known bridge master on the Mississippi, arrived back in Davenport, Iowa, on or around March 10, 1861, after having passed a month and a half in the east, under his real name of Timothy Webster, helping to save the life of the new president of the United States of America and spending weeks living with and posing as the husband of this new female Pinkerton, H.H.L. What with his original wife Charlotte, his real wife that is, the one with the children in Illinois, and Mary Ellen Bailey, his very young "wife" in Iowa, and who knows how many others, one more wife definitely made one too many. On top of all that was his budding political career in Davenport. After almost two years of building a life in that town, it was not going to be easy to extricate himself. Life was getting complicated. Something had to give.[1]

A lot of Reed's spare time was spent getting ready for the city elections of April 8. On the evening of the 11th of March, his first full day back in Davenport, he was at a political meeting in town. This from the rather biased local paper, the *Democrat*: "The Aldermanic nomination by the Democracy of the 6th Ward is a good one, and will be supported vigorously. Mr. Reed is an active man and will make a good alderman. It is the duty of the Democrats of the 6th Ward to exert themselves to elect him. The nomination was a hearty one. Let his election be no less so."[2]

But things aren't always what they seem. One may go so far as to say they are never what they seem. On Tuesday, April 2, subscribers to the *Democrat* woke up to find this open letter printed on the front page: "To the Democrats of the 6th Ward. Gentlemen, since you saw fit to nominate me as your representative in the City Council for the 6th Ward, which nomination I accepted and for which I feel grateful to you; I have given the matter due consideration, and find that I cannot do justice to my employers (M.R.R. Bridge Co.) and take such position in politics as the experiences of the case would require. I have made up my mind to decline the honor. J.R. Reed, Davenport, April 1st, 1861."[3]

There was no braver man than Timothy Webster, as Pinkerton is forever at pains to tell us, but one suspects it could only have taken a braver one to face up to the Democrats of Davenport's Sixth Ward when they got the bad news that morning. However, that was all moot: That sure bet for alderman, the one Democrat you would have put your money on, J.R. Reed, was gone. He had left town the morning before. Perhaps he was never as brave as we thought. Things are never what they seem.[4]

Tim Webster had gone back to Chicago, or back to Pinkerton, depending on how one is inclined to view his last eight months in Davenport. But one thing's for sure; he was still bridge master, even now, after all that.

On the 12th of April 1861, war broke out between the United States of America and a new country, so new indeed that it could only have come into being by virtue of that very breach of civility. Welcome to the world atlas the Confederate States of America. A week or so later, railway and telegraphic communications between Washington and the North were cut by saboteurs. On the 21st of the month, Pinkerton was called in by Chicago men who wanted to get certain very important messages to President Lincoln. The man Pinkerton chose to deliver this mail was Timothy Webster, and it didn't take long for the courier to get ready for his trip. "The services of Miss Kate Warne, my female superintendent, were requested, and in a few minutes, the important dispatches, some twelve in number, were securely sewed between the linings of his coat collar, and in the body of his waistcoat, and Timothy Webster was on his way to the capital of the country."[5]

One of the letters he carried was dashed off by Pinkerton that day to President Lincoln: "When I saw you last, I said that if the time should ever come that I could be of service to you—I was ready—If that time has come, I am on hand—I have in my Force from Sixteen to Eighteen persons on whose Courage, Skill & Devotion to their Country I can rely—If they with myself at the head can be of service in the way of obtaining information of the movements of the Traitors, or Safely conveying your letters or dispatches, or that class of Secret Service which is the most dangerous, I am at your command. In the present disturbed state of Affairs, I dare not trust this to the mail—so send by one of My Force who was with me at Baltimore. You may safely trust him with Any Message for me—Written or Verbal—I fully guarantee his fidelity—He will act as you direct and return here with your answer. Secrecy is the great lever I propose to operate with—hence the necessity of this movement (if you contemplate it) being kept *Strictly Private*, and that should you desire another interview with the Bearer, that you should so arrange it as that he will not be noticed—The Bearer will hand you a copy of a Telegraph Cipher which you may use if you desire to Telegraph me—My Force comprises both Sexes—all of good character—and well Skilled in their Business."

Accompanying this letter was the long, page-after-page "Telegraph Cipher" mentioned by Pinkerton, the code the president was to use, if he so chose. It was all very 19th-century cloak and dagger stuff, melodramatic, out of a dime novel that doesn't read so well today. One can see Lincoln chortling and slapping his thigh as he read that "Prest." had been labeled "Nuts" and that "Vice Prest." Hannibal Hamlin was "Prunes." Yes, Honest Abe, the rail-splitter, would have laughed until he died, an eventuality this code was designed to thwart. However, the silly words created by "Plums," that arch detective from Chicago, were, as history was ultimately to demonstrate, a lot more serious than they first appeared.

It is worth noting, if only as a prelude to something more meaningful, that, despite the fact that this letter and the code that accompanies it have been readily accessible for years, and that the letter has often been quoted, these agents' code names, with the exception of Timothy Webster as Peaches, have never been mentioned by historians. So, most of all, welcome aboard H.L., Hattie Lawton with her Cranberries; M.B., Mrs. Barley with her Raisins; and G.H.B., George Bangs with his Hickory Nuts.[6]

Webster handed the letters to the president personally on the 22nd. The next day he was back at the Executive Mansion, this time to receive from Lincoln certain correspondence for General McClellan and others, including a reply to Pinkerton, inviting the Chicago detective chief to come aboard in the war effort.[7]

That month, April 1861, Major General George Brinton McClellan was at Columbus, commanding the Ohio Volunteers in this brand new war that most people figured would last only three months at the most. Timothy Webster reached him there on the 24th, and that day McClellan, after reading his letter from President Lincoln, wrote one of his own to Pinkerton, entrusting it to the trusted courier who stood before him: "I wish to see you with the least possible delay, to make arrangements with you of an important nature. I will be either here or in Cincinnati for the next few days. Here to-morrow—Cincinnati next day. In this city you will find me at the Capitol, at Cincinnati at my residence. If you telegraph me, better use your first name alone. Let no one know that you come to see me, and keep as quiet as possible." This was to arrange a Secret Service. It was the first such arrangement made by the United States government. It also gives us a clue as to why Pinkerton would pick the nom de guerre "Major E.J. Allen" at this very time: "...use your first name."[8]

After delivering the packages to Pinkerton in Chicago, Timothy Webster made his way back to Davenport one more time, one final time. This was going to be a very short stay but it was going to be the trickiest part of the whole get-out.

The bridge master, and he was still bridge master, had to tell them something, and he did. "Them" included not only his "employers" but also Mary Ellen Bailey, of course. And what he told them was the truth. He gave out that he had been appointed a first lieutenant and was off to join his new regiment in New York, the Scott Guard, "a company of picked men who are going through to Washington, to be employed in the immediate service of Gen. Scott."[9]

And then the morning of May 2 came, all too quickly, at the Scott House, where Reed was now staying, and where Mary Ellen Bailey, his young and impressionable young "wife," was working in the kitchen. The two of them were going through a protracted and arduous au revoir…[10]

Not so fast, Mister!

A true word could travel as fast as a flaming lie in a town like Davenport. News of Reed's departure shot through the grapevine until, only moments later, it reached the ear of Joe Burgess, that very same cooper Reed had once hired as a watchman. The wily bridge master had stiffed Joe on a Michigan land deal, Joe had objected, and Reed had fired him. What was even more unpleasant was that Joe was still being stiffed, on the same deal. Joe now lived in a perpetual state of anger. The wrong word could get him worked up into a frenzy.[11]

It took Burgess only a few seconds to grab the one or two things he needed and dash out the door toward the office of George E. Hubbell, the lawyer who had worked on his land case and who had his own good reasons to feel that he too was being hornswoggled by the crooked Reed. The two eager men hurried over to the Scott House, where they found their quarry, Gladstone bag and Mary Ellen Bailey in hand. The lawyer and the cooper had arrived in the nick of time.[12]

The aggrieved visitors remonstrated with Reed for a few minutes, and then, after the bridge master had agreed to sign the necessary documents to end all this fuss, the three men left the hotel together and stepped out onto the street, heading for lawyer Hubbell's office. It was when they were on the sidewalk at Le Claire Row, opposite Hubbell's place of work, that Reed went back on the deal, said he wouldn't sign anything. At that point, Burgess lost his cool and called his man a rascal, which was quite something to call someone back then. Reed stared at him for a second or two, and then used the line that millions of boys have used before and since: "You say that again and I'll knock you down!" Burgess did, and Reed did. Fight! Fight! Burgess, lying on the ground, legs akimbo, a black and white line-drawing out of an old book, pulled his revolver, took aim and squeezed the appropriate mechanism with his index finger, several times. "But for the derangement of the trigger, he would have received my compliments," said Joe, a few days later, just like millions of boys have said since.[13]

After the fracas on the sidewalk, J.R. Reed walked on until he got to the depot, where he caught the 10 a.m. mail train heading east.[14]

On that very day, May 2, 1861, as J.R. Reed, bridge master, disappeared into a small room on the train to emerge a few minutes later as Timothy Webster, Pinkerton man, things were happening in the District of Columbia. Lincoln shot off a quick note to Secretary of State Seward from the Executive Mansion: "My dear Sir, Our Chicago detective has arrived and I have promised to have you meet him and me here at 8 o'clock this evening. Yours truly, A. Lincoln." By "Our Chicago detective," the president meant Allan Pinkerton.[15]

What happened to Mary Ellen Bailey? With an accusing fist, the *Davenport Democrat* of June 6, punched out the headline, "Betrayal, Desertion, Suicide." The actual article runs thus, spelling mistakes and all:

> It was generally reported, and to some extent believed, that J.R. Reed, late bridge master here, married several months since, a girl by the name of Mary Ellen Daily, who was living at the New Pennsylvania House, where Reed was boarding. There was something mysterious about it. Some weeks ago, as will be remembered, Reed left the city. Our readers will recall the almost fatal circumstances which took place on the morning of his departure, between him and Mr. Burgess. A few days after, his wife followed after, and went to Paducha, Ky., where she expected her husband had gone, to search for him. She arrived there, and made diligent inquiries for Reed, but did not find him.

The lady with whom Mary Ellen was boarding in Paducah noticed that the girl was sinking rapidly in spirits. On or about May 24 the dejected girl "proceeded to the high bank of the river and was seen to throw herself into the water. Efforts for her recovery were of no avail." By the time the lady with whom she was boarding wrote to the Davenport newspaper, Mary Ellen's body had not been recovered. It was believed that she had some relatives at or near Iowa City. "The lady wishes to be informed on that matter, as she may send her trunk back. There is evidently much black-hearted villainy at the bottom of all this."[16]

Less is often more poignant: "J.R. Reed, late bridgemaster at Davenport, deserted his wife a few weeks since. She followed him to Paducah, Kentucky, but not overtaking him, she committed suicide by throwing herself into the river from a high bank."[17]

On the third day of May, a "Department of the Ohio" was formed, consisting of the combined forces of the states of Ohio, Indiana, and Illinois, and this department, by order of General Scott, was placed under the command of General McClellan.[18]

Pinkerton hurried back to Cincinnati from his interview with Lincoln and Seward, and reported to McClellan at the general's home there, on Ludlow Street. The two men thrashed out the details of the new Secret Service, and then, over the course of the next several days, Pinkerton busied himself with implementing it, taking a suite of rooms, where he opened up his Queen City office. He "was given a free hand, and it was left to his judgment what detectives and how many to employ and what regulations should govern them."[19]

8. Hattie and Tim Join the Secret Service

It was always a good feeling to know you owned the newspaper with the largest circulation in town, and even if you didn't, you could always claim to. You wouldn't have been the only one. But, either way, one of the drawbacks was that you had the legal obligation to print a regular once-a-week list of letters waiting at the local post office. It's always interesting for historians to see certain names jumping out at them as they cast an eye down a list, and it can be reasonably useful in tracking a particular lady or gentleman, placing that person in general time and space. In other words, someone thought the addressee would be in town at roughly that time, otherwise they wouldn't have sent a letter. However, sometimes it gives a researcher more questions than answers. For example, on March 30, 1861, there was a letter waiting in Washington, D.C., for "Hattie." That's it, just Hattie. No last name. What good's that? Probably no good at all, but it is rather mysterious, that one name; and Hattie Lawton was a Pinkerton operative, and therefore, by virtue of her calling, mysterious. "Hi, my name's Hattie, and I've come to pick up a letter." On May 11, there was a letter waiting in the same city for Mrs. H.H. Lewis. Is this H.H.L.? So, more questions than answers. But it is far better to have no answers than no questions.[1]

Tim Webster arrived in Washington on or around August 8, 1861, from a two-week spying trip in Memphis. He went to the District of Columbia rather than Cincinnati because world events had moved fast while he had been traveling, and things were not the same in North America anymore. The battle of Manassas had been fought at Bull Run, Virginia, in late July, and the Yanks had lost, much to their surprise. Their whole attitude to the war, and that of the rebs too, had changed overnight, and McClellan and Pinkerton were now based in the capital of the newly delineated, greatly reduced United States of America. The general had been summoned east from Cincinnati to take command of the Military Division of the Potomac, the main Union force protecting the District. The Secret Service force of the Department of the Ohio went with him, headed by Pinkerton, who would make his headquarters in Washington. The agreement was that while in the capital he would be under the command of the secretary of war and the provost marshal general, but when in the field he would come under the orders of McClellan.[2]

The very day Webster got to Washington, he and Hattie were added to Pinkerton's new government payroll. They were not so much detectives now as Secret Service agents working not for the Department of the Ohio, as previously, but for the United States of America.[3]

Not everyone in the North was ecstatic about Pinkerton heading up the new U.S. Secret Service. A detective on the District of Columbia police force, A.R. Allen, objected to the Chicago detective code-naming himself E.J. Allen, but reserved his bitterest opprobrium for when he put forward the proposition that the "services of Pinkerton and his gang will hardly remunerate the Government for the expense of keeping them."[4]

9. The India-Rubber Doll

Allan Pinkerton, along with his two agents, Pryce Lewis and John Scully, arrested Southern spy Rose Greenhow in Washington on August 23, 1861, confined her in her own house in the city, and placed her under the guard of a woman operative. This is what Mrs. Greenhow herself wrote: "Shortly after[wards] the female detective arrived. I blush that the name and character of woman should be so prostituted. But she was certainly not above her honorable calling." This observation on the part of Mrs. Greenhow may be tart but it is also astute. She hasn't finished: "Her image is daguerreotyped on my mind, and it is an ugly picture. I would willingly obliterate it. As is usual with females employed in this way, she was decently arrayed, as if to impress me with her respectability. Her face reminded me of one of those India-rubber dolls, whose expression is made by squeezing it, with weak grey eyes which had a faculty of weeping. Like all the detectives, she had only a Christian name, Ellen."[1]

One has to admit this leaves a lasting imprint on one's mind. What is rather puzzling is that for decades now there has been a growing need among historians to identify this female detective. Even if the story is true, surely Ellen was just an anonymous Pinkerton agent who got the short end of the beauty stick given to her for posterity by a vengeful Rose Greenhow. One should probably let it go at that.

It all started with Jim Horan and Howard Swiggett in their 1951 book, *The Pinkerton Story*, when discussing the moment Allan Pinkerton invaded Rose Greenhow's house: "With him went his operatives, Lewis and Scully, and a female detective whose name we do not know." But we do know her name, don't we? It was Ellen, wasn't it? After all, this story originated in the book by Mrs. Greenhow, and it is she who tells us the detective's name was Ellen. Horan & Swiggett conclude: "It is fascinating, as we shall see, to believe, she may have been Hattie Lawton and it is probable that it was."[2]

Given that Pinkerton employed several women at that time, one has to wonder what led Mr. Horan to the use of the word "probable." Regrettably, he doesn't tell us. In the end, though, it's really moot because it couldn't possibly have been Hattie Lawton. A quick glance at Timothy Webster's August 23, 1861, report shows that not only was H.H.L. working for him in Baltimore on that day, the very day Rose Greenhow was being confronted by Ellen in Washington, but that she was already living with Tim at Millers Hotel, on the corner of German and Paca streets, in the western section of Baltimore, and had almost certainly been there for at least two weeks, working full-time on another case.[3]

Another thing: Six months later, in Richmond, Pryce Lewis would run into Hattie in Timothy Webster's room at the Monument Hotel. In his so-called "memoirs," written in 1888, he says, "I recognized a lady I had before seen with Webster—Miss Hattie Lewis." Surely if Hattie had been on the Greenhow watch back in August of 1861, along with Pryce Lewis and John Scully, Lewis would have remembered her with very different wording.[4]

Hattie was not involved in the Greenhow detail.

10. The First Trip

Timothy Webster's opening mission to Richmond began on October 14, 1861, when he left Baltimore with fellow operative William H. Scott. On the 22nd, the two agents arrived at Eastville, Virginia, on what is called the Delmarva Peninsula, where they parted, with Webster waiting at Eastville until October 25, when he crossed the Chesapeake Bay in a dugout canoe, bound for Richmond.[1]

On the evening of the 28th, a full two weeks after he left Baltimore, Timothy Webster arrived at Richmond, and checked into the Spotswood House. The *Richmond Dispatch* mentioned the arrival of, among others, "Capt. Timothy Webster." As far as we know, this is the first time Tim was ever in Richmond in his life.[2]

He awoke to a frosty morning. His first full day in the Confederate capital, October 29, was spent delivering letters. Freshly arrived, new boy in town, with a product to sell—himself—Tim needed a teaser, so he could establish bona fides, get himself noticed very quickly and favorably in the right circles, in the highest echelons of the Confederate hierarchy. Merely being a mailman was not going to cut it. He needed something explosive. And he had it. On the 30th, "Capt. T. Webster" received $40 from the Confederate Ordnance Department for 10,000 Hicks hat caps at $4 a box. These were percussion caps for rifled muskets, tiny hat-shaped pieces of metal filled or soon to be filled with mercury fulminate. They were almost impossible to get in the South, now that there were international boundaries and prohibitive tariffs. A musket is not much good without percussion caps. Yes, this was a good titillator, considering that the caps were designed to kill Yankee soldiers.[3]

On the last day of the month, along with one William Campbell, Webster visited the artillery batteries that were on the hills around Richmond. He had just met Campbell, a German-born Baltimorean, 31 years old, to whom he had an introduction by means of a letter from Mr. Campbell, the young man's father. William Campbell & Bro. was a manufacturer of leather and canvas goods, and had a factory in Richmond that employed 35 to 40 people. One of their big customers was the Confederate government, which readily and continually bought up large quantities of knapsacks, saber belts, bayonet scabbards, and the like.[4]

John Beauchamp Jones was a Southern novelist of note who, when war broke out, offered his services to the Confederate War Department, with the understanding that he be allowed to keep his own daily record of events and thoughts, and out of it make literary capital when the appropriate time came. *A Rebel War Clerk's Diary* was published in 1866, and became a classic. Jones died before seeing the work published.[5]

In the evening of October 31, Timothy Webster and William Campbell visited the rebel war clerk, who gave them a pass to visit Manassas. The two men returned to Richmond on November 5, and Webster checked back into the Spotswood House. After a lot of traveling in the distant Confederate countryside, and having spent a not so grand total of five days in Richmond itself, the spy made it back through the Union lines, and on the evening of November 14, 1861, was back in his chief's office in Washington, where he made his detailed report, which Pinkerton then wrote out for McClellan the following day. Now that Webster was back in the North, Pinkerton "deemed it best that he should again visit Baltimore, and mingle once more with his rebel friends in that city."[6]

The spy was gone from Richmond, but he would be back on a second trip soon enough. Meanwhile, in his absence, he left a paper trail, for among the advertised letters waiting in the Richmond Post Office on November 18, were two for T. Webster.[7]

---

11. The Miller's Hotel Caper

Something of a sensation was created in Baltimore early in the morning of Wednesday, November 20, 1861, when the provost marshal sent a large detachment of the Western District police to Miller's Hotel. They secured all the keys and seized and took possession of the whole establishment and everything in and around it, including the contents of the bar-room, the safe and the vault, and even a number of horses. The guards whom they placed at the hotel's entrance and exit would remain in charge of Miller's for the greater part of the morning.

The ostensible object of this whole exercise was to break up the illegal mail ring being operated by rebel sympathizers out of this hotel. The proprietors, the brothers McGee, who had taken over the establishment from Joseph Miller earlier that year, had not been suspected themselves and therefore, being regarded as loyal men, were not compromised in any way; but it was supposed that certain employees or lodgers had been receiving and transmitting letters south. A number of letters were seized and taken to the Western station house.

John (or William) Hart and his wife Mrs. Hart (actually Tim and Hattie), as well as John Earl, the barkeep/clerk of the hotel, were arrested and confined in the station house to answer the charge of treason in holding communication with persons in the Confederate states. The authorities soon found out Tim's right name, and from then on the press would refer to him as T. Webster or Thomas Webster, "a citizen of Kentucky, but left there in the early part of April, and since that time has been residing in Baltimore." Hattie would henceforth be known as Mrs. Webster.[1]

John Earl, an avowed Union man, was released that same day. Mrs. Webster was searched, but nothing incriminating was found on her beyond mere suspicion, and she was let go as well. But the government agents hung on to Thomas Webster because in his baggage they had found a bunch of alleged treasonable documents, along with several secession prints and a Confederate flag. There are some things a good reb just can't travel without. About 11 o'clock that night, by order of General Dix, a group of Western District police started out with Webster in a buggy to take him to Fort McHenry. When in the vicinity of the fortress, Webster, who was not manacled, sprang from the vehicle, and aided by the darkness succeeded in making his escape. All the following day and night they searched for him, but nothing. Timothy Webster, dangerous Confederate spy, had effected a clean getaway.

However, this episode, this entire thing, was a set-up, including and perhaps especially the escape, all of it dreamed up, planned, organized, and arranged by Pinkerton, and executed to a T by T. Webster.

Tim eventually got to the house of a secessionist friend of his, Sam Sloan, spent the whole of Thursday the 21st there, and then in the very early hours of the 22nd made his way to the train station, where he caught the 4:30 for Washington. At seven o'clock he was reporting to Pinkerton.[2]

The odd thing is, although Pinkerton devotes an entire rip-roaring chapter of *The Spy of the Rebellion* to this episode, he never mentions Hattie, even though, according to the press, she was a fundamental part of the whole adventure. Again, Pinkerton was being driven by his peculiar set of sensibilities.

12. The Second Trip

It must have been toward the end of the first week of December 1861 that Timothy Webster, now seen as a very minor Confederate hero somewhat in the Robin Hood mode, left Washington to begin his second expedition to Richmond. There can be little change from that. This was the trip on which Webster met a defecting U.S. Army surgeon named James C. Herndon, who had been serving out in California. Only two or three weeks earlier, Herndon had arrived back in New York on the *Champion*, in the same cabin as one of the company commanders of the Third Regiment of U.S. Artillery, the newly promoted Captain William A. Winder, who, unlike Herndon, would remain loyal to the Union in the years to come. Webster guided the doctor across the lines and was rewarded with a letter of introduction to one of the most powerful men in the Confederacy, Brigadier General John H. Winder.[1]

When war broke out John Henry Winder had only very recently made the rank of major, and he was sixty years old. For a West Point man, with his aristocratic Maryland background, after a lifetime spent in the army, and with a notable record in the Mexican War, that was not very good. It was not good enough. Whatever the technicalities of the promotion system were that slowed an officer's progress during peace time, there was another reason John H. Winder was doomed to the lower field-officer ranks, and that is that he was what was called in published books of those days a son of a b—, but only behind his back. So, he went South, behind their backs, and almost immediately became an acting brigadier general of volunteers in the Provisional Army of Virginia.[2]

June 25, 1861, was a very strange day in Richmond, almost eerie, in that no one was arrested. It was as if the city was intuitively saluting the coming man, John Winder, for that very day he was assigned to duty as acting inspector general of posts, with his headquarters at Richmond, his job being to inspect the several camps in the vicinity of the Confederate capital. It was while in this important position that he would take on more and more responsibility for the city of Richmond; other officers would send things his way, things they couldn't be bothered with, until, very quickly, and before anyone had time to realize what was going on, General Winder had built up a substantial power base.[3]

For John Winder's career, this all dovetailed nicely into the dangerous fact that the Confederate army was now so busy fighting out in the field that they could no longer handle one of the absolutely critical jobs they were charged with: the defense of Richmond and keeping order within the capital. So, on October 21, 1861, the Confederate War Department created a separate government organism to handle that: the Department of Henrico, meaning the city of Richmond and the surrounding Henrico County. The man placed in charge that same day, as the commandant of the department, was General John H. Winder. Included in his responsibility were garrison troops, city guard, militia, police, hospitals, prisons, warehouses, training camps, government administrative buildings, and the Passport Office. John Winder was now, in effect, the lord protector of Richmond, defending the capital from within and from without. With this position came immense power, so much so that who was going to defend Richmond from General Winder, if it ever came down to that?[4]

As Tim was crossing the lines he was stopped by a Confederate picket, and arrested on suspicion. He talked his way into an interview with the officer of the post, to whom he showed packages of quinine and percussion caps, which he claimed he had been empowered by the Confederate government to purchase in the North. The officer sent him to the commanding general, who in turn sent him under guard to Richmond, where he was released. Later that night he went to the offices of the *Richmond Enquirer* and

Gen. John H. Winder (Library of Congress).

gave the foreman there a bundle of Yankee newspapers in exchange for copies of the *Enquirer* and other Richmond journals.[5]

One reads this from the December 11, 1861, entry in *A Rebel War Clerk's Diary*: "Several of Gen. Winder's detectives came to me with a man named Webster, who, it appears, has been going between Richmond and Baltimore, conveying letters, money, etc. I refused him a passport. He said he could get it from the Secretary himself, but that it was sometimes difficult in gaining access to him. I told him to get it, then; I would give him none."[6]

From his wording J.B. Jones does not seem to remember Webster from that occasion when he first met him just over a month earlier. Mind you, he saw a lot of men each and every day, and could hardly be expected to put a name to every face.

If the clerk was truly writing in real time, on that date, then one has to wonder why he was so hostile to Webster, a man who could charm Confederate buzzards out of the trees. And why be hostile at all if Tim was in the company of several of Winder's detectives? And why hadn't he been hostile that first time he met Tim, the previous month? It makes no sense at all. On a good day one shouldn't trust the rebel war clerk, for, as he himself admitted, he tinkered with his book in 1865–66, just before publication. So, the reason this diary entry doesn't make sense is that it was doctored after the war, for his own reasons. "Doctored," that is, not "created"; the essence of the entry is undoubtedly true because December 11, give or take a few days, has to be the date Tim arrived in Richmond. A pass would be the most pressing thing on his agenda; without that little piece of stiff brown paper he couldn't travel anywhere. So that would be one of the very first things he would attend to upon reaching Richmond.[7]

We know that, soon after arriving in the Confederate capital on this particular occasion, Timothy Webster met General John H. Winder for the first time, and that the two men hit it off immediately. So much so that Winder entrusted Tim with a very important message to take North. Verbal or written, we don't know, but it was for his son, the Artillery captain, William A. Winder.[8]

After a very brief trip, including only three complete days at the very most in Richmond, Tim got back to Washington on December 16. The following day Pinkerton, after transcribing his operative's field report into a more readable form, sent it off to his eagerly waiting boss, General George McClellan. Six days later, on the 23rd, Tim Webster found Captain William

Winder, U.S.A., at Mrs. Hutton's boarding house and gave him his message from the dictator of Richmond.

One may wonder why it took a week for Tim to get that message to Captain Winder. One would have thought he would have delivered it a lot earlier, by, say, the 18th of the month at the latest. We don't have the answer to this question. He might have been delivering his messages alphabetically, or, since it was imperative that Tim be physically present at that meeting with the captain, a more likely scenario, in view of later developments, is that he had just been lying comatose in bed all that time.[9]

13. The Third Trip

It was Christmas morning in Washington City. The momentous year of 1861 was coming rapidly to an end, which is a lot more than can be said for the bad will among men that had ruined that great dream the Founding Fathers had had four score and five years earlier. Now, Union troops were encamped around the capital to protect it from the ever-present threat posed by their Southern brethren. So much for a ninety-day war. As it turned out, it would be the quietest and most orderly Christmas Day the capital had seen in ages. At Pinkerton's headquarters, Timothy Webster was busy making final preparations for his third trip to Richmond.[1]

On his previous two trips Webster had fallen into the routine of courier-spy, carrying "numerous letters from Northern residents to their Secessionist relatives in the South, and then, upon returning, he had delivered communications from Southern people to individuals north of the line." More boring letter-carrier than exciting spy, as it would turn out, when all was said and done at the bitter end; and not so much spying, rather a great deal of mundane social intercourse and lying dangerously sick in bed. But life has its built-in compensations; otherwise secret agents couldn't survive as a species. Not long from now this particular U.S. mailman would just die from all the excitement.[2]

So, Pinkerton's number one male operative left the District of Columbia on December 25, bound first for Fredericksburg, Virginia, where, par for what would very soon become the course, he spent New Year's Day prostrate in bed. Lying there, with nothing to do but doze, gave him the opportunity to examine for the first time a package he had stumbled across in a cabin at Monroe's Creek on his way down. It turned out to be a set of very revealing maps of Washington defenses quite obviously given to some Southerner or other by a traitorous Union officer. It was immediately clear that this package had to be gotten to Pinkerton at the first opportunity. How extraordinarily lucky that the reb had just left it there, in that cabin, to be discovered, and that it should have been found by none other than Timothy Webster, Pinkerton man. How clever of Tim to have picked up a package that might well have contained nothing but a dead fish. How strange that he hadn't at least opened it a little bit back there in the cabin, just a corner perhaps, and taken a sniff. Or maybe he had. The next day, January 2, Webster was out of his sick bed and on the train to Richmond. After making arrangements to obtain passes from the Confederate secretary of war, to enable him to travel to Nashville and to Manassas, he went to the Monument Hotel, that well-established hostelry fronting immediately on the west corner of Capitol Square, at the corner of Ninth and Grace, where he engaged a room for himself, and "where he found Mrs. Lawton, who had remained in the city during his absence." Why not the same room? Ah, one has to fight, and push, and shove, in order to clear a path through Pinkerton's phony prudery.[3]

The Monument Hotel, no more than what today would be called a bed and breakfast, but with a good view of the lower city and a great view of the river, had been known as the Washington House until proprietor Major John Talman, a "monument of good old-fashioned landlords," renovated it, changed its name in honor of the nearby Washington Monument rather than of himself, and re-opened it for boarders and visitors on Wednesday, August 10, 1853.[4]

Later in his book, when discussing Webster's fourth and final trip, Pinkerton refers to Hattie as "my resident operative, Mrs. Hattie Lawton." By "resident operative" it is clear that what Pinkerton means is that Hattie had, over the course of the last few months, actually lived in Richmond, on and off. And Beymer's article in 1910, fed to him by Billy Pinkerton, says: "Hattie Lewis, a young woman member of the Secret Service. She had already been in Richmond several times and had been of help to Timothy on one of his previous visits." By "one of his previous visits," Billy is presumably referring to Webster's third trip to Richmond. And the phrase "several times" implies, well, "several times."[5]

And one can tell by Allan Pinkerton's wording, when discussing Tim's third trip, that Hattie had been there during at least part of Webster's second trip and ever since then. She "had remained in the city during his absence." The question is: When did Hattie become a resident agent in Richmond? The answer has to be around the time of Tim's very brief second trip. She might even have actually accompanied him South on that occasion. This is what Billy Pinkerton has to say in his *Inter-Ocean* interview in Chicago in 1897: "At the request of Webster, Hattie Lewis, a woman of great capacity, was sent to Richmond to help in the work. She posed as his niece, and in his absence gathered many important items of information. I recollect staying up all night on many occasions for the purpose of copying letters that had been brought through the lines, which we opened and re-sealed with counterfeit seals." Or, as Billy put it in his 1898 interview: "Hattie Lewis, a clever federal operative in Richmond."[6]

Now, on January 2, 1862, at the Monument Hotel, Mrs. Lawton informed the newly arrived but depressingly sick Webster that she had just received a visit from Mr. Stanton, another Pinkerton operative. This Stanton had arrived at Richmond from Nashville after a spying tour of the South and was going to attempt to leave for Washington that night. Tim sought Stanton out, found him, gave him the very important package to give to Pinkerton, then went back to the hotel and to bed.[7]

When Tim Webster awoke next morning, he was unable to move, and was forced to remain in bed for the next four days.[8] Tim was suffering from an undetermined illness that would affect him severely in the coming months.

As a follow-up to the adventure of the stolen defense plans, we find, in *The Spy of the Rebellion*, that operative Stanton succeeded in getting through the lines with the package Tim had entrusted to him, the result being that, thanks to the sheer genius of Allan Pinkerton, James Howard, a clerk in the provost marshal's office in Washington City, was found to be the traitor and the Union was saved. This case should be of monumental importance, but oddly, not a single mention of it is to be found anywhere in the hugely long January 31, 1862, report written by Pinkerton to McClellan on the subject of Webster's third trip to Richmond, not even when he talks about Tim's activities at Monroe's Creek. The truth is, this whole episode with the package is a fiction created by Pinkerton during an all-too-common fit of self-glorification. No such package ever existed. No Stanton ever existed. And no such traitorous clerk existed; well, not exactly.

Back in February 1861, in Chicago, Pinkerton had been forced to bring charges against his bookkeeper and operative, a clerk named—yes, you guessed it—James Howard. Mr. Howard, an Englishman, had been with Pinkerton for four years, had been a long-term guest in his house, had shared his meals, and wound up embezzling over $800 from him. Pinkerton was memorializing his treachery.[9]

Finally, on January 7, Tim managed to get up and set out for Nashville, in company with William Campbell, who had concluded a deal with the Confederate government to furnish "5000 Knapsacks to be made of canvas & painted black with leather straps; together with the Belts, bayonet Scabbards &c; said Campbell then being on his way west for the purchases of leather from the extensive tanneries in Knoxville, Chattanooga & Nashville, to enable him to complete his contract with the rebel government." That same day, or very close to it, Hattie also left Richmond, but going the other way: North. She had been ordered on another mission, to Leonardtown, Maryland, where she "assiduously cultivated the acquaintance of the most important people in that locality, whose sympathies were with the Southern cause, and whose assistance to Webster and herself would be valuable in time of need." One of these wealthy and highly placed Secessionists was "Washington Gough ... who was one of the most active in his efforts to assist the Southern blockade-runners in crossing over into Virginia, and in eluding the watchfulness of the Federal pickets." Gough seems to have been an old friend, and a very good one, of Timothy Webster, and it was now at Gough's enormously impressive home that Hattie was invited to stay while she was in town. Using her "charms of manner and conversation" she was "enabled to acquire much valuable information from those who sought the aid of Mr. Gough in obtaining the facilities for reaching the rebel lines in safety." Webster and Campbell meanwhile arrived at Lynchburg at the end of their first day's traveling.[10]

The two boon companions arrived at Abingdon, Virginia, in the very early hours of the morning of January 8, with Tim so ill he had to lay over there for 24 hours. After he had recovered somewhat, they continued their peregrinations, finally returning to Richmond on January 21. Tim left the Confederate capital on the 24th. He had spent only two complete days in Richmond during which he wasn't lying flat on his back in bed, sick. He got back to Washington on January 30, 1862, to complete his third trip, and reported to Pinkerton, who that very day wrote a brief report to McClellan of Webster's latest adventure.[11]

14. The Fourth Trip

Give or take twenty-four hours, the last day of January 1862 was when Timothy Webster set out on his fourth trip to Richmond. He decided to take Hattie Lawton with him, but first he needed Pinkerton's permission. He "received his chief's ready assent" and set out for Leonardtown to ask his trusty partner if she would like to come. She did. And so, under cover of dark they made their way to the banks of the Potomac. An oyster boat was waiting there, as arranged, and in it was an oysterman with pole in hand. Hattie was wearing one of Tim's overcoats and felt hats. She looked like a man, at least to the untrained eye.[1]

There was no traffic that night, nothing on the water at all, and so Webster and the girl, as Beymer calls her, were able to cross the river together in safety. However, just as the boat was nearing the opposite bank the moon broke through the clouds and there they were, on a brightly lit stage, with nowhere to hide, three characters in search of an audience. But there were, indeed, theatregoers out there that evening, or at least there were meant to be. Rebel pickets by trade. Friends of Webster's. It had all been arranged; they would help him unload from the boat, and then ease him and his companion on their way. So it should have been peachy. But it wasn't. Something had gone wrong. Bad reviews, perhaps.

By the lights on shore they could make out the picket stations, and Tim yelled, "Pickets! Pickets!" But there was no answer, and not a soul was to be seen. The silence was eerie, and unexplainable. And then suddenly, in one swift and dangerous second, the lights went out, and the oysterman went into hysterics, assuming this to be his last moment on earth. Webster calmed him down and then continued shouting for the pickets. Still no response from the shore.

It was now obvious, as the boat bumped up against the side of the river bank, that they were on their own, and so Tim was forced to help the boatman off with the trunks. That didn't take very long, and then the vessel slid away into the night.

Trunks, in the plural, is what we're told. That means two at least, but exactly how many we don't know for sure. And they must have been big and heavy because it took both men to unload them from boat to bank. These trunks contained not only the mail but articles that Tim had promised to acquire for several Richmonders, Fredericksburgers, and other people along the way. He was no longer just a letter carrier, he was Santa Claus. Two spies lugging large, unwieldy trunks with them into enemy territory! It's almost a joke. Two Yankee tourists on vacation in the Sunny South. Taxi!!

With the oysterman now out in the middle of the river, on his way back to the other side, that left only Tim and Hattie, standing there, on a cold night just as February was rolling around, not really knowing where to go or what to do. No one was there. It was pretty lonely by the river that night, especially with the picket station lights having been so mysteriously extinguished. And what made it worse was that they had these infernal trunks. Let's hope, for their sake, that it was no more than two. But even two; how the deuce were they going to handle that?

"Webster and his companion wandered about for more than an hour, and it was nearly midnight when they came to a farmhouse." Unfortunately, we're not privy to the method they used to overcome the overwhelming logistical problem of the trunks, but everything in this tale points to dragging. Tim was a strong lad, all right, but not so strong that he could carry two trunks. And Hattie certainly couldn't have carried even one. So they had to have dragged them, over whatever terrain presented itself. One thing's for sure: Pulling the trunks like that, even if they had been on wheels, there's no way, in that sixty minutes, that they could have covered any more than a mile from where the oysterman had dropped them off.

So, there they were, approaching the farm house, hauling those ridiculous trunks. No wonder the dogs were going crazy. Sooner or later a very pumped-up farmer was going to appear on the scene with a shotgun, and was going to shoot first and ask questions later. After all, this was 1862, there was a war going on, and it was night time. But that's not what happened exactly. "The noise of the dogs brought the farmer to his door, who demanded in no very gentle terms, to know who they were and what had brought them there at that unseasonable hour. In a few words Webster explained the situation, and the genial farmer bade them welcome, and safely bestowed them for the night."

They had hardly even collapsed on the bed when there was a loud knocking at the front door. It was the "pickets from the adjoining camp." They had been ordered to find out who these two strangers were and to bring them before an officer of the guard, who was two miles away.

"Why didn't you tell them that, when they called out to you before?" That's the farmer speaking "in a contemptuous tone" to the soldiers. It's his first recorded dialog in this French farce, and he's speaking English.

"Well, we didn't know who they were, and we didn't think it was safe."

"Oho, you were afraid of them, were you, and ran away."

Then Webster appeared at the door. "Tell your commander that I will not stir from this house until morning. My name is Timothy Webster. I am in the employ of the Confederacy, and if you had answered my call there would have been no difficulty."

And so the men obligingly left, presumably to face the ire of their officer of the guard. As for the farmer, he seems to have been a rare man indeed not to have been panicked into saying something like, "Now look here, I'm sorry, you two, whoever you are, you'll have to leave this house now. I will not put up with this sort of thing." One wonders what happened next between the farmer and his two guests. Tim had a beard, sure, that's fine, but what about the other fellow? Fresh-faced, hmmm, something else about him too, a few things, in fact, hmmm. The farmer must have thrown a surreptitious glance here, a furtive look there. He wouldn't have been human if he hadn't. Yes, things were certainly not quite what they seemed here. But, this Webster was a big boy, and perhaps it was best to let sleeping dogs lie. And so they all went to bed.

The following morning Tim presented himself at the army camp, and, obviously finding no satisfaction from the officer of the guard, demanded to see the commander, Major Beale. But Beale himself was actually stationed twenty miles away, and so the Confederate uniforms had to telegraph him. Happily, they had access to a telegraph. And so, equally fortunately, did Beale, for the reply came back, "Let Webster go where he pleases."[2]

Later that "cold and stormy day," Tim and Hattie set out for Fredericksburg. We are not told how they got there, but it was presumably not by walking along the roads, which, as Pinkerton tells us, were "in a wretched condition." In Fredericksburg Tim made deliveries of "letters and merchandise, which he had brought for residents there," showing that, yes indeed, he and Hattie had managed to haul those trunks along. Ah, to be a secret agent!

The next segment of Tim and Hattie's adventurous and hazardous trip to the Confederate capital is covered by Pinkerton in these words: "He pushed on to Richmond."

They checked into the Monument Hotel and resolved to do nothing until the morrow, when they would begin their operations. During the night, Tim's "old malady" came upon him again, so much so that come morning he was unable to move. This time it was for good, that is if what Pinkerton has led us to believe about the malady is true. The next time Tim would get out of bed for anything much more meaningful than a trip to the bathroom would be three months hence, and that would be for a far more bracing walk, the last walk of his life, a walk to the gallows. For Webster, 1862 was rapidly turning into a bum year.[3]

"This was the state of affairs on the last day of January.... From this time I heard nothing further from him directly."[4]

15. Lewis and Scully

From then on the days went by slowly for Tim and Hattie, cooped up in their Richmond hotel room as they were, but for Pinkerton time changed its shape as it normally relates to the universe, so much so that, as he waited impatiently in the North for messages from his two agents, each day stretched out into an eternity to threaten his integrity as a story teller. He claims that "for weeks" he remained utterly ignorant of Webster's movements or condition. He then goes on to say, of his spy: "Hitherto his visits had not occupied more than three or four weeks," and "As the days and weeks passed, and brought no tidings from him, my apprehensions became so strong that I resolved to send one or two of my men to the rebel capital, in order to ascertain the cause of his unusual and long-continued absence."[1]

On the surface what Pinkerton writes sounds reasonable, but only because the tone is so authoritative. He makes it sound as if Tim and Hattie had been missing in action for six or seven weeks, even a couple of months, but it's all a Pinkerton sleight of hand. The reality is that, by the time Pinkerton started to panic, according to him, anyway, it could only have been a week or so since his star agent had arrived in Richmond. That's no time at all, under any circumstances. So the question should not so much be: Why should Pinkerton begin to grow alarmed?, but: Is there something else behind this story, something we're not being told? Is this a blind? Was there another reason he decided to send men down to Richmond? The answer is yes, and he's going to tell us what that reason was. But beware! He's going to top even himself. He's going to give us not one reason, but two, and then another and another, until all we can do is laugh grimly as we stumble, fatigued, along the Via Ridicula.

"My anxiety was equally shared by General McClellan, with whom Webster was a great favorite, and who placed the utmost reliance on his reports. One evening, early in February, the General called on me and advised the sending of one messenger, or two, for the sole purpose of hunting up Webster, or finding some trace of him." Well, well, so now it was McClellan's fault. But was it, really? Is this just another Pinkerton deception? The same argument applies to McClellan as it did to Pinkerton: Why should either one of them have had any anxiety at all about Tim's silence if Tim had only been away such a short time? But the way Pinkerton tells it, it sounds feasible, since McClellan was about to make a forward movement at last, and would have welcomed up-to-date information, probably information of such a nature as would have given him justification for not making that much-talked-about forward movement. A clever lie always and obviously has the ring of truth to it.[2]

And that leads to a question that has often come up, one that serves the additional purpose, here anyway, of clearing our brain for a few minutes before we resume the strenuous task of trying to penetrate Pinkerton's:

Gen. George McClellan (photograph by Mathew Brady, 1861, Library of Congress).

How effective were these Union Secret Service agents during the first year and a half of the Civil War, particularly in their estimates of Confederate troop strength at any given time? Did Pinkerton and his spies so shockingly overestimate the Confederate numbers as to scare McClellan half to death? Is that why the Union general didn't march until March of 1862? Could the war have been won there and then, in late 1861 or those first couple of months of the following year, if only Little Mac had been Big Mac and just marched? Debate rages, but that's nothing new. The May 3, 1862, issue of the *National Republican*, one of the major District of Columbia newspapers, would report the execution of Timothy Webster in Richmond, and then go on to say, in answer to the question, What if the Federal Government should commence hanging spies?: "If our Government commences hanging, they had better begin with some of their own, who acted last winter in the interest of the rebels, by making false reports of the enemy's strength." It is clear that this press barb was being launched at Pinkerton. And that makes one think about war crimes. Should a man be hanged simply because he is inept? That's a bit draconian under normal circumstances, probably, but in the case of Pinkerton, whose misinformation almost certainly prolonged the war for four unnecessary years, and caused half a million deaths...[3]

So here we get a bird's eye view of Pinkerton trying to shift the blame onto McClellan, or at least some of the blame, for what happened next; and what happened next, according to Pinkerton anyway, was a tragic example of peer pressure and human weakness. It would be no surprise to learn that the general was, indeed, pushing the detective chief for information, but Pinkerton was quite capable of resisting pressure, from absolutely anyone, including his boss McClellan. We have several examples of this. So why did he buckle now? It is, in fact, hardly likely that he did. Another sleight of hand.

That means there was another reason for all this. The digging continues, it has to, the uncovering of one layer of Troy after another, until you begin to wonder if it will ever end. But here's another layer. It could not have escaped Pinkerton's attention that Tim was a disastrously sick man, terminal even, so perhaps Pinkerton had a nasty presentiment that his agent had died out there in the field. One has to wonder. But, whether something like that was running through his mind or not, to send another agent or two into Richmond, just to check, was criminally irresponsible. One must remember that Pinkerton had several agents, resident and otherwise, in Richmond. One of them would have been able to get a message back to

Washington, surely. If Tim was dead, then he was dead; there was nothing Pinkerton could do about it except adjust plans. But if Tim was alive, then he probably wouldn't be for long, not with tourists breezing into Richmond looking for him. It was obvious that Pinkerton was quite possibly signing the spy's death warrant. But Pinkerton did it, and paid the price in guilt and remorse for the rest of his life. Or did he? Is this just another layer of lies?

Another question that has long been asked is: Why didn't Hattie, specifically, get a message out to Pinkerton, letting him know what had happened? But that question has always been predicated on some degree of belief in Pinkerton's written word, a belief we all have to maintain, to some extent, in this case at least; otherwise there's not much of a story. Thomas Kane Harnett was one of the first to try to provide an answer: "Perhaps she was too frightened, or perhaps she feared sending a message through uncertain emissaries." But the inescapable fact is that not even two weeks had gone by, so why would it have even crossed Hattie's mind? Especially with the medical emergency she had on her hands right then.[4]

Pinkerton sent for two of his agents, Pryce Lewis and John Scully, both men in their early thirties. They "knew Webster well, and were experienced spies, men who had already proved their worth in the service." Scully, an Irish cop by mentality, married with a growing family, had been with Pinkerton since the late 1850s. Pryce Lewis was single, an immigrant from Wales. He had been on at least one spying tour south of the Mason-Dixon Line. As for why Pinkerton had brought these two men into his office, it was all about Webster and his mysterious silence, according to the Pryce Lewis "memoirs," which have Pinkerton explaining: "I think he is sick." Lewis and Scully's job was to find out what had happened to Tim and Hattie, and also to gather the latest information to help General McClellan's planned forward movement. After that, their missions were to become separate and distinct. Scully was to bring the military information back to Pinkerton immediately, while Lewis was to go off on an extended jaunt around the South, just spying in general and providing good cheer as only a man with a Welsh accent can do. At least this is the account we're given in *The Spy of the Rebellion*, an account which is parroted by the Pryce Lewis "memoirs."[5]

On or around Tuesday, February 18, 1862, Lewis and Scully, dressed in their newly purchased ready-made suits, left Washington for Richmond. They were accompanied part of the way by operative William H. Scott, who was acquainted with the Federal commanders, and who was to get the two men across the Potomac into the South. This was the opening gambit of the latest significant move in the Great Game.[6]

Lewis and Scully would have been gibbering idiots had they not been fully aware that what they were doing was the height of folly. The Pryce Lewis "memoirs" claim that he, Pryce Lewis, hero, stood up to Pinkerton, told the old man it was too dangerous to go down to Richmond, that they were bound to be recognized sooner or later, he and Scully, and then the fat would be in the fire. But you either stand up to someone or you don't.[7]

As the two spies were making their way South, each carrying a large valise with a six-shooter in its outside pocket, Webster was confined to his bed at the hotel in Richmond, suffering excruciating pain and unable to move, his only consolation being Hattie. Through "the long, weary days and sleepless nights, no patient ever had more careful nursing, or more tender consideration than did Timothy Webster, from the brave, true-hearted woman who had dedicated her life and her services to the cause of her country and its noble defenders."[8]

Again, with this whole Lewis and Scully episode, we find ourselves at the mercy of that arch-fabricator, Allan Pinkerton. We have dug through layer after layer of lies, and still nothing sounds even halfway right. In so many instances in Pinkerton's books we have no other source to go to, yet fully aware of the dangers of this, we go on with the story anyway because we have no choice. It's either Pinkerton or no story at all. Sometimes however, there are other voices, and occasionally they contradict *The Spy of the Rebellion*, especially if the possessors of those voices hated Pinkerton's guts. That's not to say that there weren't thousands and thousands of persons who hated Pinkerton, it's just that there haven't been many who have taken up the pen to express themselves publicly. And of those who have, not all are particularly intelligent. One of these, perhaps the most strident, is Pinkerton's son Billy.

Billy it is who gave us the name Hattie Lewis, and there's nothing wrong with that. He also gave us Harry Knipe, as well as the names of a bunch of other operatives. Billy is not afraid to say what's on his mind either. Billy Pinkerton was not a particular believer in that old saying, "If you don't have anything nice to say about someone, don't say anything at all." That's a plus in many ways; it can benefit historians, anyway. In 1883, when he was interviewed for the article that became "Famous Detectives," this is what he had to say about how Lewis and Scully were brought into the tragic picture: "By 1862 the business which Webster had to attend to had increased to such proportions that it became necessary to send him some assistance." Lewis and Scully were "instructed to act in conjunction with Webster." Billy continues: "It was through this necessity, and the circumstances accidentally growing out of the arrangements made by the Detective Agency, that Webster's real character and business became known, and he made to suffer the extreme penalty."

Fourteen years later, in his 1897 *Inter-Ocean* interview, Billy said this: "In the spring of 1862 Webster found that his work was getting too heavy, and suggested that assistants be sent to him." A year after that, in his 1898 interview with the *Chicago Evening News*, he expanded upon his version: Webster's "work as a secret service agent of the Confederacy was assuming large proportions, and he asked Secretary Benjamin to allow him a few assistants. This request was readily granted, and he was authorized to choose two helpers. His selection was, of course, made from among the trusted agents of the federal secret service bureau." It is interesting to read, in the *Richmond Examiner* of April 22, 1862, that Lewis and Scully admitted having been sent to Richmond by the Washington government to act as Webster's "aids."[9]

Billy shows no signs of hesitation, let alone shame, in telling a version so at variance with his father's that it could almost be two different stories. No one has ever questioned *The Spy of the Rebellion* on this issue, and so it's a luxury to have one more perspective. In this instance, it is one of those unsettling pronouncements that starts off looking like a joke but which, upon closer and closer inspection, becomes more and more credible until one winds up being prepared to believe it. At which point, what happens to your old view, the story you've never had reason to question until now? In a very small way it's like having your faith shattered; the good thing is, in this case there's another faith to replace it if you get stranded: The Gospel According to Billy.

In 1910, when Beymer was writing the story of Timothy Webster for *Harper's Magazine*, he was being spoon-fed material by his interviewee, Billy Pinkerton. This was only a dozen years after Billy had last promulgated his remarkable version of the story of Lewis and Scully, but that version is nowhere to be seen in the *Harper's* article, at least not with the naked eye. It's Allan Pinkerton's version all the way. Instead of wondering why Billy changed his story, it is much more comfortable and less time consuming to wonder why, in this instance, Beymer chose *The Spy of the Rebellion* over Billy Pinkerton.

So, on the one hand we have Allan Pinkerton's canonical version of how it came about that Lewis and Scully were sent to Richmond, and on the other we have the Gospel According to Billy, which we find in the Apocrypha that hitherto no modern historian has seen. The two accounts are very different. Which one is true? Well, surely the Pryce Lewis "memoirs" provide the unequivocal answer. They are, after all, Pryce Lewis's memoirs, aren't they? And Pryce Lewis was the man on the ground at the time. He would be the perfect arbiter, wouldn't he? Let's just see what the "memoirs" say. Ah, yes, if everything were that simple, we wouldn't have to put up with these difficulties.

16. The Pryce Lewis "Memoirs"

The Pryce Lewis collection, numbering about 200 items, was donated to St. Lawrence University by the St. Lawrence County Historical Association, who had, in turn, received it as part of a larger collection of the papers of history professor Harriet Shoen. The main feature of this collection is the Pryce Lewis "memoirs" as dictated in 1888 to David Cronin, the famous illustrator, and brought to light only in 1949, by Miss Shoen, a friend of Pryce Lewis's daughter. Miss Shoen spent a good part of her life trying to get these "memoirs" published. The "memoirs" consist of three notebooks, handwritten, presumably by Cronin as he listened to Lewis, with an astonishing amount of editing, both regular editing and copy editing, done by various hands, including Cronin himself, either on his own initiative or at the behest of Pryce Lewis. It is obvious that some fact-checking has been done as well, by someone.

At some stage someone made a typescript of all this. Well, not exactly "all this." It is a typed copy of the manuscript, yes, but it is a typed copy of the edited version of the manuscript. As always, it is best to go for the original document, so you can see what's been crossed out, what's been discarded, what's been changed, if different ink has been used and when, if there has been cutting and pasting of paragraphs. A warning about pagination: At the very best of times a manuscript and its typescript are two different animals, but in the case of the Pryce Lewis "memoirs," with so much editing having been done, not only is the typescript quite different from the original manuscript, the page numbers differ wildly. I use the manuscript page numbers.

Even before these "memoirs" are inspected, they warrant quote marks, to warn the reader that any such work, whether it be memoirs or a "diary," that takes a hundred years to surface has to be deeply suspect. That's not to say the basic draft of the Pryce Lewis "memoirs" wasn't written in the 19th century. It clearly was; you can tell by the spelling, if nothing else.

The university is the only place the general public can go to access the Pryce Lewis "memoirs"—manuscript or typescript—so it comes as a shock to discover that they do not have the original manuscript, merely a copy. This wouldn't be so bad if all of the original had been copied, but, unbelievably...[1]

Each page of the original handwritten text had at one time, to its left, a corresponding page of handwritten notes. This is obvious when you look at the manuscript owned by the university; the extreme right inch or two of the left-hand pages all managed to find their way under the lamp of the photocopying machine, so you get a taste of what's there. On some of these corresponding pages there were a lot of notes, on others there were merely some, and on others there seem to be none at all. The right-hand text-pages themselves were copied, of course, but whoever did the copying felt that the note-pages on the left were not worth the trouble. And maybe they weren't. It's just that it would have been nicer to have photocopied them so future readers could make their own mind up. The upshot is, we don't have those left-hand pages. On one or two occasions there were so many notes that they constituted more than one page; oddly these have been copied, being slipped in at the appropriate moment of the text, with no accompanying explanation, so that today, with no recent thought ever having been given to their purpose, a vague and uncomfortable puzzlement looms over them.

A good amount of these particular "memoirs" is nothing more than crude plagiarism of *The Spy of the Rebellion*, and is therefore useless, even as an entertaining read, and it's certainly not that. However, sometimes the "memoirs" depart from Pinkerton's book and go off into a unique Pryce Lewis narrative. When this occurs, it is usually for one of three reasons. The first is to narrate at extraordinary and tedious length some silly adventure populated with characters who are impossible to substantiate. This has obviously been done to flesh out the manuscript in order to make it of marketable length. The second is a rather sickening attempt to glorify and exculpate Lewis, mostly at the expense of Pinkerton and especially Scully. As will be seen, both Lewis and Scully, in 1862, behaved in a way that was less than honorable, so it would be greatly surprising to find that the dominant motivating theme of the "memoirs" was anything other than "Pryce Lewis: Hero." The third reason is when the writer, probably Lewis dictating to Cronin, tells something worthwhile. It doesn't happen often.

One may ask: If the author of the "memoirs" was, indeed, Pryce Lewis, as we're told, then why did he have to plagiarize? Why should he be reduced to such foul play? After all, he was the man on the ground, not Pinkerton. Why couldn't he have just told the truth? The answer is twofold: One, given his despicable behavior in Richmond in 1862, the truth would have hurt him and forced him to remove the word "Hero" from "Pryce Lewis: Hero." No publisher would have touched such a book, about such a miserable blackguard. And, from Lewis's standpoint, one must remember that to demonstrate himself as Hero was the whole raison d'être of the "memoirs." Well, aside from the possibility of picking up a dollar or two in royalties, and that brings us to the second reason. Pinkerton's book had already come out five years before Mr. Lewis is purported to have dictated these "memoirs," and since no one would have believed an account that differed in any substantial way from Pinkerton's, the compilers of the "memoirs" felt that they had little choice but to plagiarize. As can be seen at a glance, Lewis made an attempt to cover up his plagiarism, but like all but the most talented who commit this sort of theft, he was inept. He didn't realize that it's not so much the words that give the plagiarist away, it's the structure. One feels sorry for Lewis. He was caught in an impossible situation. He was a prisoner of his own impotence. In the end, though, his "memoirs" remain unpublished, simply because they are unpublishable.

It is beyond the mandate of this book to investigate the provenance of these "memoirs," but a researcher is certainly tempted to do so, if for no other reason than to set the record straight. It would be an easy enough task, if one had the will to undertake it. But until someone does, the item known as the Pryce Lewis "memoirs" is merely a source, and a crippled one at that, to be quoted or not, and so it doesn't really matter who, per se, wrote it, who edited it, or how many people contributed to it, and when. What makes the whole thing so depressing is (1) we have only half the "memoirs," (2) so much of it is plagiarized from Pinkerton's *The Spy of the*

Rebellion, and therefore almost useless, and (3) as a literary work, the writing is so bad, it's no wonder Pryce Lewis, David Cronin, Lewis's daughter, and Miss Shoen were never able to get the thing published.

17. The Two Most Inept Spies in the World

Lewis and Scully arrived in Richmond by train at about one o'clock in the afternoon on the 26th of February and checked into the Exchange Hotel. From there they set out on their mission to find Webster. The first place they made for was the offices of the *Richmond Enquirer*. Not too long before in the overall scheme of things, Tim had acted as courier for the proprietors of that newspaper, and now Pryce Lewis was carrying them a gift from the North, bringing new meaning to the expression "letters to the editor." The publishers were now in a position to repay all those kindnesses by putting Lewis and Scully on the right track.[1]

The two Pinkerton men were so elated at how easy their mission was proving that, fresh as a daisy and happy as a lark, and with no thought whatsoever for who might be watching, they proceeded along the sidewalks of old Richmond, straight to the Monument Hotel, demanding to be shown to Webster's room. It was what Pinkerton referred to as "a precipitate and unheralded appearance." A "negro boy led us up to his room, rapped, and opened the door." It was a "long, narrow room," and at "the farther end was a bed upon which Webster lay."[2]

"I recognized a lady I had before seen with Webster—Miss Hattie Lewis." This is from the Pryce Lewis "memoirs," and it's meant to be Pryce Lewis himself speaking. He has chosen a very strange way in which to introduce Hattie to his readers. It's as if he doesn't know she's a Pinkerton. The "memoirs" have her "sitting in a chair at the foot of the bed," but Billy Pinkerton, via Beymer, has her seated by the window, sewing. There was a third person in the room as Lewis and Scully burst in, a Mr. Pierce, who, according to *The Spy of the Rebellion*, was a "warm Southern friend, whose friendship for Webster was of long standing, and whose visits to the sick man were of daily occurrence." This Pierce was sitting at the side of the bed, says Beymer, and trying to cheer the invalid up. Pryce Lewis "advanced to Webster's bedside and we shook hands as old friends. Webster then shook hands with Scully," and introduced the two newcomers to Mr. Pierce. With Pierce just squatting there, right there, like a big toad in the middle of the road, and not going anywhere, the rest of them were forced to pretend they were just little frogs hopping around mindlessly, with nothing to do, and nowhere to go, barely alive stylized stage props who hardly knew each other.[3]

"I have a letter for you," Pryce Lewis finally told the sick man, and handed it over. The toad took the hint, and with Scully and Hattie "withdrew to a side window," while the Welsh postman "sat down beside the bed" and nattered to the English postman. "Lewis, why in h— did the old man send Scully here?" Lewis and Scully stayed an hour or more.[4]

The following day Lewis and Scully, "with rare fatuity" returned to Webster's hotel room. These fellows must have been pretty dim, that is if we're going to stick with Pinkerton's story. And, sick as he might well have been, what about Webster? How many mental pistons was he firing on? If it was so dangerous to be so overdosed by Lewis and Scully, did it never occur to him the previous evening to say to Lewis something like, "Never show your damned face here again"? And what about Hattie? If Tim couldn't demand that they leave, why didn't she take charge? Yes, Pinkerton has Tim warning Lewis and Scully to get out of Richmond, but not until the second day. Two and two are not adding up to anything like four here. According to the Pryce Lewis "memoirs" Scully alone went in the morning of that second day and spent hours and hours in Tim's room. Far too long. Again, why didn't Tim throw him out? That afternoon Lewis went for his turn, and found that Tim was entertaining a visitor, not the mysterious Mr. Pierce this time but Captain Samuel McCubbin, Jr., the head of General Winder's detective force, who, after the hello-how-nice-to-meet-yous, informed Lewis that he, McCubbin, was the occupant of the room next to Tim. It must have been nice for Tim to have such a good friend living right next door, stethoscope to wall if the need should ever arise, and a stalwart Confederate policeman at that. But worse was to come that day, in the form of a proclamation from President Davis that martial law had been declared in and around the cities of Norfolk and Portsmouth, not far away from Richmond, not far at all. Ominous in that the odds were it was going to happen in Richmond itself very soon, and that portended evil for any Yankee spies who might happen to go and get themselves caught.[5]

18. Things Go Horribly Wrong

It was the last day of February, Bad Friday. This wasn't the first time the president of the Confederate States of America had proclaimed a day of humiliation, fasting, and prayer, and it wouldn't be the last, by any means. And so, for this Friday fast, as for all such humiliation days, Richmond closed up, tight as a drum. It felt just like a Sunday, even down to church attendance, which was overflowing, of course, since the Richmond ramadaners, with no alcohol to sustain them through their trial, had nothing to do but get down on their knees and pray. It was on this day, for Lewis and Scully, for Tim and Hattie, for the whole U.S. Secret Service spy system then lurking in the South, that things started to spin out of control.[1]

The actual spin can be said to have had its origin a year before, on February 4, 1861, with the opening of the first session of the Provisional Congress of the Confederate States of America. Deputies and delegates traveled to Montgomery, Alabama, from seven of the Southern states, to establish the new country, to draft a constitution, establish a government, and to vote on issues such as president and vice president. Arriving two days late owing to traffic was the honorable gentleman from Florida: Jackson Morton, known to his friends as Billy.[2]

A lumber man, enormously wealthy, with a vast number of slaves, Billy Morton had been a U.S. senator back in the 1840s and '50s. He still maintained a home in Washington, at 288 Eye Street, and it was there that his wife and four children were living when war broke out in April 1861. Being the daughter of the late Colonel William Archer of Virginia, Mrs. Elizabeth F. Morton was as dyed in the wool a Confederate as Billy, and like a great many aristocratic Southern women living in the District of Columbia in 1861, and men too, she felt herself above the law and just couldn't keep her mouth shut. No wonder Pinkerton's Secret Service men searched her house. Operatives Lewis and Scully didn't find anything, but it was a very big house and took a long time to search. In that time the two detectives got to know the family quite well. That fact alone would, as it turned out, have terrifying consequences for everyone. Shortly after the search, Mrs. Morton was encouraged to leave the North, and in August 1861 she and the children took a flag of truce boat South, to meet up with her husband in Richmond, the new capital of the Confederacy.[3]

On February 17, 1862, the Provisional C.S. Congress was replaced by a more permanent C.S. Congress. The group of newly elected and re-elected members did not include Billy Morton, and it took the family several months to pack their things up and return to Florida. In the intervening time, on February 28, Mrs. Morton and one of her two daughters were walking along a Richmond street when they just happened to spot two men they knew only too well: the Pinkerton agents who had searched their house in Washington not too long before, Mr. Lewis and Mr. Scully. The two ladies rushed to Mrs. Morton's son, Chase, and he, in turn, made a beeline for General Winder's office. Spy alert. Spy alert. Confederate police officers were immediately put on the trail, and ran their quarry to earth in a private house. Here young Chase Morton was introduced into the presence of the guilty parties, much to their discomfort and chagrin. The two bumbling spies became so confused that they took off, leaving their overcoats behind. They ran fast, without swerve or falter, straight for the Monument Hotel, pursued by General Winder's detectives. The arrest at the hotel was made so discreetly that it would be another four days before even Tim and Hattie realized it had taken place, and they were in their room upstairs in the very same building when it happened.[4]

General Winder, "seating himself at his desk, made out a commitment consigning us to Henrico County Jail." In the early morning, just as February was ticking over into March on the calendar, Officer George W. Clackner and his men escorted the two prisoners to their new lodgings. When they arrived they found that the jailer was away uptown and had the keys with him, so, after some discussion, Lewis and Scully were put up in the guardhouse. For beds they were given soldiers' bunks, where they remained until daylight. They were awoken by some rough-looking enlisted men bearing coffee and breakfast, and at ten o'clock Clackner appeared, alone, to take them to the jail. Later that day Scully was committed to a place that, just at that very moment, was being born again as a prison, with the medieval name of Castle Godwin. Pryce Lewis was luckier; he got to stay where he was, in the granite and iron jail house.[5]

Castle Godwin, the "snug institution" hitherto known as McDaniel's negro jail, had been selected as a "secure retreat for the Unionists of Richmond, and for politically dispeptic [sic] characters from other portions of the State," and was located in the obscure Lumpkin's Alley, off Franklin

Street, opposite Wall. It contained thirteen clear and well-ventilated rooms, which had been provided with comfortable beds and other conveniences, "far surpassing in cleanliness and in comfort the accommodations offered at nine-tenths of the cheap boarding houses of Richmond." The establishment, which was of brick and of recent construction, was presided over by the brand new warden, George A. Freeburger, one of Winder's Baltimore boys, while an armed sentry kept guard over the main entrance to the prison. The prisoners were supplied with meals from Bradford's Eating Saloon.[6]

Daylight brought with it other activity, the most talked about being the fully expected presidential proclamation enacting martial law in Richmond; suspension of habeas corpus and civil jurisdiction in Richmond and for ten miles around the city. If Lewis and Scully had had any hopes of being tried as civilians, those hopes had just been dashed. They would now have to face a court-martial arranged by the newly appointed provost marshal.

Far worse than any of this, for the man on the street at least, was that martial law took away his booze, a drug without which he couldn't function. He couldn't function with it either, but at least he could get through the day. Now, with Jeff Davis demonstrating yet again his ignorance and intolerance of the human race, not only was it forbidden to distill liquor but the saloons were being closed as well. In order for a man to get a drink within

Jefferson Davis (Library of Congress).

the Department of Hen-rye-co he was now placed in the iniquitous position of having to make an effort. Stress on the "eff." Stress on the rye.[7]

Effective that very day, March 1, 1862, the office of provost marshal of Richmond was created by General John H. Winder, as one of the several sections of his Department of Henrico. As his first p.m. he named Captain Archibald C. Godwin, a Virginian, who, until then, had been the efficient commandant of the Confederate States prisons at Rocketts, just outside Richmond. At the same time, Samuel McCubbin, another Baltimore man, and hitherto leader of Winder's private police, was appointed Chief of the Provost Marshal's Police. In effect, he became what today might be termed Richmond's police chief. McCubbin's boys would take their first martial swagger out onto the streets of the city, complete with muskets, complete with imported percussion caps, on the night of March 3, 1862.[8]

Captain Godwin wouldn't last long in his new job. Three days; not a world's record, but close to it. On reflection, General Winder felt that Richmond, as a city, would be easier to run if it were split into two halves, the Eastern District and the Western District, with an assistant provost marshal in charge of each section. So Godwin took the east and Captain John C. Maynard the west, both men reporting to the new overall p.m. of Richmond, John C. Porter, who had been appointed a colonel only a few days earlier. This new arrangement went into effect on March 4, and news of it was promulgated on March 7.[9]

Of those who were wondering just what President Davis meant by the suspension of civil jurisdiction, none were giving it more thought than the jurists themselves. For one thing, would the civil courts cease to function? The Confederate States District Court, the Hustings Court, the Mayor's Court, the Appeals Court, and, to some extent, the Circuit Court of Henrico. It hardly seemed likely, given the depressingly large number of crimes of all sorts that needed to be prosecuted in the city every day, but it's all in the wording, and the wording on the proclamation scared the legal men; the last thing they wanted to do was get on the wrong side of Jefferson Davis. But it wouldn't be long before clarity came. Every Richmonder was awakened in the early hours of the morning of March 3 by the tremendous lightning and thunder and amazing volume of rain that fell in just two hours. Whether the judges in Richmond took this as a sign from Mr. Davis or not, they did suspend court until the morrow, when they hoped that someone or something might just get around to resolving the issue. Of course, everything worked out all right. It's all in the wording.[10]

Martial law, the press whipping the people up over spies, it was not a good time to be in Richmond if you were a Pinkerton operative. "The free and unrestricted access of Federal spies to this city ... exposed every act of the Executive, every movement of our troops." And this, much more menacing: "To ferret out these lurking foes and to prevent the prosecution of their operations here in future, was a matter of vital importance."[11]

19. That Letter Has Sealed My Fate

It wasn't just martial law the people of Richmond learned about when they opened their newspapers that morning of March 4, it was also the names of the captured agents: "Two Lincoln spies, giving the names of John Scully and Pryce Lewis, were arrested at the Monument Hotel on Friday last, and are now in prison. The proof of their connection with the secret service of the enemy is most positive." Both men protested that they were British subjects and that they were now claiming the protection of their government. Under ordinary circumstances, being a foreign national would have availed them little, if at all, but in 1862 the Confederate government was rather optimistically courting the British and the French, in the hopes that one or both of those powers would come into the war on the right side. In reality there was little chance of either doing so.[1]

Allan Pinkerton, aided by his creative dialog, covers the fateful moment that morning when two particular *Enquirer* readers learned of the arrest: "One day, Mrs. Lawton came into his room—as was her custom—but this time there was a gravity about her manner, which, to Webster's quick perceptions, boded no good. Finding him receiving some friendly visitors, the lady withdrew." Webster got rid of those friendly visitors as fast as he could and Mrs. Lawton again entered the room. Webster was impatient to hear the news.

"Be calm, my dear friend," said the devoted little woman, "what I have to tell you calls for the utmost calmness."

Webster was champing at the bit.

"Well," replied Mrs. Lawton, "I learned this morning that Lewis and Scully have been arrested, and taken to Henrico jail."[2]

Webster wanted to know when the arrest had actually taken place. "The very day they were here last."

Not having seen them for the last several days, and not knowing why, Tim had been afraid of this. At that moment he knew the jig was up for him too. "Then all is lost." Pause. "And now the time has come I will meet it manfully." He goes on, "It will be only a short time before I share the same fate."

"Why do you think so?" anxiously inquired Mrs. Lawton. "Surely they cannot connect you to these men."

Just at that moment, a cue in a play, Hark! I hear a knock on the door. And Captain Samuel McCubbin enters, stage right. He demands to be given the letter Lewis and Scully have brought Webster from the North, and Webster asks Hattie to give it to the detective. McCubbin exits, and Webster utters those six immortal words: "That letter has sealed my fate."[3]

20. Alone but for Specters

"That letter has sealed my fate."

If we go along with Allan Pinkerton's story and accept the existence of the letter, then that letter must have been designed to act as a bona fides, to prove to all and sundry Lewis and Scully's true gray colors. If so, it couldn't have been so much the letter, per se, that had sealed Tim's fate, since there could hardly have been anything compromising in it, either en clair or in code. What Tim must have meant was "McCubbin's taking of the letter like that has sealed my fate." But, when one is under pressure, one doesn't always strive for grammatical perfection. Of course, it was the taking of Lewis and Scully that really sealed Tim's fate, whether one subscribes to *The Spy of the Rebellion* or Billy Pinkerton's alternative version of this story. In Billy's version, the letter would not be needed, of course, since it was Tim who handpicked Lewis and Scully and Confederate Secretary of War Judah Benjamin who implicitly approved that choice. What better bona fides than that? With Lewis and Scully having been outed as Pinkertons, however, a similar fate was not far behind for Tim, no matter which way you look at it now or looked at it then. Regardless of whether one is an adherent of Pinkerton père or Pinkerton fils, Timothy Webster knew he was a dead man walking, or rather, in his case, a very sick man lying virtually comatose in a bed at the Monument Hotel in Richmond. Hattie too was a gone goose, unless she were to get out of Richmond immediately, out of Dixie while she still could. So why didn't she get out? That rhetorical question has been asked many times by insensitive scholars. A better question is: How could any operative, female or male, possibly have just taken off and left their dying comrade all alone to be captured by Hog Winder? What sort of person, aside from an insensitive scholar, would do that?

Once Tim heard of the arrest of Lewis and Scully, his "physical condition seemed to improve, and although depressed with fears for the fate of his companions, he gradually became stronger, and was at length able to leave his bed and move around his room." These things do actually happen.[1]

"The visits of his numerous friends had now almost ceased." He had become a social leper. That's because everyone knew: Don't be seen with this man, and if anybody asks if you're a friend of his, deny it, deny it, deny it. The black spot had been placed on his door. "From General Winder's officers, with whom he had previously been so intimate, he heard nothing, nor did they make inquiries about his health, as had been their custom." Only two friends still came by: The completely shadowy, as-if-he-never-really-existed Mr. Pierce and the awfully convenient "Mr. Campbell, with whom Webster had traveled for some time, and his family." This dropping away of old acquaintances, and the breaking up of old associations, "was significant to Webster of impending danger. It must be that he, too, was suspected, and that the favor of the rebel authorities had been withdrawn." Again, we don't know precisely where we are timewise, but it must be at least toward the end of the first week in March, maybe into the second week.[2]

"Day by day during his convalescence, did the brave little woman who had nursed him back to life, endeavor to encourage him to a hopeful view of his situation, and to impress him with her own sanguine trust for a favorable outcome from this present dilemma. Webster listened to the bright promises of his devoted companion, but he was too profoundly aware of the danger that threatened him to permit himself to hope that the result to him would be a beneficial one."[3]

On March 8, 1862, the day the Confederate Senate removed the word "acting" from Brigadier General John H. Winder's rank designation, the *Richmond Dispatch* lamented the fact that martial law, with its new regulations of search and seizure, had not been imposed earlier: "They would have kept from the Confederate capital a number of prowling Yankee spies who have passed with impunity from point to point throughout the South." Hang 'em.[4]

21. Mrs. Taylor

In the middle of March 1862, on or around the 14th, Tim and Hattie left the Monument Hotel after a residence there of a month and a half, and took a room at a rental house on 4th Street, in the block between Clay and Leigh, water and gas included.[1]

Mr. Walter Hanson Stone Taylor worked in the Second Auditor's Office, part of the Confederate Treasury Department. His wife, Harriet Beall McKall Taylor, managed the family's rental property; from the Taylor home on 7th Street, north of Leigh, it was only a short walk away, three blocks over and a block down, within sight of St. James Episcopal Church. Each and every room she rented out at the 4th Street house was entirely adequate for two persons.[2]

The Taylors, despite having eight names between them at all times, had managed to reproduce on several occasions, their most visible success being the twenty-five-year-old twins, Ann and Martha, who, in the most genteel and dignified way possible, ran about town doing good deeds and performing noble works because that's what ladies of quality and virtue did with their day. But, with energy and spare time outstripping the number of worthy projects currently available to them, the Misses Taylor stood in need of more solid substance to sink their teeth into. And so one can only imagine their relief when, at 4 p.m., on March 24, the great and the good of Richmond gathered together in the basement of the Broad Street Methodist Episcopal Church and formed the Ladies' National Defense Association. That very evening the association's board of directors appointed a committee, the Ladies' Gunboat Association, and these formidable women, including the twins, began to put into action a plan to go around the city, door to door, raising money to pay into a special fund in the Confederate Treasury Department, so that they could, in cooperation with the Navy Department, build a gunboat and place it in the James River in order to defend the capital against the Yankees if and when the time came. These two young defenders of the Cause would have been dreadfully annoyed to find that two Yankee spies had infiltrated not only Richmond but—ultimate insult—their mother's boarding house.[3]

22. Scully's Trial

William Wood Crump was forty-two, a colonel in the Confederate States Army, and, being judge advocate, a man upon whom it fell to act as state prosecutor on his share of courts-martial in his native Richmond. Two upon which he acted thus in the month of March 1862 were those of John Scully and Pryce Lewis, in that order. As for the other side of the table, for the up-front payment of $100 each in gold, both spies would be represented by John Harmer Gilmer, a prominent and very well-off defense lawyer.[1]

Beymer says, "Scully was the first to be placed on trial, and Webster was called on to testify; but Webster was too ill to be moved, and the court adjourned to his bedside to take his evidence." Pinkerton tells us that Tim had been staying at his new residence a mere two days when one of General Winder's men arrived to see if the invalid was sufficiently recovered to go out, "as his presence was imperatively demanded, at the court room, as a witness in the trial of John Scully." The officer told Webster that the request had come from Scully himself. But Tim wasn't up to it, so the officer left. The mountain would come to Muhammad; Tim's testimony could and would be taken at bedside.[2]

Two days later the court filed one by one into Tim's boarding house room. One of the group was the man under grill, John Scully. "Seating themselves around the bedside of the invalid, the court was formally opened, and Webster was requested to state what he knew of the antecedents of the accused. Though very weak and speaking with considerable difficulty, Webster made his statement." He had first met the man in Baltimore in April 1861, he told the court, and he, Scully, "was always in the company of known secessionists, and was considered by them to be a good friend to the South." Tim had always assumed that to be the case, he said, but did express surprise upon learning that Scully was now in Richmond. He had no idea that the man had ever been a government spy, which was a very good thing to volunteer, under the circumstances. "This was all that he could say, and although closely questioned by the president of the court and the attorneys present, he insisted that his knowledge of John Scully was confined to what he had already stated." Finding it impossible to obtain any further information upon this subject from the sick man, the court, in a body, left the room, and departed from the house. Mrs. Lawton, who had been compelled to retire on the entrance of the Confederate authorities, and who had been in a wild state of excitement and apprehension during their visit, instantly went back into the room, where she found that Tim had fainted, that he was limp and inanimate on the bed.[3]

There is nothing in the press or any documentation available to us to corroborate that this bedside testimony ever took place. We just have Pinkerton and his disciples to go by, and that's always dangerous.

As for Scully's court-martial in general, records of the event no longer exist, "and there is no other known account of Scully's defense"—other, that is, than Pinkerton's in *The Spy of the Rebellion*.[4]

23. Pryce Lewis's Trial

Thomas A. Staples was fast approaching the half-century mark, an epochal point in the average man's life when he is apt to do anything because nothing is surprising anymore; he has seen it all, but never done a damned thing. But Tom Staples was not your average man. For one thing, he was married to a woman half his age. On the morning of March 19, 1862, Mr. Staples set out, as usual, for his place of work. It is just possible that had his private life been more conventional, the enormous shock that awaited him when he got to the Henrico County Jail might have been averted. He discovered that there had been a mass breakout at about 9 o'clock the previous night. Nearly half of his guests had broken the lock off the door and simply walked out. One of the men who got away was Pryce Lewis, described as an Englishman, a very important prisoner about 22 or 23 years old, six feet tall, dark hair and whiskers, and a noted Abolitionist. It was the last-named feature that was sure to identify him, especially in the dark.[1]

By March 24, those escapees who had managed to remain at large after the first sweep of the keeper's broom were finally caught in the bushes, and that included the notorious "Price Lewis, New York spy" who, in recognition of his efforts, was taken from the jail on the 26th and committed to the more secure Castle Godwin.[2]

As soon as it was humanly possible, Lewis was "conducted to a room in the Court House," at City Hall, where the court-martial was already assembled. "The Court consisted of seven officers, besides the Judge Advocate. The President of the Court was a Colonel, the rest field officers of lower rank and line officers, some of them quite young. All were in full uniform, and impressed me as being intelligent and refined."[3]

The charges and specifications against Pryce Lewis were read. "The principal charge was being an alien enemy in the employ of the Lincoln Government, followed by a specification that on a certain day named, I was 'found within the fortifications of Richmond taking a plan thereof.'"[4]

The Pryce Lewis "memoirs" protest that this "specification was so false and absurd that I felt justified in pleading 'not guilty' to all of the charges and specifications which were of a similar tenor." One has to wonder what those other charges might have been, given that the lads had only been in town less than two days before they were bagged.[5]

The first witness examined was Mrs. Morton. Then came her daughter, and finally her two sons, Chase and Howard. "The taking of their testimony occupied the first day. They all swore to the circumstances [under] which they had met me in Washington." The next day the Military Governor of Richmond, General John H. Winder, appeared on the stand. "I was greatly surprised at his manner while testifying. He appeared confused and all mixed up—a blundering old man. His memory was very infirm; he told nothing straight, and testified to remarks made by me which I never uttered. I do not think he intended to lie, for he excused himself once for his inconsistent answers, and remarked that he could not remember all I said."[6]

The Pryce Lewis "memoirs" then go on to tell us who else appeared as witnesses at the trial: The detectives, George Clackner, Philip Cashmyer, and Samuel McCubbin. "Clackner testified as to the letter brought by Lewis to Webster and signed by Scott." The author of the "memoirs" then goes on to say that Clackner "swore that he knew Scott in Baltimore and that he was loyal to the South. This was the only evidence favorable to me."[7]

"Mrs. Morton was recalled and said I had behaved gentlemanly in her house."[8]

At the next session of the Court, Pryce Lewis was called as a witness in his own defense. His counsel asked him very few questions, "through the Judge Advocate, confining himself to our theory of defence." The prosecution was also satisfied with a few inquiries.[9]

The trial lasted only "four days," and Lewis felt that, aside from the rather strange Winder testimony, he had received a fair trial. On April 1, a couple of days after getting back to Castle Godwin, he was taken down the hallway of the prison to Scully's cell, to look after the Irishman, who was either ill or faking it, depending on whom you read. The next day Lewis too had reason to feel sick when he learned that he had been found guilty at his own fair trial, and that he, like Scully, would hang on April 4.[10]

24. The Priest, the Consul and a Deal

If they were to avoid the noose, the two boys needed all the help they could get, and that help would have to come fast. There were a few ways in which this could be achieved, but in none of them were the odds much in favor of Lewis and Scully. One of the ways was to wait and see if a presidential pardon arrived in the nick of time. But that was no way to run one's life—or death. Scully, being a Catholic, put his faith in God, and, according to the Pryce Lewis "memoirs," had Lewis dash off a letter for him to John McGill, Bishop of Richmond. As for his own salvation, Lewis, unfortunately, was a lapsed Baptist, and was reduced to writing to F.J. Cridland, the British vice consul.[1]

The man from the consul's office came, but, in matters of policy, a consul did not have his own voice; he merely represented his country. And, as far as the question of the American Civil War went, Queen Victoria's policy was neutrality. Sorry, old boy.[2]

That avenue being closed, there was still God. And then, suddenly, there he was, the man in black, standing in the doorway, offering the way. Or was he? Having come in on the wrong cue, the apparition vanished. But he had served his purpose. The appearance, premature or not, real or a mere literary device, was the only way the man in black, or anyone else, could reconcile the differences between Pinkerton's account and that detailed in the Pryce Lewis "memoirs."

Pinkerton: "You will not tell him what you know of Webster, and his connection with this matter, will you?" Did Pryce Lewis really say that to Scully when he learned that the Irishman was about to confess to a Catholic priest?[3]

Or did he say what Beymer has him saying? "Do not speak of Webster, John!"[4]

Pinkerton: "I don't know what I will tell him," answered Scully. "I have not decided what to say, nor do I know what I will be commanded to relate."

But, verily, Scully was lying. In very King James English too. For he had seen the way…[5]

Pinkerton: "For G-d's sake, Scully, don't say anything about Webster; we can meet our fate like men, but to mention his name now, would be wrong indeed."[6]

This reads like a joke today, just as it would have done in Victorian days.

Pinkerton: "I tell you," said Scully, "I don't know what I am going to say. I don't want to do wrong, but I cannot tell what I may have to do yet."[7]

Pinkerton: "Lewis argued with his companion long and earnestly upon this matter," and when at last the priest really and truly arrived, "and Scully followed him to another cell, the warning admonitions of his fellow prisoner were ringing in his ears."[8]

This is how the Pryce Lewis "memoirs" tell it, with Lewis as overweening hero: "Now, Scully," said I, "I do not want to interfere with your religion, but what about this confession? You are not going to say anything about Webster, are you?" He replied solemnly, "Let come what will. I shall not say a word about Webster." I believe he was sincere in this declaration. "That is right," I responded, "for it will do us no good, we are as deep in the mud as he in the mire. He had nothing to do with placing us in this condition. But if Allen [sic] Pinkerton were here I would not suffer for him an hour, for it was his downright outrageous lying that brought us here."⁹

The man in black was not God, of course, but neither was he one of General Winder's detectives posing as a man of the cloth, a silly rumor put about by Billy Pinkerton in later years. Augustine L. McMullen was actually a linguist, a former professor at Georgetown University, in the District of Columbia, a Marylander who'd gone South, a Jesuit priest not unused to being in a cell. On April 2 Father McMullen found himself in a new one. It was John Scully's. The British consul may not have been of any use to Pryce Lewis, but McMullen was the answer to Scully's prayer. One Irishman sent to another in time of great need. Forget last rites, Father, just get me the h— out of here.¹⁰

Bishop John McGill (Library of Congress).

The next morning, April 3, the day before they were to hang, the two great spies, without any torture being applied to them whatsoever, offered General Winder a bargain designed to save them from the hangman's noose. Winder heard them out, and accepted the offer. The deal was struck. And so Lewis and Scully spilled their guts, confessing that, yes, they were spies, but only little ones in the great game of cat and mouse. The big rat was

Webster, a spy of the first water. The two of them had merely been sent "by the Washington government to act as his aids." They intimated to Winder that the big rat "was playing a deep game."

Worse was to come. The two judases, in order for the deal to be consummated, had to be the star witnesses for the prosecution come trial time. Much worse, they would have to vomit their testimony all over the courtroom floor in front of the accused. Worse even than that, more than likely, was that General Winder was playing a deeper game than any of them. Things were not going to work out well for anyone. They never do when you ignore your Chaucer: He who sups with the Devil should have a long spoon.[11]

25. The Day They Came for Tim and Hattie

"Several days of anxiety and solicitude now passed. Unable to learn any tidings of his unfortunate comrades, Webster tortured himself with all manner of vague fears and doubts as to their probable fate, all of which had their effect in retarding his recovery, and keeping him confined to his room."[1]

This is Pinkerton writing, so one should automatically default to distrust. Given what we know about Webster, how amoral he was, how callous he had been over the well-being of Mary Ellen Bailey in Davenport, for example; his unfaithfulness to his wife, Charlotte, and to his kids; the mere fact that he was a spy; the only reason he would have tortured himself over the fate of Lewis and Scully, even if they'd been his best friends, would have been because he felt that their predicament might affect him, that they would squeal. But, having said that, why didn't he, Tim, do something about this fear, something proactive, instead of lying there in bed like a landed fish, doing nothing at all but waiting for the police to come? If he truly was sick all that time, why, Hattie was there to be used, and possibly other agents as well. But most of all there was Hattie, the trained and experienced resident agent. Surely, even under the difficult circumstances that obtained, one of them could have dreamed up a way for them both to get out of Richmond. If one relies on Pinkerton's narrative, it's as if Tim had given up. It's as if Hattie had given up too. Two agents of their caliber giving up at the same time? Hard to believe. These are just things to think about; to pursue them further would be to whistle in the dark.

It didn't make the Richmond papers, and there was no little cake with twenty-nine candles dotted around the top of it with red-faced everyone screaming "blow," but March 28 was Hattie's birthday. Mrs. Timothy Webster, Pinkerton agent. Stuck in a lousy boarding-house room in Richmond, Virginia, with a dying man, day in and day out, waiting for the sound of the measured tread on the stairs outside, the muffled footsteps of the undertaker's minions or, worse still, the jackboots of Winder's Germans.

Hattie brought the *Richmond Examiner* to Tim on the morning of April 3. The relevant item indicated that as a result of the court-martial, the two spies would hang on the morrow, April 4.[2]

"This filled the cup of Webster's misery to overflowing, and, sinking on a chair, he wept like a child. Refusing to be comforted, although Mrs. Lawton exerted herself to the utmost, Webster paced the room, half frantic with his grief, at the evil fate which had overtaken his friends. Slowly the day passed, and when the shadows of evening were falling Webster was at last induced to lie down, and attempt to catch a few hours sleep. He was soon slumbering quietly, although ever and anon he would start nervously and utter an inarticulate moan." A twelve-hour crying jag is a long one for anyone, especially a spy.[3]

If he could pace the room all day, crying like a baby, he could have escaped. If he was half as good an agent as we have been led to believe, then he could have waltzed out of Mrs. Taylor's house with Hattie on his arm, whistling Dixie, and been back in Washington within a week. But no. Pinkerton, our sole source for all this, has him behaving like a spoiled child, weeping, sobbing, going limp and inanimate or throwing self-indulgent and time-wasting tantrums, feeling sorry for himself, failing Hattie totally, not to mention himself and his boss, and possibly his country as well.[4]

No. No. There's something else here. This really doesn't make sense, doesn't add up, the way Pinkerton tells it, all this stuck in a guest room business, week after week, just waiting for the axe to fall. There's something going on we're not being told about. Is there something horribly unsavory about Webster that Pinkerton decided the world should never know? Something Pinkerton had to bury so deep underground that not even the left hand of God, plunged into the earth, could retrieve it?

General Winder's police, in the ominously Bavarian form of Philip C.

Cashmyer and his henchmen, arrived that night at Mrs. Taylor's boarding house on 4th Street. They had come for Tim and Hattie.[5]

The actual details of the taking of the two spies are recounted only by Pinkerton. We are totally at his mercy on this. There is no corroboration or account from any other source. One thing's for sure, though: Pinkerton has Tim and Hattie being taken at William Campbell's house. Forget that. That's a Pinkerton invention. But who knows, maybe the details themselves are more or less genuine.

So, striving for as much accuracy as we can by transmuting Herr Campbell into Mrs. Taylor, here we go, *The Arrest of Tim and Hattie*, a short play in one act, by Allan Pinkerton:

> [Tim lies prone on the bed, attended by Hattie Lawton. Mrs. Taylor suddenly enters the room, stage right, with a look of fear upon her face, which fills Hattie with alarm. The actors must be careful not to allow this scene to degenerate into cheap melodrama.]
>
> Hattie (hurriedly ejaculating) [Note: This is Pinkerton's stage direction, not mine:] What is the matter?
> Mrs. Taylor: One of General Winder's men is below, and I fear his presence indicates misfortune for Mr. Webster.
> Hattie: Who is it?
> Mrs. Taylor: Captain Cashmyer. He inquired for Mr. Webster, and says he must see him at once.
>
> [Melodrama piano music, "the villain approacheth." Webster, disturbed by this conversation, and probably by the music too, is awake in an instant and inquires what is wanted.]
>
> Mrs. Taylor: Captain Cashmyer has called and wishes to see you.
> Webster (hoping that Cashmyer might be bringing some tidings of Lewis and Scully): Let him come up at once.
>
> [Mrs. Taylor departs, and in a few moments returns with the Confederate officer. Cashmyer's salutation is cold and formal.]
>
> Cashmyer (without any preliminary): I have a painful duty to perform, Mr. Webster. I am directed by General Winder to arrest you, and convey you at once to Castle Godwin.
>
> [Cashmyer, being 21 when he immigrated to Baltimore in 1847, will still, after the intervening fifteen years, have a marked German accent. As he is speaking, two soldiers appear at the doorway.]

> Hattie: You cannot wish to take him away in this condition, and at this hour of the night. Such an action would be his death, and would be the worst of inhumanity.

[Webster stands silent and unmoved. He does not utter a word, but gazes fixedly at Officer Cashmyer, whose visits heretofore have been those of sympathy and condolence.]

> Cashmyer (looking at Hattie:) I cannot help it, my orders are to take him dead, or alive, and those orders I must obey.
> Hattie: Then I will go too. He needs care and attention; without it he will die, and no one can nurse him so well as I.
> Cashmyer (gazing at the brave little woman for a moment, probably out of admiration for her perfect grammar. A shade of pity comes over his face:) I am sorry to inform you that my orders are to arrest you also, and to search your trunks.
> Webster: This is infamous. What can Winder mean by arresting this woman, and what am I charged with that renders your orders necessary?
> Cashmyer: Webster, as God is my witness, I do not know. I only know what my orders are and that I must obey them.

[The end.]

Without further parley, Webster and Mrs. Lawton prepared to accompany their guards, and Cashmyer, demanding their keys, commenced a search of their trunks, which resulted in his finding nothing that would incriminate his prisoners.

A carriage was procured, and Webster was assisted into it, while Mrs. Lawton, under the escort of Cashmyer, was compelled to walk.

It was quite late when the carriage pulled up at Castle Godwin. Coincidentally, at that very moment, Pryce Lewis just happened to glance out of one of the prison windows and see Tim and Hattie get out of the carriage and walk through the gloomy portals of the prison. If this is true, then the carriage must have stopped en route to let Hattie in. She had, after all, started out on foot with Officer Cashmyer, as one is bound to recall. But the question remains: Why didn't Hattie get into the carriage at the very beginning of the trip? Pryce Lewis noticed that Webster "was well dressed but looked very pale and ill," and had to be helped from the carriage.[6]

General Winder was present when the two new prisoners arrived, and after a hurried examination, Webster, "pale and emaciated, and scarcely able to walk"—to quote Pinkerton—was remanded to a room in which a number of Union prisoners were already confined. Mrs. Lawton was conducted before the General, but she stoutly declined to answer a single question.[7]

Hattie was placed in a cell on the first floor of the prison, a room already occupied by "a rather fine looking lady" about 25 years old, Annie Scott, who despite her claim to be a Virginian and to have a brother in the Confederate army, had been caught crossing the Confederate lines around Leesburg and communicating with the enemy. General Hill had quite rightly ordered her arrested and sent down to Richmond. It is said that she was the first woman ever to be arrested as a spy by the corporate entity known as the Confederate States of America.[8]

Since March 4 Annie had been Castle Godwin's only female inmate. Now, all of a sudden, she had company. The two ladies would have plenty to talk about. Like Annie, Hattie had a brother in the army, except it was the other army, the Union army. No, it wouldn't be a good idea to chat about Harry. The jig would soon be up if she did that. But in the privacy of her own mind she knew the reality, and the way the war was going Harry might be dead by now. He might even have been shot by Annie Scott's brother, if she truly had one, that is.[9]

26. The Gag Order

When it came to the court-martial of John Scully in mid–March 1862, the Confederate government slapped a gag order on the Richmond press, and they kept that somewhat soiled handkerchief stuffed in the mouth of the newsmen until after Pryce Lewis's trial at the tail end of the month. Finally, on April 3 the *Examiner* had had enough and spat out the undigested parts of the rag, publishing what it had learned through the grapevine, that the two spies had been tried by court-martial and it "is said that they will be hung tomorrow, although the finding of the court is subject to the President's review."[1]

26. The Gag Order

Later that evening and over into the small hours of April 4, Tim and Hattie were taken into custody.[2]

There no longer being any need for it, the gag order was retracted, in time for all the other Richmond newspapers to offer up their voices in more or less exactly the same collective song.

The *Whig*'s vocal offering was a harmless little ditty: "For satisfactory reasons we omitted to mention in yesterday's paper that two spies named John Scully and Price Lewis had been tried by court-martial, convicted and sentenced to be hung this forenoon. The President has granted respite. The prisoners claim to be Englishmen, no doubt of Puritan stock."[3]

They could make all the little jokes they wanted to, but no one this side of dementia was laughing. It was a tame report toadying to the government, and offering little except a weak excuse for being beaten to the punch by the more ruthless *Examiner* of the day before. The *Dispatch* of April 5 wasn't so cringing: "For reasons satisfactory to ourselves, the principal one being the fact that the authorities were averse to any publicity being given to the affair, we have refrained for several days past from mentioning that two men, Pryce Lewis and John Scully, had been tried before the court martial, now sitting at the City Hall, and condemned to be hung as spies." The execution was to have taken place the day before, the 4th, at 11 o'clock in the morning, at the New Fair Grounds, the gallows having been erected there, but the grand event had been postponed for a short time on a respite granted the parties by the President, "but we are assured [it] will come off at an early day." The paper goes on to say, "It is intimated, and we believe on good authority, too, that the condemned have made disclosures affecting the fidelity of several persons, one or more of whom have been apprehended. Rumor had it yesterday that one of the parties thus implicated was an officer holding a place under the Government."[4]

The *Richmond Enquirer*, in its piece written on April 5, offered the bluntest of all the explanations: "We were informed, by undoubted authority, a few days since, that the two Lincoln spies, Price Lewis and John Scully, captured some time since in this city, were to be hung on [sic] yesterday, but being requested not to mention it in print, we refrained from doing so. As other city journals, however, have not observed the same secrecy, we now feel free to state that, though the condemned men have been respited for a few days by the President, they will certainly be hung. We learn that they have made certain important revelations implicating some very high functionaries in our government. This, however, we merely mention as a rumor."[5]

It wasn't just the Richmond newspapers that were making up for the lost time and opportunity that the gag order had imposed upon them; also living in the capital, either temporarily or more or less permanently, were special correspondents working exclusively for the larger provincial papers. The press corps they would be called today. No Yankees, of course. These reporters would write news articles of their own and send them off to their home paper using the quickest method possible. Such a man wrote his report on April 4, 1862, for the *Memphis Appeal*, in the days when the *Appeal* was still being published in Memphis. "The testimony so far given by the spies is not fully known to the public, but it is said to implicate persons in high position never before suspected of disloyalty." The only arrest the correspondent had heard of as having been made in consequence of these disclosures was "of a man named Webster, who has been engaged for six or eight months past in conducting a mail line between this city and the Northern States."[6]

The *Appeal*'s correspondent then goes on to explain how the underground railroad operated. Letters, sealed or unsealed, were left at the counting room of the *Richmond Enquirer*, he says, with seventy-five cents in silver to act as postage on each, "and were carried off in some mysterious way to Maryland. Persons desiring answers were bid to request their correspondents to direct to some street and number in Baltimore, where the agents of Webster would call. The return mail, upon the arrival of the enterprising conductor in Richmond, was dropped in the Post Office and distributed in regular manner as drop letters." Occasional numbers of the *New York Herald*, the *New York Times*, the *New York Tribune*, and the *Baltimore American* were brought in this way to the various newspaper offices in Richmond. "It is now supposed that Webster's underground mail line was gotten up by Seward, and that all the letters forwarded by it in either direction were examined in Washington, for the double purpose of obtaining information from the Confederate capital and of criminating Southern sympathizers at the North. The statement of the spies is that the whole body of Yankee detectives and news collectors in Richmond had their instructions to communicate with Webster, and that he carried off periodically what they were able to pick up during his absence." The correspondent predicts: "We may look for startling revelations in two or three days, and the scaffold erected at the Fair Ground for the two already under condemnation may have to be enlarged." The first voice in the wilderness to cry out, Webster's going to hang.[7]

26. The Gag Order

But why the gag order?

An item in the *Richmond Examiner* of April 22 gives us the all-important corroboration that Webster was a witness at Scully's trial, and at Lewis's too, and that he, Tim, "excited suspicion by the character of his evidence." The *Examiner* reiterated this in their issue of April 28, when they wrote that Webster "first excited suspicion by the character of his evidence on the trial of Scully and Lewis." They mean "trials" rather than "trial," since Lewis and Scully were court-martialed separately, but what was it in Webster's statements, in his testimony, that could possibly have excited suspicion? Pinkerton, in that book of his so constantly in need of corroboration, *The Spy of the Rebellion*, goes into Tim's bedside testimony at Scully's court-martial, yes, but there is nothing in his account that suggests anything untoward. But there may have been something, something Pinkerton is not telling us. Something perhaps he never knew about his gray-eyed boy, about his star operative, the man he called Peaches.[8]

The *Examiner* item goes on about Webster: "On that occasion he is said to have conducted himself more as the advocate than as the disinterested witness." That sentence appears harmless when taken in isolation and arouses no particular suspicion in a reader beyond wondering what it means, but read in conjunction with other newspaper items, it takes its place in the growing line of sinister undercurrents.[9]

The *Dispatch*, in its April 30 issue, says of Webster: "Suspicion was first excited against the prisoner by the style of his evidence against Lewis and Scully, and they let the cat out of the bag on him after their conviction."[10]

"Against Lewis and Scully?" Surely they mean "for Lewis and Scully," don't they? After all, Tim Webster was testifying *for* Lewis and Scully, wasn't he?

The *Enquirer* of May 2, 1862, tells us that Webster was a "vigorous witness against" Lewis and Scully. One realizes this could merely be the *Enquirer* plagiarizing the *Dispatch*, but...[11]

We're going into unexplored territory here, uncharted seas. Only a few historians of the 21st century have seen any of these old press items, and the general reaction has been not that the papers made an error but that it was all a vicious lie, typical Confederate propaganda, perpetrated by the Richmond press, individually and collectively, a conspiracy to force Timothy Webster into the test-tube of history as a double-dyed villain who would stoop so low as to betray his own colleagues. According to our collective historian (OCH, let us dub this unified voice), what the *Enquirer* really should have said, in this case, was "vigorous witness for," not "vigorous witness against." Yes, OCH has seen one or two of these old newspaper reports but not enough to be less sure of himself, not enough to prevent emotion from clouding objectivity. But suppose it's not propaganda, vicious lies, a conspiracy continued by Southern newspapers month after month, year after year, century after century, merely in order to defame and keep defaming the memory of the noble Yankee patriot, Timothy Webster. What if it's true? Can it be that the *Dispatch* and the *Enquirer* were actually telling it the way it was? Is that what the *Examiner* of April 28 meant when it said that Webster "excited suspicion by the character of his evidence?" The original item, the one in the April 22 issue of the *Examiner*, the one that started this chain of investigation, reports that Webster was a witness at Scully's trial, but it never says "witness for."[12]

Furthermore, the May 6, 1862, issue of the *Western Democrat*, out of Charlotte, North Carolina, says of Webster that he had been the "principal witness against" Lewis and Scully "on their trial."[13]

Finally, the *Richmond Dispatch* of December 11, 1862, when discussing the possible flag of truce exchange of Lewis and Scully, has this to say: "It will be remembered that it was principally on the testimony of a man named Webster that they were found guilty."[14]

Years later, in 1903, the *Richmond Times-Dispatch*, in their Magazine Section, ran a chunky article called "Webster the Spy." In it they say that Timothy Webster was the "principal witness" against Lewis and Scully.

That's seven individual and separate pieces of hard evidence presented. Hard, not circumstantial. Men have been hanged on less. But, in this case, one is aware that none of this argument would hold up in a court of law, and that it could well be simply a case of one newspaper copying another and adding their own spin, but...

There is another piece of evidence that wouldn't stand the ghost of a chance in a courtroom, so flimsy as hardly to be worth mentioning, yet so tantalizing that it has to be mentioned. On March 17, 1862, Judah Benjamin resigned as Confederate secretary of war, and moved on to become secretary of state. This shift was ratified by the Confederate Senate on March 24. Why did this happen? Why did Benjamin get moved? The generally received answer is that after blunders on the battlefield, especially after the fiasco at Roanoke Island, where reinforcements failed to arrive, an investigation of his office was conducted, and he was found wanting, and so he was forced out of War and bumped upward into State, where his bungling wouldn't hurt the Confederacy so much. A variation of what would become known a hundred years later as the Peter Principle. Benjamin would stay in State, some would say lie in state, until the end of the war.

All that may be true. In fact, it is true. But then there is this, from the *Richmond Examiner* of April 28, the day before Tim Webster was hanged: "Webster has been here for many months, running to and from Washington at pleasure under the special permit of the former Secretary of War and has, no doubt, done the southern cause an incalculable amount of harm."

Judah Benjamin (Library of Congress).

And this, from the *Richmond Enquirer* of May 2: "Webster was [at the time of his arrest] and had been for some time before, employed by the Confederate States War Department to carry letters to and from the North." In previous newspaper accounts one had seen the accusing hand waving in the general direction of the War Department, but now the much more specific finger-pointing had begun, and it was pointing right at Judah Benjamin. But, whether or not Benjamin was guilty of anything more than bad judgment, he would never pay the price. Not even close. The price would never be discussed. Jefferson Davis didn't have many friends, but Benjamin was one of them.[15]

Sometimes one is made to think and re-think by sheer repetitive exposure to something, almost like advertising. In this particular case, did Timothy Webster do a deal with John Winder two weeks or more before he and Hattie were arrested? It is not proposed to go into this much further, because there is simply not enough hard substance under one's feet, but another question, with the same possible answer, does raise itself.

What was it that got Lewis and Scully the death sentence? That they were absolutely identified as Pinkertons? That, in itself, wouldn't be anywhere near enough to get them hanged, even in those early spring days of 1862 when anti-spy hysteria was sweeping Richmond. These two rather silly fellows should have just been slapped on the wrist, made to sign a parole, and sent packing back North. Paroles could say whatever the writer wanted them to say. In this case, "If you ever appear in the Confederacy again, you will be hanged." And that's fair enough. But no, for an execution to be imposed there's obviously something more, a lot more. Pinkerton tells us that it was because they were lurking around the fortifications of Richmond. However, nowhere else, aside from the Pryce Lewis "memoirs," can one find a specific charge against Lewis and Scully.

No spy had yet been hanged in this war, and there had been plenty of spies who had done a lot worse than Lewis and Scully had done. Pinkerton may be right about the lurking, but if he is, why didn't the writer of the Pryce Lewis "memoirs" tell us the full story? This would have been a perfect opportunity for Pryce Lewis, dictating in 1888, to tell us all about his crimes against the Confederate States of America. He could have gone to town on the details, could have dined out on the story for the rest of his life, with no adverse effect on himself by so doing, except perhaps indigestion. He wouldn't have lost his "hero" status over this issue. On the contrary, it would have increased it, and consequently helped his chances to get those very "memoirs" published. In this instance, he was free to write what he wanted. But no. Again, he reverts to boring plagiarism. So, why did the two spies get the death sentence? It doesn't make sense, unless…

…there never was a death sentence imposed upon Lewis and Scully at all. Suppose Winder made it up in order to put intolerable pressure on the two lads, to get them to sing. Suppose the court-martial's real sentence had been merely a prison term. This is all very vague, one appreciates that, but perhaps it's as good as can be done given the shockingly spongy substance under one's feet.

But why the gag order?

Suppose, back in March before his arrest, Tim sang from Mrs. Taylor's boarding house, a squeal rather than a pleasant melodic air. Suppose he was not giving evidence on behalf of Lewis and Scully after all, as everyone has always assumed, but against them. Just as the papers say. What if Webster was a witness not for the defense, but, instead, a secret snitch for the prosecution. What if he'd cut a devil's deal with Hog Winder.

But if Tim sang, what was the song? What possible deal could he have cut with Winder? What could he have told Winder that the old general didn't already know? Lewis and Scully had been recognized on the street as Pinkerton men, and they had been apprehended. Simple as that. Given their association with Webster, if Lewis and Scully were Pinkertons, then, in all probability, so was Tim. There seems to be nowhere to go with this, but there are two realities that won't go away: (1) the seven pieces of hard press evidence suggesting that Tim did, indeed, croon, and (2) the gag order.

If Tim did betray Lewis and Scully somehow, then the sine qua non is that the two boys didn't know it. If they had, they would have sung right back, of course, immediately, and ad alta voce. Their voce would have been so alta that we would have been hearing it to this day. No, if this happened at all then Webster sang to a house that had two reserved but ultimately empty seats in the front row. The names on the seats were, "Lewis and Scully."

In the end, the best that can be said, perhaps, is that there was a lot of panic and treachery going on in the court and in back rooms, with Webster, Lewis, and Scully all sobbing, weeping, and spilling their guts all over the place, and with General Winder holding in one hand a carrot, in another a miniature replica of the scaffold, and in his third a huge barf bag with the words "Deep Game for Big Rats" stenciled on its side.[16]

As the *Memphis Appeal* man reported, they had made extensive preparations for the hanging of Lewis and Scully out at Camp Lee. It was a fine, manly gibbet, one upon which a spy could certainly die like a, well, like a man, and it reared its hideous form over what only a year before had been peaceful fair grounds. The ropes had been prepared and tested, although not, of course, on the real thing. Four companies of infantry had been selected, and they had been practicing forming a hollow square immediately around the gallows. To each of the other hundred or so companies at the encampment a position had been assigned. With perfect order secured, and fair play guaranteed by all parties, the event would go off like a ceremony. And now they'd done gone and canceled it.[17]

27. The Trial of Tim

Timothy Webster's trial as a spy began toward the end of the first week in April 1862, in the immediate wake of his arrest. This is what we are told: At first, owing to Tim's extreme infirmity, the court-martial convened in his cell at Castle Godwin, but at some point he was able to get out of bed and belly up to the bar, which, as a consequence, shifted to City Hall where it belonged. The proceedings were presided over by Nat Tyler, a newspaper publisher by trade, one of the three owners of the *Richmond Enquirer*, and only recently, at the age of 34, appointed a lieutenant colonel in the Wise Legion. One recalls Judge Advocate W.W. Crump, state's prosecutor in the Lewis and Scully trials; well, here he was again. The accused was defended by Nance & Williams, a reputable law firm since November 1855. Eaton Nance and John G. Williams didn't work for nothing, nothing but hard gold, and why should they?[1]

There were two specific charges: The first was that Webster, being an alien enemy, and in the service of the United States, had been lurking around the armies and fortifications of the Confederate States in and near Richmond on April 1, 1862. The second charge contained the same wording, except that the lurking had been in Memphis about July 1, 1861, in other words a full nine months earlier.[2]

When Pryce Lewis was placed on the stand, he was asked if he knew Webster. Of course, he had to reply in the affirmative, but added that he knew very little of him.

"Do you know of his carrying mails between Richmond and Washington?"

"No I do not. I never saw him carry any."

"What! You don't know?"

"No."

"Didn't you ever hear a rumor to that effect?"

"Yes. It was rumored that he carried a mail. Of my personal knowledge, I know nothing of it. I couldn't swear to it for I never saw him carry any letters."

Pryce Lewis stuck to his disingenuous story. They tried to browbeat him into something more to their liking, but he behaved like a man. Like a Welshman, indeed. "My examination was very short."[3]

"Webster sat by me on the opposite side of a long table. He was very pale, and his dark hair and moustache seemed black. His gray eyes observed me closely while I testified. He put some question, so unimportant that I have forgotten what it was. I replied to it."[4]

That's it, as far as the Pryce Lewis "memoirs" are concerned.[5]

Nance & Williams, notwithstanding the esteem in which they were held as members of the Richmond bar, and despite bringing a number of

27. The Trial of Tim 99

witnesses on Webster's behalf, failed to stanch the tidal wave of hard evidence against the accused. And yes, there was very hard evidence against Tim, much of it coming from Lewis and Scully.

"Webster had been in the employment of one of the Departments of the Government at Richmond, in running the underground railroad"; i.e., "in carrying letters to and fro between the Department and friends of the South residing in the North." It was the War Department the *Raleigh Register* was talking about, with Judah Benjamin as secretary of that department, but the paper didn't want to come right out and impugn anyone in print, not at this stage anyway. Now, whether they were just speculating about Tim being Benjamin's actual employee or they had evidence of that we don't know, but it is worth observing that the *Richmond Enquirer* of May 2 had this: "Webster was ... and had been for some time before, employed by the Confederate States War Department to carry letters to and from the North."[6]

"It was proved on his trial that he was a spy in the pay of the United States Government and that all the letters he carried to and brought from the enemy's country were first carried by him to Washington and copied by the Yankee Government officials. It is stated that by this means many of our Northern sympathizers have been detected and thrown into prison."[7]

Yankee spy, brave engineer of the underground railroad, the mail train, Tim Webster at the throttle. Hero. No doubt true. If you're a Yankee. But what if it was your son, brother, cousin, aunt, who was one of the folks up there that Tim caused to be arrested, or worse? You wouldn't see him as such a hero then. You'd want to stomp the son of a b—. You'd want to see him hung. Just put the boot on the other foot, turn a blind eye, and keep on stompin'.

And, it must not be forgotten in the choppy sea of sentimentality that Timothy Webster was, indeed, guilty. Guilty of being a spy, in general, that is. And certainly guilty of causing considerable damage to the Confederacy by his letter-carrying activities. But, according to the newspapers, he was being tried on two specific charges. We know, from his reports to Pinkerton, that Tim was guilty of Charge No. 2, the Memphis caper, early on in the war. The prosecution should have been able to prove that without much problem. But, no, the court-martial acquitted him, "the charge not being sufficiently sustained." That is odd, indeed, but what is a lot stranger is that they nailed him on the first charge: Hanging about Richmond on April 1. But surely Nance & Williams would have been able to refute that easily in a matter of a few seconds, even if they had been lukewarm pro bono public defenders just out of law school and merely going through the motions.

April 1 was just a few days before the trial. Surely Webster was sick as a dog in bed in his room at Mrs. Taylor's house on Fourth Street. Any number of witnesses could have been brought forth to testify for Tim on that score, from Mrs. Taylor herself to Tim's good and loyal friends, William Campbell and the mysterious Mr. Pierce, the toad. So why would the court-martial even bring such an easily refutable charge, let alone find him guilty on it when there was obviously no possible way he could have been? No matter how off-key Lewis and Scully's crooning was, it was effective, but their evidence against Webster could have had nothing to do with the specific charge in question, because on April 1, the date relating to the charge, the two super-spies were behind bars and could have had no knowledge of Webster's movements. They couldn't have known where he was or what he was doing on April 1.[8]

But perhaps we've been led up the garden path. Held hostage to bulls' droppings. Perhaps Tim wasn't as sick on April 1 as Pinkerton has made out. Perhaps this is the old man's idea of an April Fool's joke. After all, the story of Tim being confined to his bed for the entire month of March has one source and one source only: Pinkerton. And Pinkerton is Civil War literature's most persistent and irritating liar.[9] We must consider which source to trust: a court-martial or Pinkerton?

Timothy Webster's trial came to an end on Saturday, April 19. The only business left for the court-martial to conduct now was the verdict and, if guilty, the passing of sentence. The bleak outlook was, perhaps, aggravated by press items such as the one printed in the *Richmond Enquirer* of April 15: "Last night some of our men caught a spy two miles above Falmouth on a stolen horse. He had on a Federal uniform under his outside suit. He left Washington a week ago. He was brought to town to-day. Hang him." The *Enquirer* was part-owned by Nat Tyler, and Nat Tyler was the man presiding over Tim's court-martial. "Hang him." And hanging was in the air. On April 5, about the time Tim's trial was getting under way, Judge J.D. Halyburton sentenced Louis Napoleon to death, despite the efforts of defense attorney John H. Gilmer, the same legal brain who had failed Lewis and Scully. The European celebrity was due to be hanged, not in absentia as one might expect, but in Richmond on May 9. After two respites from President Davis, they would finally get around to stretching his neck on August 22, in the gully east of the new alms house. When all was said and done, hanging Louis Napoleon was the best thing for everyone, even for the man himself. The world is full of lunatics strutting about, hand stuck in coat, pretending

27. The Trial of Tim   101

to be one emperor or another. That wasn't a crime in itself, but passing Confederate treasury notes was. Fausse monnaie, the French called it, false money. Louis Napoleon should have stuck to his previous occupation—walking around Richmond selling fruit from a basket.[10]

One reads in several books, perhaps most, that Hattie was sentenced to a year in prison. Not true. She was never sentenced. She never had a trial. There was no need for a trial, since it was assumed by the authorities and everyone else that she would do a few weeks behind bars and then be sent home. No, she was just thrown into Castle Godwin and left to wait.

If anyone was keenly aware of the meaning of "suspension of habeas corpus," it was Hattie Lawton. For the entire time of Tim's court-martial, he and Hattie were never allowed to communicate with each other, "and the noble little woman" was "compelled to suffer in silence, while Webster was undergoing the painful experience of the investigation."[11]

The *Richmond Examiner* of April 23 managed to get in a sneak raid on Hattie's reputation: "Since the arrest of Webster, it has been discovered that the woman claiming to be his wife, and who, at the time of the arrest was living with him at a respectable boarding house, is nothing more nor less than a common and notorious prostitute." What made them write something like that, about Hattie being a prostitute? Was it just cruel slander, or did they know something?[12]

That interesting correspondent for the *Memphis Appeal* wrote another report from Richmond, on April 23: "There are three persons under sentence of death here," and he identifies them: The "two Washington spies of Seward, and a poor, wretched Italian, who stole blank sheets of Confederate money from the lithographer's, signed them, and passed them." That was John Richardson, aka John Richards, aka John Dailey. All great names for an Italian. Even better for a nephew of the great Napoleon Bonaparte. Then the *Appeal* man gets down to "Webster, the underground post-route man, has had his examination, but the sentence has not been rendered. He will probably hang with the rest." Dixie was not just a good correspondent, he was a minor prophet. But since he was one who merely reflected the views of everyone else, he was a cheap prophet, not one crying in the wilderness, by any means.[13]

The *Examiner* might or might not have known anything, but one thing's for sure: The rebel war clerk was as capable of invention as the *Examiner* or anyone else. This from his "diary," the entry dated April 24, 1862: "Webster has been tried, condemned and hung." Which shows how unreliable the war clerk is. The results of Tim's trial wouldn't be arrived at until the following day, Friday the 25th, when, with two-thirds of the court concurring, a guilty verdict was announced. John Winder, the commanding general of the Department of Henrico, approved the proceedings and findings the same day, and ordered that the sentence be carried out under the direction of the provost marshal sometime in the morning of April 29, between the hours of 6 and 12. The sentence was final, irrevocable, and as harsh as could be imposed by a court in a civilized country. Tim was going to hang.[14]

28. Post Trial

Things had very definitely gone south in Richmond after the arrest of Lewis and Scully on the last day of February, and they immediately got worse. What with the press acting not only as state prosecutor, judge, and jury, but also as furious provocateurs spurring on the lynch mob, any and all Union spies still in Richmond were tripping over each other, sauve qui peut, to get out as fast as they could.[1]

"A day or two after Webster's trial, Scully was returned to the cell I occupied." So says Pryce Lewis in his so-called "memoirs." "He said he had been a witness on Webster's trial, but I did not ask him what he had testified to—the subject was too painful." This, of course, defies belief, the editor of the "memoirs" rightly deleted it, and the whole passage was reworked, complete with spelling mistakes: "The day Scully returned, Capt. Freedberger came into our cell."[2]

Pryce Lewis said to Warden Freeburger, "I suppose poor Webster blames us for this matter."

Freeburger turned to Lewis: "Lewis, Webster hasn't a word to say against you. He blames the priest and Scully here."

"This was said before Scully, who turned away towards the window."[3]

Warden Freeburger says: "Lewis, I must say one thing. I never saw but one man go through so well what you have gone through. That was a man who was executed in Mexico." Thanks a lot, Georgie.[4]

Varina Davis (Library of Congress).

After the day of execution had been fixed, Mrs. Lawton was permitted to visit Webster in the room to which he had been assigned. Pinkerton makes it sound as if he, Pinkerton, was actually there. Another talent. But too much Pinkerton, as we know, can be the equivalent of sitting in the saddle for three days on end, the maximum exposure to the man without the appropriate prescribed salve being three short paragraphs: "The meeting between Webster and Mrs. Lawton was a most affecting one. Tears filled the eyes of the faithful woman as she gazed at the pale and emaciated form of the heroic patriot. Their hands were clasped in a warm pressure, and her words of heart-felt sympathy and grief were choked by the sobs which shook her frame. Even in the excess of his despair, Webster's fortitude never for a moment forsook him. He bore the burdens which had been imposed upon him with a courage and firmness that impressed all who witnessed it."[5]

"Under Mrs. Lawton's direction, the room in which he was confined was soon made cheerful and clean; with her own hands she prepared for him such delicacies as he needed most, and her words of comfort were of great effect in soothing his mind, and in preparing him for the dreadful fate which he was called upon to meet."[6]

"Nor did Mrs. Lawton stop here. She sought an interview with Jefferson Davis, but finding him engaged with General Lee, she obtained the privilege of visiting the wife of the Confederate president. With Mrs. Davis she pleaded long and earnestly in behalf of the condemned man. Besought her by every holy tie of her own life to intercede for the pardon of the poor invalid, whose life hung by so slender a thread. All in vain, however. While fully sympathizing with the fate of the unfortunate man, Mrs. Davis declined to interfere in matters of state, and Mrs. Lawton left the house utterly hopeless of being able to avert the dreadful fate which impended over Webster."[7]

29. The Fatal Day Draws Nigh

The hours flew swiftly by, Pinkerton assures us, and even as the day of execution drew near, a ray of hope still glistened through the cobweb of Gothic gloom and inertia that surrounded Timothy Webster and Hattie

29. The Fatal Day Draws Nigh

Lawton. If only General McClellan could capture Richmond in the next few days, everything would be all right. McClellan was, indeed, on the move, and heading their way as part of his Peninsula Campaign, but as each precious day was succeeded by the next, it became ever more apparent that there was a better chance of dodging wingèd hogs passing overhead than Little Mac advancing upon the walls of the Confederate capital. With the flickering ember of hope dying, Timothy Webster prepared to meet his fate like a man.[1]

According to Pinkerton, one thing impressed the doomed man more than anything else, and that was the "thought of being hung." This is not startling news, since the thought would impress anyone, frankly, bad grammar notwithstanding. Any other mode of punishment would have been accepted with joy, Webster informs us through his rather unconvincing Pinkerton mouthpiece, "but to be hanged like a murderer was a disgrace which he could not bear to think about." And then comes the very day before the execution. Pinkerton decides that an anecdote is necessary here, one of his own making, one he can control, so he provides one. As he sat at his desk in 1882, pen in hand, he had in front of him an old newspaper, not merely for inspiration and historical reference but for more mischievous reasons as well. The April 30, 1862, *Richmond Examiner* article covers the scenes leading up to and including Tim's hanging on the morning of the 29th. Pinkerton lifts one particular detailed scene out there at Camp Lee, changes the location, a few of the words, some of the players, omits bits and pieces that make Tim look bad, and, hey presto!, we have this: Tim, still in his cell, making a request to see General Winder, "and that officer, evidently expecting a revelation from the lips of his victim, soon made his appearance at the prison." The scene thus fabricated in *The Spy of the Rebellion* is not very well thought through, so a first-time reader must overlook the holes in Pinkerton's plot.

"Webster, you have sent for me; what is it that you desire?"

"General Winder, I have sent for you to make an appeal to your manhood; my fate is sealed; I know that too well—I am to die, and I wish to die like a man. I know there is no hope for mercy but, Sir, I beseech you to permit me to be shot, not be hanged like a common felon—anything but that."

"I am afraid that cannot be done," said Winder, coldly.

"It is not much to ask," pleaded Webster, "I am to die, and am prepared, but, Sir, for G-d's sake let me not die like this; change but the manner of my death, and no murmur shall escape my lips."

"I cannot alter the sentence that has been ordered."

Mrs. Lawton, who was present, and unable further to restrain herself, exclaimed, "General, as a woman I appeal to you—you have the power and can exercise it. Do not, I pray you, condemn this brave man to the odium of a felon's death. Think of his family, and his suffering. Let the manliness of your own heart plead for him. It is not much that he asks. He does not sue for pardon. He seeks not to escape your judgment, harsh and cruel as it is. He only prays to be allowed to die like a brave man in the service of his country. You can certainly lose nothing by granting this request, therefore, in the name of justice and humanity, let him be shot instead of the dreadful death you have ordained for him."

While she was speaking, the hard lines around the rebel's mouth grew still more harsh and rigid. He did not attempt to interrupt her, but when she had finished, he turned coolly upon his heel, and, as he reached the door, he said, "His request and yours must be denied. He hangs tomorrow."

"Then," ejaculated the undaunted woman, "he will die like a man, and his death will be upon your head—a living curse until your own dark hour shall come."[2]

Without deigning to notice them further, General Winder passed out of the cell, slamming the door behind him, and probably wondering why his victim, if he objected so much to being hanged, didn't arrange some other form of death for himself. After all, there were plenty to choose from.[3]

Pinkerton hazards a guess as to what Webster might have been thinking. "Then, unable to bear the agony of his thoughts, he would start to his feet, press his hands to his ears, as if to drown the fearful sounds, and pace rapidly the narrow cell. Mrs. Lawton never left him; ever alert to his needs, ever ready with sustaining words, although her own brave, tender heart was breaking, she did her utmost to strengthen and sustain him. Gradually he became calmer. The slow-moving hours passed on, and he resolutely performed the last duties that devolved upon him. Messages were confided to his unwavering nurse for the dear friends at home; expressions of love and regard for his kindred, and unswerving breathings of devotion to his country." One refreshing thing, anyway: For once, Tim doesn't faint or sob or go limp and inanimate. And another good thing: The hours, which before General Winder's appearance were flying swiftly by, were now moving slowly. Time warps when you're reading a Pinkerton novel.[4]

We can recognize easily enough the bits and pieces that Pinkerton plagiarizes from the *Examiner*, but, as can seen in the above paragraphs, there is a lot more happening in this scene. Trouble is, it sounds fake. Too many generalizations and not enough specifics. If he had the *Examiner* of April 30, 1862, in front of him as he wrote, which he undeniably did, then it is hard to believe he didn't also have the *Dispatch* of the same date, in which there is an article with its setting in Tim's cell on the eve of the execution, when the condemned man, upon learning "there was no show for him, became completely unnerved." Yes, that really has to be Pinkerton's source for his rather flowery paragraph. It's not much of a source, but how much inspiration do you need when you're a creative writer like Pinkerton? The phrase, "no show." What does it mean? It means Tim was hoping for a reprieve, the chance of which is always of such huge importance in the thoughts of a condemned man. How do we know all this? Pinkerton never mentions a reprieve. But that's only because he never knew that on that very day, the 28th of April, Nance and Williams, Webster's lawyers, had applied for a new trial. If Pinkerton had been aware of this he would have been the first to make literary capital out of it, out of the show that never came.[5]

Instead, Tim to Hattie: "Tell Major Allen that I met my fate like a man. Thank him for his many acts of kindness to me. I have done my duty and I can meet death with a brave heart and a clear conscience." One never stops being shocked and stunned, even dismayed, at Pinkerton's almost desperate arrogance.[6]

That night Webster gave Hattie a sizable quantity of gold and Confederate Treasury notes. After all, he wouldn't be needing that sort of thing where he was going, since the streets there were already paved with gold, if not with Treasury notes. Pinkerton does not cover this story, which is hardly surprising. If it is a false story, merely a newspaper rumor turned tale, then there's nothing to cover. If, however, it's true, then it offers a lot of room for thought, notably: Did Hattie carry any of it out of the Confederacy when she was released later that year? And, if so, what did she do with it?[7]

30. The Morning of the Big Day

April 29, 1862, is not necessarily a day that will live in infamy but it was certainly one that provided Allan Pinkerton with a great opportunity to sicken us with his most purple prose to date, complete of course, with the invented dialog.

"The first, faint streaks of the early dawn came in through the grated window; the sun was rising in the heavens, brightly and gloriously lighting up a day that should have been shrouded in gloom."

Or this, still on the subject of the sun and its beneficence: "Its beams illumined the little chamber, where Webster lay calm and wakeful, his hands clasped by the woman who had so nobly shared his captivity. A silence had fallen upon them. Each was busy with thoughts which lips could not utter, and the death-like stillness was undisturbed save by the tramp of the guards in the corridor. Suddenly there came the sound of hurried footsteps. They paused before the door. The heavy bolts were shot back and, in the doorway, stood Captain Alexander, the officer in charge. The little clock that ticked upon the wall noted a quarter past five o'clock."

"Come, Webster, it is time to go."[1]

There was no sympathy in the rough voice that uttered these words.

"To go where?" inquired Webster, starting up in surprise.

Victorian readers must have roared with laughter at this, and slapped each other's outer thighs when their own were smarting too painfully. By this time they were as ready for this response as they would have been for something like "Who, me?"

"To the fair grounds."

"Surely not at this hour. The earliest moment named in my death warrant is six o'clock, and you certainly will not require me to go before that."

"It is the order of General Winder, and I must obey. You must prepare yourself at once."

Webster, having uttered his fill of useless not-for-profit words, arose from his bed, and began his preparations. Not a tremor was apparent, and his hand was as steady and firm as iron. When he had fully arranged his toilet, he turned to Mrs. Lawton, and, taking both her hands in his, he murmured, "Good-bye, dear friend, we shall never meet again on earth. God bless you, and your kindness to me. I will be brave, and die like a man. Farewell forever."

Then, turning to Captain Alexander, who stood unmoved near the door, he said, "I am ready."

Brave Tim. Never a trembling lip. Never a doubt. Die like a man! Die like a man! The callous observer, rendered speechless by choking on his tears of mirth, was unable to declare that if Tim had lived like a man he wouldn't now have to die like one.

30. The Morning of the Big Day

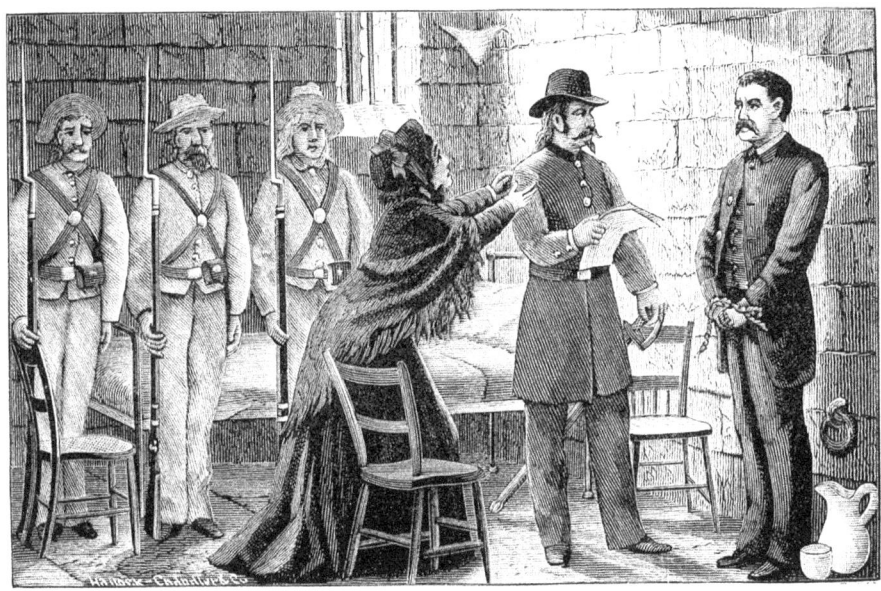

Hattie Lawson with Timothy Webster before his execution (from *The Spy of the Rebellion* by Allan Pinkerton, 1883).

As they went out through the door, a piercing shriek rent the air, and Mrs. Lawton fell prostrate to the floor. No Victorian melodrama would be complete without it.

Down the stairs, to the main entrance of the prison, and out into the morning, where Webster and his guards found a company of cavalry drawn up before them, and a carriage, procured by Mrs. Lawton, awaiting their appearance. Webster crossed the pavement with unfaltering step and entered the vehicle, the order to march was given, and the procession started for the scene of execution.

This entire anecdote comes from *The Spy of the Rebellion*; well, almost all of it. For the final segment we have an alternative source; two, if you want to be generous: The *Richmond Examiner* and Captain Samuel McCubbin, Jr., chief of the provost marshal's detectives.

Many years later, McCubbin was holding court for the press with tales of those war days, and in a jovial, reminiscing mood, told a reporter from the *Richmond Dispatch* that just as Timothy Webster was getting into the carriage with the guard, Hattie leaned out of the window and yelled out, "Die like a man, Tim!" to which the condemned spy shouted back, "You bet I will." At which the tumbril rumbled off down the shady avenue of history.[2]

McCubbin had been there at the time, all those years earlier, and might well have actually heard that dramatic interchange in person, but come 1879, seventeen years after the event, was he remembering off the top of his head, or is it simply that he had in front of him, as he was being interviewed, the very issue of the *Richmond Examiner* that came out the day after Tim Webster's execution?: "It is said that, on taking leave of him, Webster's wife exhorted him, 'to die like a man'; in how far he obeyed her exhortation, our readers can judge." One can hardly wait to get to the hanging, to see how Tim manned up to the scaffold.[3]

Yes, McCubbin could certainly pillage from a newspaper, but then so could Pinkerton.

31. Tim Swings

Everyone was pretty well used to calling it Camp Lee by now, and to thinking of it as a virtual synonym for what they used to refer to as the New Fair Grounds, and before that the Central Fair Grounds, a mile out of town as you went west on Broad. It was a couple of years ago now, before the war, on an unexpectedly rainy November 8, 1860, to be historically exact, that the First Virginia Regiment, with fifteen companies of horsemen, had opened up the new cavalry camp there, to much, much fanfare and tons of wet horse manure. But it would dry out, and despite the disappointing turnout on opening day there would be great tourist opportunities, every day. Run 'em out there for fifty cents on the R & F. Night and day. Day and night. Or at least within Christian reason.[1]

Now, on the morning of April 29, 1862, there was some classic entertainment of a different type coming up. It was a good day for a hanging. And it was always an enriching experience to see a man dangle up close. If it wasn't you, that is. And that's why it was always a treat; because it wasn't you. Yet.[2]

If this had been just any old hanging, you might not have been able to get a train ticket, so crowded might it all have been, but on this occasion, the citizenry of Richmond felt fairly much the way the press did about the object of this morning's exercise. Stay away in droves and show your contempt for a d——d Federal spy.[3]

The star of the smallest show on earth, the one they were waiting for, was Tim. The carriage bringing him from the prison duly arrived at Camp Lee and out hopped not one passenger as expected but two. Nothing wrong with giving a hitchhiker a lift to a hanging, provided he's a doctor of divinity and rector of the Monumental Church. George Woodbridge was a good man, they said, and he was too, if you yourself were a white man and not one of his brutalized slaves. Of course, Tim being white, George genuinely tried to help him, to cure his soul. But Tim wasn't a religious fellow at all, and had no use for that sort of mystical mumbo-jumbo. The prisoner was placed in a small room in one of the buildings near the north boundary of the camp, with a bunch of Provost Guards to make sure he didn't try to disappoint the executioner one way or another. The Reverend Woodbridge stayed with his mark for about an hour, realized he couldn't close the sale, and then left. At that point Tim lay down and went to sleep for about thirty minutes.[4]

This from the *Richmond Examiner*: "The hour of ten having come and past, and there being no signs of a reprieve, the convict's whole manner and carriage underwent a sudden change. He dropped his determined and defiant air, and gave way to tears, moaning, and crying out aloud against the ignominious death he was about to suffer. He asked his attendants to call the chaplain of the post to pray for him. The chaplain—the Rev. Moses D. Hoge—immediately went in to the afflicted man." Die like a man, Tim.[5]

Hoge, the famous Presbyterian minister of Richmond, would have been more than happy to grant the doomed wretch the inestimable favor of being able to share his last platform with a celebrity.

The *Examiner* goes on to tell us that Webster "besought and entreated Dr. Hoge to intercede with the authorities and have his sentence commuted from hanging to being shot. He said he did not mind death, but the idea of being hung was horrible." This all sounds awfully reminiscent of the words Pinkerton uses in *The Spy of the Rebellion*, in the previous night's scene where Tim and Hattie are trying to persuade General Winder to change the method of execution. In fact it is the very same scene.[6]

Then Tim expressed dismay that there were so few people there to witness what he considered the great event. He had prepared a speech, and was irritated that it wouldn't be heard by any but a tiny knot of spectators.[7]

Although "the doomed man eventually resumed his look of composure and indifference," he was "pale and looked in feeble health." However, "his eye was clear and steady, and not a muscle of his face betrayed his emotions." Nonetheless, he had to be helped, or perhaps encouraged, into the carriage by the Reverend Hoge and Warden Freeburger, for the short ride to the scaffold, the same one that had been erected for Lewis and Scully but never used. Even his gallows had not been custom-built. The ultimate insult. It was almost the public gibbet, in fact; anybody could swing on this damned thing, it seemed. At about 11:10 a.m., Hoge accompanied him up the wooden steps onto the eternal plank. Ah, but only part of the way, Reverend—this time. Tim's hands were bound behind his back, his silk dress hat was carefully removed, and the executioner adjusted the noose and slipped the black hood over his victim's head, the color all the better to match Tim's outfit. Because they didn't have a real, trained hangman to do the job on Webster, they had brought in John Caphart, their "acting" jack ketch, whose real job was as a detective at the military prison. Jack's training had been as a policeman in Norfolk, which, for his current customer at Camp Lee, was rather unfortunate, given that suspending a man by the neck correctly is a very definite skill, one you learn as you go along. And Caphart hadn't really hanged a lot of men, not all the way, anyway. But public executioner is an occupation that is so spiritually demoralizing that one needs support just getting through the day. Finding such a man, a professional, is almost impossible, at the best of times, hence Caphart, who was helped greatly by being a heavy-set man with a long white beard, hard facial features and cold, cruel, gray eyes.[8]

The trap was sprung, but the noose slipped and Webster crashed to the ground. Some said it was the fault of the cotton. No hemp ropes available. He was picked up and brought back onto the scaffold. As the trap was set once more, Tim calmly said, "I suffer a double death." This time the hangman's knot was tied so tight that the rope was too short. "Oh, you are going to choke me this time." This was all great fun for the tiny crowd of spectators, and, as far as they were concerned, the series of botched attempts could have gone on all day. And they probably would have if it hadn't been for the unexpected: A successful drop. At 11.22 a.m., Tim swung and died quickly, probably within a minute, which, at the hands of an amateur such as Jack Caphart, was tantamount to getting away with it almost scot free. The dead man swayed gently in the breeze for half an hour before being cut down and taken back into the city. Some of General Winder's detectives cut the rope into souvenir pieces and stuffed them in their pockets.[9]

Even if he hadn't been hanged, Timothy Webster might not have had long to live. He had been very sick for a long time, if what we are told is true, and had been prostrate for three solid months, February, March, and April. All of which smacks of a terminal condition. Although the hangman did not intend to put his victim out of his misery, death per se must have come as a relief to Tim from his physical ailments.

The day after Tim was executed, Hattie lost her cell companion: "Mrs. Ann E. Scott was released from Castle Godwin yesterday, on taking the oath of allegiance. It is understood that she will stop in Richmond." On top of everything that had just happened—the arrest, the imprisonment, Tim's execution—Hattie was now all alone.[10]

As a coda, one hears that John Caphart, the acting hangman, died on November 10, 1864, of "gradual decay." He was 66. Another rumor is that the very second he died his grandson was born in the adjoining room. Life goes on.[11]

32. Post Gibbet

There is no published primary evidence, let alone proof, for what happened in the immediate wake of Tim's death. Perhaps the two books that come closest to offering us anything like that are *The Spy of the Rebellion* and David D. Ryan's *A Yankee Spy in Richmond*. The subject of the latter is Elizabeth Van Lew and the following all-important quote about Timothy Webster and Hattie Lawton is represented as being from Miss Van Lew's "occasional journal": "When this poor fellow was hung, I went, accompanied by a friend, to Castle Thunder to ask permission for his wife to stay with us. Poor agonized creature. The wife never forget [sic] the heartless murder." One must bear in mind here that this event took place on April 29, 1862. Castle Thunder did not come into existence until mid–August of that year. This particular Van Lew story shouldn't be dismissed merely because the lady couldn't spell, or because she got the name of the prison wrong, or because her wording is so trite, or because it's a post facto journal, or because she herself may well not have even written it. And even if this story is made up, that's no reason to dismiss the entire journal. Or is it? This last observation, while not to the point exactly, is needed here to set the tone for the Van Lew "diary" in general, and, of course, without prejudice; merely jaundice. Back to the point: The Van Lew "journal" goes on: "During our visit it was announced that the body of Webster had been brought back and we were politely invited with the poor wife by Alexander to see. I think we could hardly have done this. Alexander would not let her stay with us; said she would be immediately sent off. Took her under his special care."[1]

We are told by Pinkerton, in *The Spy of the Rebellion*, that early in the afternoon, Captain Alexander returned to the prison, and informed Mrs. Lawton that it was all over. He found her deathly pale but now firm, and giving no other outward sign of the agony of the past few hours.

"May I see him before he is taken away?"

"There is no objection to that."

The two of them, the officer and the lady, went to the room where the body lay in the metallic coffin Hattie had procured for the occasion. Death had not discolored Webster's face in the least.

Several rebel officers stood around the coffin. All of a sudden Hattie turned on them and, facing Captain Alexander, she screamed at them, in a burst of passion, "Murderers! This is your work. If there is vengeance or retribution in this world, you will feel it before you die!"

As if stung to the quick by this accusation, Captain Alexander stepped up to the coffin, and, laying his hand upon Webster's cold, white forehead, said: "As sure as there is a God in Heaven, I am innocent of this deed. I did nothing to bring this about, and simply obeyed my orders in removing him from the prison to the place of execution."

It does look very much as if Miss Van Lew, or whoever wrote her "journal," did have Pinkerton's *The Spy of the Rebellion* in front of them on the table as they wrote. Why not? Everyone else did. One understands Mrs. Timothy Webster's wish to see her husband's body once more before he was buried, and one understands Captain Alexander acceding to that request. But why would Alexander have invited Miss Van Lew and friend, total strangers to Tim Webster, one would imagine, to be participants in this very private last moment? Especially when Tim's wife, Hattie, had to ask permission.

Application was made to General Winder for the privilege of sending Webster's body to the North, where it might be buried by his friends; but this the rebel officer peremptorily refused. A petition was then made for Tim to be placed in a vault in Richmond, with no better success.

Pinkerton then sheds some light upon Winder's character. But is it a true light, or is it a false beam, shining obliquely through the prism of second-hand revenge? Could it be that Pinkerton is not an honest lamplighter at all? Could it be that the light falls on him instead of on the man he is intending to vilify? He snarls as he writes that "in dead hour of the night" the rebel general ordered the remains to be carried away and buried in an obscure corner of the paupers' burying-ground.[2]

If true, or even if it is untrue, this whole sad chapter could only have been pieced together by Pinkerton after his debriefing of the one person who could provide him with the information: Hattie Lawton. And even then, what did she really know about what went on with Tim's dead body? She couldn't possibly have been privy to the events of that night. She might have heard something later. That's the best she could have done. Whatever information she gave to Pinkerton was then used faithfully or unfaithfully by the old man to forge this part of his narrative. In 1871, years after the war had ended, Pinkerton sent his No. 2, George Bangs, to Richmond on a special mission, one of monumental importance to all of them, one in which timing was the key. That Bangs was able to go straight to Tim's grave suggests that the *Richmond Dispatch* of May 3, 1871, was right when it wrote of Tim that "his remains were interred properly." After a quick check of the baggage car, to make sure that what he had come for was secure, Bangs took his seat as the train pulled out of the Richmond depot on April 29, right on schedule, heading north by northwest, bound for Chicago. It had been nine years to the very day since the infamous execution. Tim Webster was finally going home.[3]

33. The Languishing of Mrs. Timothy Webster

Just in case Allan Pinkerton was slow to catch the latest Richmond press concerning the late Timothy Webster and his "wife," the *Argus*, in the city of Rock Island, Illinois, just across the bridge from Webster's old quarters in Davenport, Iowa, reproduced in their May 2 issue an item from one of those very newspapers. Within a few days this piece was everywhere in the country, but the *Argus* was one of the very first provincial newspapers outside the Confederacy, if not absolutely the first, to carry news of the execution, a claim that brings with it a certain sense of ironic satisfaction in that, for the couple of years that Webster, alias J.R. Reed, had been master of the Rock Island bridge, he had never once received as much as a mention in the *Argus* or any other rag in that town. Now, after a long year of war and other more mundane events, few in Rock Island, or, come to think of it, in Davenport, probably even remembered the man. So much for fame.[1]

The boys at the *Democrat*, over in Davenport, dreamed up many headlines for their May 5 issue, of course, as they had to do every day. But some came ready-made via the AP. It doesn't really matter now who wrote "Hung as a Spy"; the subjoined Associated Press article had winged its way through the telegraph lines the day before, and when it hit the front page it brought to the Iowa river town the news that Timothy Webster had met an ignominious end at Richmond a few days since. Piggybacking on the item, the *Democrat*'s editor wondered how many readers could possibly have had any idea that this had been their old fellow citizen, J.H. Reed (*sic*), the bridgemaster, "or that he had for several years been a resident of this city, and had mingled with the people generally?" The *Democrat* goes on to give a bit of local history, which is not unblemished by error: "Immediately after the desperate attempt made by the enemies of the railroad bridge here to burn it down—which occurred, we believe, in the spring of 1859—there came to this town a man by the name of J.H. Reed, who immediately took charge of the bridge. This same man was no other than Timothy Webster. Reed was not his name, at least not his real name." The article was surprisingly accurate in its summation, letting the readers know that for several years before coming to Davenport Tim had been in the secret police service, not only in Chicago but in New York, and that while in that service he was in the habit of changing his name to suit circumstances. When he arrived at Davenport he was acting in two capacities, superintendent of the bridge and member of the secret police, there to ferret out the projectors of those schemes against the safety of that structure. "He was here nearly two years, we should say, and during that time was known by the name of Reed." The paper continues: "When he left this city, which we are bound to say was under rather questionable circumstances, he reported that he was going to enter a company then forming in New York for Government service. Aside from this he informed a citizen that he was in fact about to join an organization in that city for the purpose of acting as spies." From the time he left, no one had heard of the "daring young man" who, just a few days earlier, "had died by the halter in the enemy's capital. That he is the same man known here as J.H. Reed, there is probably no great room for doubt. Mr. Webster had a family living in the State of Illinois, somewhere on the line of the Peoria and Oquawka Railroad. We believe that he had a wife and two children there." The editor now had to face a certain unpleasantness, and he was man enough to do so: "The report that he had his wife with him, and that she was in Richmond at the time of Webster's execution, is a matter very easily understood and explained by those who understand the workings and intricate machinery of the secret police service." That may all be true, about it being easily explained by those who knew how to explain that sort of thing, but the editor who wrote this wasn't one of those who knew, or if he did he couldn't find it within himself to commit that knowledge to public paper. He could only get as far as "We doubt not that some female, passing as his wife, was with him," before he found himself so embarrassed he couldn't continue in a coherent manner. Instead, he gave up, and finished with "Webster was a man about forty years old, we should judge—of good personal appearance and pleasant address." The paper expressed regret that Tim had been thus brought to the end of his career.[2]

The day after this article, the *Democrat*'s rival, the *Gazette*, ran this on their front page: "The *Democrat* of yesterday contains a cock and bull story about J.H. Reed, formerly bridge master here. It maintains that a man recently executed as a spy at Richmond, Va., under the name of Timothy Webster, was none other than the identical J.H. Reed, who so suspiciously disappeared from this city about a year and a half ago. Our neighbor's sensational story sounds very much like some of the telegraphic dispatches we occasionally receive, and presume is quite as true."[3]

The *Intelligencer*, in Washington, says, in its May 7 issue, when talking of Webster the hanged man: "His wife is under arrest as a spy, and will be sent out of the Confederacy." This was copied by several papers. Not in any way intending to minimize Hattie's plight, she must have had little doubt by now that she was in no real danger of being hanged, and that sooner or later she would be repatriated.[4]

The citizens in Davenport, Iowa, awoke on the morning of May 12 to a news item that must have made at least some of them contemplate the mysterious way in which the universe moves, or at least the fourth estate: "The *Chicago Times* says it is currently reported in Chicago that the federal spy who was hung in Richmond a few days ago was once connected with the detective police of Chicago. This corroborates what we published one week ago. Reed, alias Webster, was once engaged in that capacity, and we are strong in the belief that he and the man hung are the same persons. It will take some time yet to develop the matter further."[5]

By late May, back in Richmond, Virginia, there were about sixty inmates in Castle Godwin. George Freeburger had been removed as warden, and Fred Shaffer appointed as his replacement. "Among the prisoners are Miss Anna Scott, of Leesburg, and Mrs. Webster, who will, no doubt, be sent to their respective homes as soon as opportunity serves. This prison, owing to the care and vigilance of Assistant Provost Marshal Alexander, is a model of neatness and good order. It might well serve as a pattern for all other places of confinement."[6]

"The Secretary of War has ordered that, when time and opportunity serve, Mrs. Webster and Miss Anna Scott, now in confinement at Castle Godwin, shall be sent home." With regard to Hattie, this was not at all unexpected. Nevertheless it must have come as a welcome bit of news for her on June 6. What is unexpected is Annie Scott. Recalling the May 1 issue of the same paper, one was under the impression that she was already free. Apparently not.[7]

At the very time Pinkerton was visiting his family back in Chicago for a few days, Mrs. Timothy Webster, a prisoner at Castle Godwin, wrote to Jefferson Davis. The letter was referred by the President to the Secretary of War.

Castle Godwin, July 22d, 1862.
Mr Jefferson Davis, President C.S. of America.
Dear Sir,
I write this to appeal to you to consider my Effections & I prey mercy at your hand, that you will grant me permicion to return to Boltermore and from there to go to my Relitives in Kentucky. noble Sir, I am a heart Broken wife, bereft of a husband. I am now allone here in Richmond and a Prisoner in the Castle. Pardon me, Sir, for persuming to address a letter to you. I have been to Genrial Winder to see if I cannot be sent home. at first he told me I should go. Weeks pasted by. I was not sent. I went then to the Secretary of War and he wrote me an order for the Genrial to send me home. I waited but all in vain. I then went once more & the Genrial told me that he could not send me home, said that people from Maryland had come & reported I would hang the people—theirfore I could not be allowed to go. I do not understand it. all the People that I do know is Southern People in

33. The Languishing of Mrs. Timothy Webster

Boltermore. I now appeal to you—to grant my last prayers, to command that I be sent to my friends. I am retched, and miserable. But rather to have my People to Harbor a thought as wrong as me that I would ingure any one in any way, I perfer to remain here among my people & suffer being detained as a Prisoner. I cannot believe my husband was guilty. No power on earth can convince me. Sir, if I am doomed to remain here, I beg one favor at your hands, let me be allowed the Privelage of having my room excluded from being occupied by any one but my self, and I will be content to remain. I beg of you, kind sir, to consider my prayer, & I remain, with Respect,

Mrs Timothy Webster[8]

A remarkable letter, written in a clear and distinctive hand. First, the spelling is so bad, worse even than the late Timothy Webster's, that everyone who came into contact with it must have known she was faking it. Wouldn't it have seemed odd to the reader that she couldn't spell Baltimore, yet she could spell Kentucky? And where does she get Kentucky? Hattie had relatives in Lee County, Illinois, but that's not Kentucky. Was it because Tim often posed as a Kentuckian? Was it to appeal to President Davis, who himself was from Kentucky? If so, that ploy would never have worked. Every day for a year now, Davis had been bombarded with letters and notes from favor seekers who had come to Richmond from Kentucky, whether they had or not.

With the suspension of habeas corpus and, more importantly, of civilian jurisdiction, the military court dockets had become so overcrowded and action on them so sluggish that Castle Godwin could no longer hold the backlog of prisoners awaiting trial. In an effort to overcome this problem, General Winder commandeered three huge buildings sharing a block on the northern side of east Cary Street, at the rear of 18th Street, right on the James River. These buildings had been used up until now for housing Yankee prisoners, but Winder had them converted into the new, bigger, improved principal military prison of the district of Richmond. Greanor's Tobacco Factory would hold Confederate deserters and political prisoners; Whittock's Warehouse would house the black and female prisoners; and Palmer's Warehouse would continue to be home to Union soldiers who, for one reason or another, found themselves in the Confederacy. The entire conglomeration, located only two blocks from Libby Prison, looked for all the world like a giant four-story upscale block of brick row-houses, except that pieces of tobacco-related machinery were still to be found in some parts of the complex. On August 13, 1862, Captain Alexander, in his role as assistant provost marshal in charge of the Eastern District, transferred his headquarters there, and as he did so you could almost hear Castle Godwin subside into oblivion. The new premises could hold about a thousand inmates, they said. Some even said 1400. Long live Castle Thunder![9]

On Monday, August 18, every prisoner then in Godwin was transferred to Thunder, 221 miserable souls in all, including Mrs. Timothy Webster, who went into Whittock's Warehouse, which could hold 350 persons. There were two other women spies in Castle Thunder at that time: Mrs. Tabb, of Portsmouth, Virginia, and Frank Abel, a Baltimore prostitute cum part time dick trying to make a buck the hard way working as an undercover agent for Washington spymaster Lafayette Baker. Going by the name of Mrs. Francis F. Jamieson of Orange County, New York, Frank had been arrested on horseback in the vicinity of Culpeper Court House, but that's because she was so obviously a spy she might as well have been wearing a neon hat and a flashing patsy nose.[10]

The Pryce Lewis "memoirs" go into some detail as to what the conditions were like in Castle Thunder, but that information is not especially germane to Hattie, being a woman. Charlotte Gilman, a prostitute but not a spy, who came to Castle Godwin a few days after Hattie, and who transferred with her to Thunder, would, months in the future, on April 15, 1863, be called upon as a witness for the Confederate government, to testify at a Congressional hearing put together to inquire into the treatment of prisoners at Castle Thunder. Miss Gilman claimed she had always been well treated, and that all the ladies spoke of Captain Alexander in the highest terms. Most if not all of the women who were incarcerated there and who were later interviewed said the same thing.[11]

There was some excitement in early September when they captured the notorious renegade Dr. William Rucker and threw him into Castle Thunder. Guarded day and night, there was no way this infamous spy could even have made a successful break for the bathroom. Something not quite as exciting as Rucker but entertaining nonetheless, as well as being practical, was that, at that very time, General Winder was cracking down on the new capital-wide epidemic of loafing, seizing all such idlers and committing them to Castle Thunder for a short taste of what might await them if they continued with their experiments in the Devil's workshop.[12]

On October 10, Castle Thunder received a visitor who was just that; in other words not a criminal bound for the slammer. William P. Wood was, of all things, keeper of the Old Capitol Prison in Washington. He was in enemy territory, openly and on a semi-secret mission, sent down into the

33. The Languishing of Mrs. Timothy Webster

Castle Thunder (Library of Congress).

Confederacy by General James S. Wadsworth, who until very recently had been the military commander of the District of Washington. The purpose of Wood's visit to Richmond was to negotiate prisoner exchanges. It was all quite irregular, there already being an official Lincoln-administration commissioner of prisoner exchanges, Colonel William H. Ludlow, and, on the part of everyone, there was a touch of light-heartedness with which this whole Wood affair was treated. That's because both sides were looking forward to seeing what would come of it.

Wood didn't come to Richmond empty-handed, of course. He had with him 145 Confederate prisoners. In exchange for this batch, an equal number of prisoners were selected by the Confederacy to be sent back North.[13]

As part of his tour of the rebel capital, Colonel Wood was shown around Castle Thunder, accompanied by Captain Cashmyer of the Provost Guard. The two men were received and conducted over the prison by Captain Alexander, the superintendent. Wood "expressed himself highly pleased at the evidences of cleanliness, comfort and discipline of the Castle." One of the Irish inmates jokingly asked Wood if he wouldn't like to have Captain Alexander as one of his permanent guests up in Washington. Wood replied with a good-humored laugh that they'd had the captain once, but hadn't been able to keep him.[14]

According to the Pryce Lewis "memoirs," Wood visited Lewis's cell: "It's all right, Lewis. I have come to get you away, to take you to Washington." The blowhard, bombastic first stage of a cheap promise. Always the same, isn't it? Captain Alexander remained in the room, of course, so it made meaningful conversation between the two Union men very difficult, but that should have made no difference to the promise. "Colonel" Wood called on Lewis again a few days later, "said he had a hard time to get us away, but hoped still to get us released." Second stage. Again, always the same weak excuses. After a visit to Salisbury prison, down in the Carolinas, Wood returned to Richmond and sent a boy with a bundle of underclothing for Scully and Lewis. The third stage of that cheap promise. And the underwear was probably second-hand, knowing Wood. Which all goes to prove that, as the British say, he was just trying it on. Just at that very delicate moment one of the Richmond newspapers published a declaration by Federal Secretary Stanton that Wood was not authorized to act as special commissioner but that he had gone "to Richmond on his own volition." Obviously, by exposing Wood in such a manner while the man was still in Richmond, Stanton was hoping the Confederates would relieve him of the embarrassment. But Wood figured it out in a hurry, jumped on a horse, and rode like the Devil to City Point, with Winder's detectives "in hot pursuit." In a scene from a thriller, the flag of truce boat was actually moving off from the dock at the very second Wood arrived, and, without a second's hesitation, he took a flying leap... "It was a brilliant exploit," said the "memoirs," and quite right too.[15]

On October 13, only three days after Mr. Wood's visit, Mrs. Timothy Webster wrote her second letter to Jefferson Davis, this time from her new quarters, Castle Thunder:

33. The Languishing of Mrs. Timothy Webster

My Honorable President:

I say my, for I own no other; will no other own. I come to you, a poor weak woman whose future looks oh, so cheerless. I come to you the relict of him who has paid the penalty of his wrongdoing, if wrong he did, of which I know nothing. I come to you begging. I wish to go home. It was hinted an exchange. Oh Sir, exchange me, a Southern born, a South-adoring woman. No, no; rather let me remain here in my people's prison and die than exchange me for one of my countrywomen. They say I might harm someone. Does a mother harm her child, a child her mother? The South is my mother. I will not harm her. Her glory is my pride. I look to her like a bleeding bird for succor. I have suffered. Oh, you can feel for suffering; let me go home where I may seek some spot, and unnoticed pass the remainder of my dreary, dreary days. I will pray for you, do you no harm. There is nothing so ingenuous as fear but I fear nothing. I am protected here and my Holy Mother knows my heart; but I have ties in Maryland, interests there. Please let me go home.

Edwin M. Stanton (Library of Congress).

Very respectfully, your obedient servant,
Mrs T. Webster.[16]

One sees the enormous difference in the spelling between this letter and the one Hattie wrote from Castle Godwin a few months earlier. This second letter is available today, but only in typescript, and so might have been corrected; but it might not have. President Davis forwarded it for inquiry and advice to Secretary of War Randolph who, on October 17, sent it on to General Jno. H. Winder, Brigadier-General of Volunteers, for inquiry and report. Winder sent it back to Randolph with this handwritten note attached: "Respectfully returned to the Secretary of War with the report that it was decided by the Secretary some time since to release Mrs. Webster and send her home, but the Secretary having been told that Mrs. Webster would compromise many friends in Maryland, the Secretary directed she should be retained until further orders."[17]

This was certainly a blow to Hattie. But two weeks later, on November 5, came a bit of heartening news. Mrs. Tabb, the Yankee spy from Portsmouth who had transferred, along with Hattie, from Castle Godwin back in August, was released on parole, to appear in court at a future date. It gave Hattie hope that soon she would follow.[18]

Elizabeth Van Lew's journal reveals about Hattie that "only when Mr. Wood, or Colonel Wood, of the Old Capital [sic] Prison visited Richmond was she relieved from her sad fate." If this is true, then it would explain how Hattie got out. If it's true. Given Colonel Wood's rather dramatic departure from the Confederacy, surely he would have been the last man to have had any lasting influence with the Richmond authorities.[19]

34. Hattie Gets Out

By December 1862, Yankees and rebels were being exchanged across the lines on a regular basis, and the whole flag of truce program had lapsed into a well oiled and rather bucolic routine. Most of these transfers were soldiers, prisoners of war who had given their parole that they wouldn't take up arms again for a specified period of time. However, some of those making the trip on the flags of truce were, strictly speaking, not being exchanged. They were civilians, men and women, political prisoners, well-credited persons on a mission, relatives visiting the other side, and "miscellaneous"; i.e., those who for one reason or another were crossing the lines, permanently or temporarily, even tourists, as long as they had the proper passes. This whole flag of truce system suited both sides, it being cheaper than the alternative.

Those being received into the Confederacy from the North would be brought down the Chesapeake Bay by Federal steamboat to Fortress Monroe, the Union base just off the southeast shoreline of Hampton, which, like a good deal of geographical Virginia, lay, paradoxically, in the heart of Confederate territory. From there the steamer would cruise around the tip of Newport News, and proceed up the James River to City Point, where it would deliver its passengers.

Persons going in the opposite direction would be escorted under guard and travel by train from Richmond down to Petersburg, whence they would ride the short railroad to City Point. There they would board the same Yankee steamboat, which would then return to Fortress Monroe, and from there 150 miles up the Chesapeake Bay to Annapolis, where the vessel would dock at the Naval Academy Wharf to disgorge its passengers. From here the soldiers would be taken to a parole camp that had been set up on the grounds of the Academy, while the civilians, after acquiring yet another pass, were free to make their way to wherever they were headed.

The steamboats *New York* and *Metamora* would ply this route once or twice a week, back and forth, sometimes carrying a lot of passengers, sometimes only a few, and, on occasion, none at all. While they were on board, these passengers would be under the command of an assistant exchange officer, always a commissioned officer of the Third New York Infantry.

Captain John Elmer Mulford was a short man. But he more than made up for that with a dense black beard. More important than facial hair, though, was the fact that he was the exchange officer aboard the *New York* as that vessel waited at Fortress Monroe on the morning of December 9, 1862. The mail boat *Adelaide* had come down the Chesapeake earlier that day from Baltimore, carrying sixty-four rebel prisoners who had been captured at the battle of Antietam a few months before. Now those men, some wounded, were transferred to the *New York*, which left at noon, bound for City Point.[1]

The next day the *New York* arrived back at Fortress Monroe, carrying no exchange prisoners. She then turned around and, again with no prisoners, headed back to City Point, where she sat in dock all day on December 11, waiting for passengers. That very day the rebel war clerk, John Beauchamp Jones, wrote in his diary: "Scully and Lewis, condemned to die as spies, have been pardoned by the President, and are to be sent North." That may have been so, but it was months and months, almost a year, before their release would be effected.[2]

On December 12, 1862, the two Richmond newspapers, the *Whig* and the *Dispatch*, using the same common story, announced the departure of the three Abolitionist ladies: Mrs. Frances D. Jameson, arrested as a spy at Centerville some time since; Maria Underwood, of Washington, arrested as a suspicious character; and "Mrs. Sarah Webster, wife of the man executed some months ago as a spy." The ladies had been, and still were, at Castle Thunder, the papers said, but at 7:30 that morning the three left Richmond, as part of a group of 270 released prisoners, and, under the charge of Lt. Louis Juste Bossieux, of Company B of the City Battalion, they were taken to City Point.[3]

An odd coincidence is worth pointing out just to illustrate the great cosmic joke: Just over a year earlier, on October 14, 1861, the very day Timothy Webster left Washington on his first spying mission to Richmond, a card advertisement was placed on the front page of the *Richmond Dispatch*, offering Cranberries, which meant the fruit rather than, say, Hattie Lawton, even though, funnily enough, the wording in the ad, although innocent enough, and having absolutely nothing to do with the code name of a Pinkerton agent, does sound just like that which a spy would use in a dime novel: "A nice lot of cranberries, now receiving. Whole sale or retail. At 80 Main street. L.J. Bossieux." But what's really interesting is the name of the cranberry vendor. In a surreal sense, then, Tim and Hattie's adventures in Richmond began and ended with the same man.[4]

The *Richmond Enquirer* of December 13 says:

> Among the prisoners sent North on [sic] yesterday, by flag of truce, were Mrs. Frances Jamieson, a she-spy from Washington, Mrs. Webster, wife of the spy Timothy Webster, who was hung some months ago, and Belle Underwood, a half-cracked, half-Union and generally suspicious female, belonging in Kentucky, who first introduced herself to the notice of our authorities as a "bold soldier boy" who had entered the Confederate army as a substitute—having passed the usual examination—and performed picket duty before her real character was discovered.

By being so prurient as to force its readers to wonder about the circumstances under which Miss Underwood was exposed, the *Enquirer* was demonstrating its power as an organ of social advance, it being impossible, at that moment, for the average man or woman to progress to a point where they no longer needed to contemplate the thoroughness of the army's "usual examination," the one passed so handily by this young lady. The army may not have been so rigid when it came to privates, but the public was, at least the reading public.

But, of course, the truth is, as in most cases, much more mundane and less inspiring of cheap and needlessly ribald double entendres. The curious Miss Underwood first appeared in the Confederacy some months earlier, having arrived from Washington for seemingly no good reason. For this she was quite rightly lodged in Castle Godwin. At that time she was in women's clothing. They didn't know it then, but she was in the South trying to find her boyfriend. Or possibly "a" boyfriend, which, really, would have been just as absurd. In due time she was released, and on July 26, a Saturday, she presented herself at the camp of the Palmetto Sharpshooters, dressed as a soldier. Now the Sharpshooters, being a part of Longstreet's division, were not usually fooled by stunts like this, or if they were they never talked about it. She looked like a boy and indeed passed the first surgeon's examination. Either that surgeon was drunk or incompetent, or she really did look like a boy. The second surgeon, however, was more experienced in the field of human anatomy, and kindly suggested that she don clothing more appropriate to her gender.

Miss Underwood hung around the camp for the rest of the day, and then, on Sunday, went down to Richmond where she was recognized by a Palmetto captain, and she found herself up before Captain Alexander, the assistant provost marshal. He felt that a return to Castle Godwin would be a great tonic for her.[5]

The *Richmond Dispatch* of December 13 says: "Three female inmates of Castle Thunder, viz. Mesdames Webster, Underwood and Jameson, were sent North yesterday by flag of truce."

Actually, because the processing experience, from Richmond to Petersburg to City Point, took all day and most of the evening, it wasn't until well into the night that the flag of truce left City Point to go down the James to Fortress Monroe.

Certain historians, a growing number, write that "four Federals" were exchanged on December 13, 1862, for legendary Southern spy Belle Boyd. These historians usually name three of those "four Federals," Mrs. Timothy Webster, Mrs. Underwood, and Mrs. Jamieson, but nowhere, ever, is there an attempt to identify the fourth one. That's because there wasn't a fourth one, or even a first one. According to all the newspapers, biographies, her autobiography, and government documentation, Belle Boyd, who was then only 18 years old, was released from the Old Capitol Prison in Washington and sent back South over the course of the three-day period between August 29 and September 1, 1862, well over three months before Hattie's departure from Dixie on Saturday, December 13. As for Mesdames Webster, Underwood and Jamieson, there is no evidence that they were exchanged for anyone.[6]

So, that Saturday morning, then, the steamer *New York* duly arrived at Fortress Monroe, carrying the 270 paroled Union soldiers, the three freshly released lady criminals, and two other passengers worthy of note: Sally Anderson, the wife of the rebel general Joseph Reid Anderson, head of the Tredegar Iron Works in Richmond; and George Moore, the British consul, who had only been back from England a month. That afternoon the *New York* left Fortress Monroe for its climb up the Chesapeake to Annapolis.[7]

Was Hattie still aboard the *New York*, or had she disembarked at Fort Monroe? We don't know, and, frankly, it is of no importance except to suggest that she might have, but it is most probable that she carried on to Annapolis. Nine months later, Lewis and Scully would be freed from prison in Richmond, and would come out taking that same course. They went all the way to Annapolis, so it seems reasonable to assume that Hattie preceded them along that route. But either way, her destination had to have been Washington City. There could have been very little else on her mind. Find Pinkerton. Cry on his shoulder, perhaps. Kill him, perhaps. There is no way Pinkerton could have known what was on her mind. And perhaps she didn't know either.

So, Hattie was gone from out of the South now. Tim was dead. And, over the coming years, back in Richmond, people's memories, unattended and uncared for, would become corrupted and confused, weeds around a neglected tombstone. With the worms at work, it didn't take long for the rot to set in. Just a matter of months after the war ended, Captain John H. Greanor started to get his tobacco warehouse in order again, like it used to be before the trouble started. For those several years in between, though, the enormous building had been one of the three main component parts of Castle Thunder. By 1867 they were already conducting tours of the famous old prison. "Here, in the fourth story, is the gable window from which leaped Webster, the spy, with his irons on; there the steps down which he was borne on his way to his execution; there on the lower floor are the apartments of his wife." If history wasn't going to get it right, then Hattie was better off out of it.[8]

It's difficult to say with any precision where Hattie Lawton was at 3:40 p.m., on December 15, but she was probably in Annapolis, getting her pass filled out. She would need that form from the Federal authorities before being allowed to proceed on to Washington or anywhere else in the Union. She might not have made it to the District of Columbia until the 18th, but this was, of course, an extraordinary lady, and it's just possible that she was already there, or getting close.[9]

Pinkerton, alias E.J. Allen, certainly didn't know where Hattie was. He himself was in Manhattan. His connection with the Secret Service had come to an end over a month earlier, and now he was an agent for the War Department, reporting directly to Secretary Stanton, his mission being to uncover Army frauds, especially those of contractors supplying U.S. troops in New York City. On this mid-December day he was sending a couple of panicky telegraphs from 61 Franklin Street to his operative W.H. Scott, in Washington. The first read: "Look out for Mrs. Webster, as she will not know where to go also for Lewis & Scully do not send the goods yet as they may arrive by the next flag of truce." Pinkerton had obviously been looking at some false flags in the recent Richmond papers. It would be another nine months before Lewis and Scully were freed.[10]

The second telegraph bore the same date, but no time of day: "Please send this dispatch to Mr. Scott directly it arrives. W.H. Scott Washn. Do every thing in your power to keep out of the papers all mention of H H L's arrival and of any things concerning her finis E.J. Allen."[11]

Over the winter of 1862–1863, 181 Pennsylvania Avenue was still the Washington headquarters for several of Pinkerton's operatives: Mrs. Warn, Mr. Scott, Frank Warner, Henry B. Seymour. And Pinkerton himself, whenever he was in town. In the spring of 1863 they all packed up and returned to Chicago.[12]

35. Notre Dame

But then what for Hattie? After her last exit from Richmond, what sort of condition was she in? Did she remain in the employ of the Pinkertons? The answer is almost certainly yes. What else was she going to do? Break out into a new career? Go back into the prost biz? No, everything indicates that she remained a full-time Pinkerton agent until 1868, and that, even after that, she stayed connected to the company, doing the occasional job for them, until the founder of the company, Allan Pinkerton, died in 1884.[1]

On June 5, 1863, Pinkerton wrote a letter from Chicago to President Lincoln, reminding him who he was, and that, at "different times, by direction of the Commanding General," he had sent persons within the lines of the enemy, both males and females, including "four men and one woman, who were arrested early in 1862. Of these, one has lately made his escape from Richmond, and the woman, after having suffered imprisonment for nearly a year, was released and returned home in December last."[2]

The University of Notre Dame was famous even back then. It was the school chosen by Allan Pinkerton for the education of his two sons, Billy and Bobby. When Hattie L. Smith was involved many years later in the probate of the estate of her youngest brother, George W. Warn, she was claiming quite a bit of money from that estate, if and when it ever sold. This claim was largely built around her having paid young George's fees and expenses at Notre Dame when he was there as a student in the 1860s.[3]

The purpose of the exercise was to get George a good education. The four sisters took it upon themselves to make sure this was made possible and that it came to fruition. Money talked. And effort. Although nowhere in the George Warn probate papers does Hattie ever actually mention the name of the school—only that it was in South Bend, Indiana—she makes the case that beginning in March 1863 and for three years thereafter she made periodic cash payments there for George's schooling. However, Notre Dame assures us that George did not become a student until the 1864–65 season. That's a difference of a year and a half. How can Hattie have been so far out? In addition to this, the payments made as itemized by Hattie in her probate claim and those recorded by Notre Dame in their receipt records do not match even closely. At least, not most of them. But a few do, and Notre Dame does confirm that they were cash payments, for what that's worth. Actually, it's a little more muddy than that even; the Notre Dame records do have the names of the payers, George's two guardians, two of his sisters, and Hattie is not one of them, under any name. But then, neither is George's eldest sister, Angie. And to make it murkier still, a quick examination of the Notre Dame records shows quite clearly that, in the case of George Warn anyway, they, the records themselves, are hopelessly inadequate.[4]

There are various ways in which these problems can be resolved, that these questions might be answered, but we would be guessing. However, one guess is as good as another, really, for one of them is almost certainly bound to be right. As for Hattie making the payments, her claims must have satisfied the probate court, after all. They're not just going to take her word for it. One feels that she did make the payments, her share anyway, but not directly to the school. It's probable that she—and Kate Warn herself—made their share of the payments through the two other sisters. And that would make sense. The school would receive one payment every so often, rather than several small ones.[5]

What this Notre Dame adventure does tell us, as documented in Appendix B, is that Hattie and her sisters were well off enough to provide for their brother George's education at an expensive school.

36. Little Johnny and the Lost Cabin Mine

The war never really touched the town of Dixon, no great or small battles having occurred in Illinois. Unlike his brothers, John Warn managed to remain clear of the army, and in very early 1864 he waved goodbye to his wife and little E.T., and set out alone to look for gold. What he had in mind wasn't just an aimless meander throughout the west with pick and shovel in hand; he knew exactly where he was going: the new big strike up in Idaho Territory. It's all they were talking about. Alder Gulch, that's where he was headed.[1]

Johnny crossed the plains via the Bozeman Cut Off, and in the spring of the year arrived at Virginia City. City wasn't exactly the term they should have applied to this place; only a few months earlier, May 1863, there had been nothing here, not even a shack. Then a couple of prospectors hit upon the rich placer diggings in the Gulch, and men came in their thousands, Southern boys mostly, rebs from the border states, swarming over the earth.[2]

A typical western boom town, Virginia City grew way too fast. The law couldn't keep pace with the snarling animal greed, and within only a few months the violence and lawlessness of Virginia City were a legend. The perfect environment for a young man like Little Johnny. Freed from the shackles of convention, he was about to discover himself. The legend of John S. Warn, western pioneer, had begun.[3]

Johnny had only been in Virginia City a few days when there was a commotion. An old man, knocking hard at death's door, was staggering down the main street, muttering queer things about Injuns and fortunes in gold, and a lost cabin mine somewhere in the Big Horn Mountains. He was making no sense at all. Seems he had been staggering for some time, in fact all the way from the Big Horns. And that's a long way to stagger. He was raving and quite clearly insane. One could only hope it was temporary, and that a swig of water might restore his senses. However, some pronounced that he'd had more than his fair share of liquid. Men crowded around to stare at him up close as he beat a frenzied zigzag down the dusty street. All of a sudden, like a bolt from the blue, Johnny recognized the delirious old buzzard. It was none other than his uncle, Allen Hurlburt, from Janesville, Wisconsin, his mother's brother, the same man who had left his family in Rock County all those years before to head west to Californ-eye-ay to become a forty-niner, the same man who had never been seen since.[4]

Come on, Uncle Allen, spit it out! Well, it seems that Captain Hurlburt and two other prospectors had gotten themselves lost the previous fall in the Big Horns and, quite by accident, had discovered a fantastically rich ledge of gold. They built a cabin nearby and wintered over, preparing to hit the vein come spring. With the thaw they opened up a mine and were on the point of getting the riches out when the Indians killed Uncle Allen's partners. After a supreme effort Hurlburt made it back to, well, not civilization, perhaps, but to right now, crawling on his belly in the dirt of Virginia City like a snake, babbling, reduced to incoherency by the monstrous effort and the things the Indians had done, and now, dammit, he couldn't remember where the mine was.[5]

Johnny and the others cleaned the old man up as best they could and then they all headed back to the Big Horns, to look for the lost cabin, with old Uncle Allen in the lead, little nutty head bobbing on his stalk of a neck, a mild but disconcerting vagueness radiating out from between his ears, that smile just a little too wan. They didn't find the mine, surprise, surprise, but they did all emerge from that little expedition sadder but wiser men. And it's all true, the whole thing, the adventure. Little Johnny's adventure, anyway.[6]

Take a trip forward in time to December 1883, that being the first occasion on which the three little words Lost Cabin Mine ever appeared in a newspaper, at least as relating to that particular strike in Wyoming. It was such a catchy name it caught on in a hurry, and soon, in paper after paper, there was the name Lost Cabin Mine. You couldn't get away from it. But there was never any actual location mentioned, no date associated with the discovery of this mine. "A long time" and "many years since," but not even so much as a specific decade to help anyone out. No names of individuals either. Not even the whisper of a surname to guide us to the truth. The legend had voice, but it had no form, not until the middle of 1885, when John S. Warn wrote his four-part article in the Dakota newspaper, the *Bad Lands Cow Boy*.[7]

"Many conjectures and newspaper reports have been scattered broadcast over the country from time to time, in regard to the Lost Cabin mines of the Big Horn mountains. My friends have many times requested me to write the history of the mines, as my uncle, Allen Hulburt [sic], the original discoverer, told it to me. As will be seen later on, I went on the first expedition with my uncle after he was driven out by the Indians."[8]

The last thing John wrote was: "I saw Capt. Hulburt in Virginia City in the fall of '64. He was still engaged in trying to get men to go with him [to go and look for the Lost Cabin Mine], but he was always unsuccessful."[9]

So, even though Little Johnny Warn didn't invent the whole thing or even come up with the name, if he never did another thing in his life he certainly did create the entire legend of the Lost Cabin Mine, down to the tiniest detail. By the time he'd finished writing about it in the *Bad Lands Cow Boy* there was nothing else left to tell.

In May 1864, in a typical reflection of westward expansion and growth, the old Idaho Territory was reduced in size by having a huge chunk of it carved out on the maps and named Montana Territory. Not long afterwards, a new county came into being. Counties need a whole bunch of officials to run them properly, bureaucratic positions to be filled in order for the gears of local government to mesh as they should. John S. Warn was duly elected constable of Edgerton Co., M.T.[10]

37. Post Pike's Peak Syndrome

After his Pike's Peak adventure, Allen Warn, the eldest of the brothers, couldn't, for the life of him, think of anything to match that for sheer excitement, so he made his way back to Dixon to pick up Emma and the boy from the family farm, move to nearby Amboy, get a job as a blacksmith, and give family life another shot. What was that kid's name again? But Allen couldn't wait to get the hell out of there for good, and his opportunity came in July 1863, when the Lincoln administration began drafting older men for the army. Acting as cannon fodder for one's country wasn't exactly what Allen had in mind as an escape route from the tyranny of the anvil, but, in the end, it didn't make much difference really: He was dying inside anyway. Besides, the Lincoln government wasn't offering him much of a choice. He half-heartedly tried lying about his age, adding three or four years to make himself thirty-six, but that didn't work; they were taking men who were well into their fifties. On October 9, 1864, he enlisted for a year's service in Company G of the Second Regiment of Illinois Light Infantry. He went in as a private and on September 4, 1865, at Springfield, came out as a private, having failed dismally to get shot on the battlefield. There was nothing for it now but to go back home to Amboy in a desperate bid to put off the inevitable.[1]

In the late 1860s, Allen left home yet again, this time for Wyoming, as one of the hundreds of toiling and sweating blacksmiths willingly punishing themselves for the Union Pacific Railroad as they pushed ever nearer toward that great historical moment when they would drive in the Golden Spike to signal the completion of the first ever transcontinental railroad. Just as he was leaving Dixon, his younger brother Johnny was coming home. It was as if they passed each other in the night, two yo-yos in search of a string. The wife, Alice, took Johnny back, which is hardly a surprise, given the lad's agile tongue. He went into the grocery business, and rapidly did well. Hurrah! He was that sort of guy. But it wasn't the life for a budding legend and John S. Warn finally left in 1872, bound once more for the Dakotas and his true destiny.[2]

Meanwhile Emma had taken son Frank out to Wyoming to meet up with Allen and try again. While there she met her own Golden Spike and it was all over with Allen. She and Norman Potter made their way back to Illinois, and Emma got her divorce in September 1871. On January 9, 1872, she married the Spike, and they moved to Texas to begin a new life of happily ever after. Which was just as well, because that was more than Allen was capable of.[3]

38. The Death of Kate Warn

The Western Union boy handed the slip of paper to the Rev. William Corby, S.S.C. It bore that day's date, of course, January 25, 1868. The message on the telegram could not have been more urgent, or more sad: "Send George Warn here by first train. His sister is dying. If has not sufficient money, please advance it to him and I will remit. Allan Pinkerton."[1]

Father Corby had been a chaplain to the Irish Brigade during the Civil War. He was with them at Gettysburg, and on the second day of that epic three-day battle, he had stood on a boulder and given his boys a general absolution. That certainly made the news, and history too. Now, only a handful of years later, he was president of Notre Dame, as well as a member of the Society of the Holy Cross (Societas Sanctae Crucis), qualifications that definitely put him in a position to be able to lend George three dollars and send him to Chicago immediately. The boy was just in time. Three days later, Kate Warn, the world's first ever female private detective, was dead.[2]

The well and comfortably furnished top floor of Pinkerton's National Police Agency building in Chicago, at 92–94 Washington Street, was where all the female operatives were required to live when not on duty. The press, just two months before Kate's death, reported that these ladies' quarters consisted of a "kitchen, parlor, sitting, and living rooms." Considering the year of the article no mention is made of sleeping arrangements, except to say that they had to share their floor with the stationery room. It was on this floor, on the morning of January 28, that Kate Warn took her last, difficult, breath. Cause of death: Congestion of lungs. She was 38.[3]

"In this city, at the headquarters of the National Police Agency, Jan. 28, Mrs. Kate Warn, for over twelve years Superintendent of the Female Department of Pinkerton's Detective Force. Funeral from the residence of Allan Pinkerton, 554 West Monroe st., on the 30th inst., at 12 o'clock noon. Friends of the deceased and of Mr. Pinkerton are invited to attend."[4]

Undertaker James W. Wright buried Kate Warn on January 30, 1868, in Lot 555, Section C, Graceland Cemetery, Chicago.[5]

It is evident, from all the press and documents engendered by the lady's death, that Allan Pinkerton was accustomed to calling her Kate Warn. In the book *The Hoofs and Guns of the Storm: Chicago's Civil War Connections* (2003), author Arnie Bernstein reproduces a picture of Kate Warne's grave and says, "her name is misspelled Warn on the tombstone." Mr. Bernstein is not being singled out here with any malicious intent; he is merely one of many writers—most writers, in fact, and perhaps all writers these days— who use these very words, and he then goes on to say that most of the lettering on the tombstone has worn away. He's right. You can't make out much of Mrs. Warn's monumental inscription today, but it was all clearly visible in March 1959, when a letter was written telling us what it said: "In memory of Kate Warn, born in Chemung County, N.Y. Died in Chicago, Jan. 28, 1868, aged 43 years. For 13 years, Supt. of Female Detective Dept., Pinkertons National Police Agency." Graceland Cemetery has that letter to this day. Anyone can read it. However, it's not worth reading. Although it spells her name right, it has not been reproduced accurately by the transcriber. One can do better...

Here's another version, quoted from the *Brooklyn Daily Eagle* of August 31, 1884: "Kate Warn, born at Chemung County, N.Y. Died at Chicago, January 28, 1868, 38 years of age. For thirteen years superintendent of the Female Detective Department of Pinkertons National Police agency, a brave, true woman, and possessed of rare merits."[6]

Ah, how about that one, then? Surely that's going to be accurate, being 1884 and all that. But no. One look at what's left today on the tombstone tells you immediately that the *Eagle* got it wrong too.

What the stone actually used to say, before a lot of it wore away, was: "In memory of Kate Warn, born in Chemung Co., N.Y. Died in Chicago, Jan. 28, 1868, aged 38 years. For 13 years, Supt. of Female Detective Dept., Pinkertons National Police Agency, a brave, true woman, and possessed of rare merits." If you've got a choice, to get it right or to get it wrong, why not get it right?[7]

"Estate of Angie M. Warn, will proved and letters testamentary granted to Allen [sic] Pinkerton, executor, on bond of $8,200. Bond approved."[8]

Who else would she have picked as executor? There has long been a rumor that the two of them were having an affair all those years. Given the way he writes about her, it's probably true, but there has never been a shred of evidence, beyond imagination and wishful thinking, to substantiate the gossip. However, the recent discovery of what has become known as the Thomas T. Eckert papers reveals something of great interest in a telegram that was sent by Pinkerton, alias Major E.J. Allen, from Chicago to his temporary wartime Washington home, 288 Eye Street, at 3 o'clock in the afternoon on Wednesday, March 18, 1863: "Kate Allen two eighty eight I st Washn I shall prabable [sic] leave here Tuesday evening direct for Washn Robert will be with me if I make connection I shall be home Saturday morning Joan not well Allen Pinkerton."[9]

Was Kate just house-sitting while Pinkerton was back in Chicago? If so, why not address the telegram to Kate Warn rather than Kate Allen? Or to Mrs. Barley. Or Mrs. Cherry. Or Raisins.

So, after all this time, the door to Kate Warn's boudoir, always pushed slightly ajar by the finger of suspicion, has been nudged open a little more by the first ever shim of real evidence, and yes, as everyone had suspected, there is Pinkerton, dressed in his nightgown, tiptoeing his way over to the four-poster, candle in hand, wick aflame. Mind you, we can't quite see who it is in the bed, but one can make a pretty good guess. Sometimes imagination and wishful thinking are right, after all. Of course, it would never hold up in court, but that's not what gossip is all about.

As a cock-eyed coda to the life of Kate Warn, and there are always many codas, especially if the person is a cult figure, this from an 1896 article on Graceland Cemetery in the Chicago newspaper, the *Inter-Ocean*: "The grave of Kate Warren, the government spy, who was caught within the Confederate lines and condemned to die, is in the same lot. Friends had remembered her services to her country and scattered flowers."[10]

---

39. Kate Warn's Successor

With Kate Warn's death, Pinkerton was faced with the need to choose a successor, a woman who would run the female detective department, someone who would move into Mrs. Warn's old quarters at the office on Washington Street, someone who would take Kate's place. We don't want to read too much into this, and so we have to say that we don't know why Pinkerton chose Julia Ann Hubbell as his new female superintendent. She lasted only two years in the job, 1868 and 1869, and then she was gone, not only from the firm but also from Chicago. Pinkerton never replaced her, and that was the end of his female department, as such.[1]

It's not so much that Julia Hubbell is a shadowy figure; we easily learn quite a bit about her from birth to death. No, it's not that. But we do have proof that, for a while, at least, she was the shady lady of naughty lane. A rather short fling with a Mr. Bryant at sixteen produced a son, to whom she gave the rather daring name of Melvin. A marriage to George W.L. Hubbell in 1859, a music professor almost twenty years her senior, did not last long. In the mid-1860s she ran a boarding house on Clark Street. (A boarding house, eh? No, it couldn't be that type of boarding house. It just looks to be too much on the up and up for that.)

Was she a Pinkerton at the time Kate Warn died? In other words, was she promoted from within the organization? Could be. Or she might have been brought in from outside. We just don't know. And that's our fault, not hers.

What seems odd is that no one has ever mentioned Julia. Ever. You'd think, with all the books written about the Pinkerton agency, that someone would have discussed Julia Ann Hubbell, that some historian might have asked the obvious question, "Who replaced Kate Warn as the superintendent of the female department?" But no. Apparently not.

When Pinkerton took her on she was 34, about the age Kate Warn had been.

Although she grew up in Milwaukee, she was originally from Woodstock, Vermont, but both her parents, Jared Thompson and his wife Frances Hayden, were from Connecticut, just as Kate Warn's parents had been.

In the end, Mrs. Hubbell came back to Chicago and spent the last thirteen years of her life at 1439 Dunning Street, which is where she died, rich, on January 14, 1896.[2]

40. The Portrait of Kate Warne

The portrait of "Kate Warne" languishes in Paintings and Sculptures at the Chicago Historical Society's museum, an institution that, since 2006,

40. The Portrait of Kate Warne

has been called The Chicago History Museum. The item has a code number, ICHi-75012. It is stored in a drawer, "along with similar materials." It was donated to the society in 1927, and since no one seems ever to have heard of it until 2015, it would appear that it has been in that drawer for close to one hundred years.[1]

An image of "Kate Warne," something no one else had ever seen or heard of. All these decades the consensus had been that there was simply no visual representation of Mrs. Warn, of any sort. Except for the descriptions given of her by Pinkerton in his books, no one in modern times has had any idea what she looked like. In desperation, certain amateur historians had even put online a few Civil War group photos in which they claimed they could make out that such and such an unidentified young uniformed gentleman of the officer corps, usually the one without the beard, was, in fact, Pinkerton's great female operative in disguise. Hail Marys, if you like. The most notorious of these Hail Marys were finally revealed as issuing from John Babcock and Lt. Alfred Tanner, which shows how silly this phase was. Fortunately all that has died down now because finally we have a picture of Mrs. Warn. "Kate Warne 1866."

In anyone's book, to come across a portrait of the world's first woman detective would have been a scholarly coup of the first order, or more reasonably, the second order. No one ever did stumble upon such a thing, until 2015, when the image became famous, and mentions and pictures of it immediately started to appear on a growing number of websites.[2]

The portrait is of a woman, standing, holding a fan in her right hand and with her left hand on a chair. She is well dressed. She is not pretty. The museum feels justified in declaring the portrait to be of Kate Warne. That's because, at the bottom of the image, in color, is handwritten some wording: "Kate Warne, 1866." Because it says Kate Warne it must be Kate Warne.

Every website describes the item as a watercolor painting, but to me it looks like a normal 19th-century black and white photograph. I'm sure most people would feel the way I do, but what do we know? So, what does the museum itself say? They're the ones who'll know. They're the court of last resort, the experts. The museum employee I was dealing with agreed that, yes, the item is black and white, but then she told me this: "It is likely a painted photograph." That can only mean that a monochrome watercolorist painted over the original black and white photograph, to make it look like a black and white watercolor painting. So, it is both a b/w watercolor and a b/w photograph, at the same time. I've never heard of anything like that, and I can't quite get a grip on why someone should do such a thing. It still looks like a photograph to me, though.

This wording: "Kate Warne 1866." In color, perhaps burgundy. Why wasn't it written in b/w? The spelling Warne, not Warn, tells us two things: it was not written by Kate herself, as she would never have spelled it that way, and it was not written by anyone even remotely contemporaneously, as no one spelled it Warne back then.

The item measures 17 inches high by 13.75 inches wide, which, one must admit, is an enormous photograph. I did confirm with the museum employee that she was talking in inches and not, say, centimeters.[3]

As for the accession record, it shows no information other than the year it was donated. I had asked various other questions, for example:

Has it ever been examined by an expert?

Does it have a backing of any sort? Or anything written on the back.

Is what we see online what we get in real life?

In the museum itself, how is it displayed and described to the public? As a watercolor or as a photo?

I got no answers to these questions, and no further communication from the museum.

In the end, maybe it is Kate Warn in the portrait. But there's no way to know that based on the evidence we have.

41. Carrie Lawton

There is only one primary source that mentions Hattie Lawton, and that is Allan Pinkerton's 1883 book, *The Spy of the Rebellion*, which is, in effect, the biography of Timothy Webster. Outside of that book Hattie Lawton does not exist, not by that name anyway.

Exactly the same can be said of Carrie Lawton.

Pinkerton did not have enough material, fit for publication, that is, to make a full-fledged book about his hero Tim, so he padded it with anecdotes, mostly of an Abolitionist nature, featuring other operatives, some of whom—John Scobell and Stutterin' Dave Graham, for example—were just as fictional as the stories they star in; others, such as George Curtis, Mrs. E.H. Baker, and Mrs. Carrie Lawton, were real agents but with their names changed and adventures invented for them.¹

Pinkerton lumped these anecdotes all together in a section of the book that is not in sequence with, nor, indeed, has anything to do with, the main narrative. It occupies chapters 22 through 31, and might as well be called "Anecdote Dump"; there is little or no historical value in it at all, and precious little that is entertaining. Ten chapters of tedious bull dung. Worse is that, by being so riddled with Pinkerton lies, this section of the book has made real research into the subject next to impossible, as anyone can see from the results over the years. In the unlikely event that there is even one person out there who objects to hearing the great man called a liar, rather than just a harmless old fabricator, in the preface to his book Pinkerton writes, "The events narrated have all occurred." He adds: "The record is a truthful one." And, for good measure: "In detailing the various events which follow, I have been careful to offer nothing but that which actually transpired." And of course the sub-title of the book itself: "…True History…." One must always bear in mind that this man Pinkerton rates up there with the greatest egos of his century. Again from his preface, but this time referring to Abraham Lincoln and the Baltimore Plot, he writes this: "I cannot repress a sense of pride in the fact that, at the commencement of his glorious career, I had averted the blow that was aimed at his honest, manly heart." This was the first time Allan Pinkerton single-handedly saved the United States of America, but it wouldn't be the last.²

Allan Pinkerton, 1861 (photograph taken at the Mathew Brady Studio; Records of Pinkerton's National Detective Agency, Box 4, Folder 6, Library of Congress).

"It was on a beautiful morning in the early part of the month of April 1862, when a lady, mounted upon a handsome, spirited black horse, and accompanied by a young and intelligent-looking negro, also excellently mounted, rode out of the city of Richmond, apparently for the purpose of enjoying a morning ride."³

The horse wasn't the only species representing pulchritude that fine morning and blacks were not the only ethnic group being praised for physical and mental virtues. "The lady was young, handsome and apparently about twenty-five years of age. Her complexion was fresh and rosy as the morning, her hair fell in flowing tresses of gold, while her eyes, which were of a clear and deep blue, were quick and searching in their glances."[4]

These characters, who sound so god-like, were "Mrs. Carrie Lawton, a female operative on my force, and John Scobell." Pinkerton goes on to say, "These two persons had been for a time employed in Richmond, and were now endeavoring to effect their journey North."[5]

Pinkerton says, about Carrie: "Among my female operatives, however, none were clearer headed or more resolute than Mrs. Lawton, who prior to this time had been a most efficient worker and had been remarkably successful on her trips into the lines of the enemy. In each case she had escaped with rare good fortune."[6]

"Mrs. Lawton and Scobell had been for some weeks in Richmond, during which time they had obtained much important information, Mrs. Lawton taking the role of a Southern lady from Corinth, Mississippi, and Scobell acting as her servant. Having determined to leave Richmond, they were on their way to join the Union forces which, under General McClellan, had their headquarters on the Chickahominy at a point about ten miles from Wilson's Landing. Here, according to previous arrangement, they were to meet Mr. Lawton, who was also one of my operatives, and from that point were to proceed to the Union camp."[7]

Whereas Mrs. Hattie Lawton's husband—her real husband, that is; not Timothy Webster—is never mentioned in *The Spy of the Rebellion*, Mrs. Carrie Lawton's is. In true life there was no such man, nor was he based on anyone, but such a minor detail as the truth is not important in Allan Pinkerton's book of American history. In fact, Pinkerton goes so far as to make Carrie's husband a supporting character; a Pinkerton man, to boot. Welcome aboard Hugh Lawton, to this mad merry-go-round of smoke and mirrors.[8]

One of the pioneer Pinkerton biographers, Richard Wilmer Rowan, in 1931, misinterpreted a passage in *The Spy of the Rebellion* where Hugh and "the audacious Carrie" suddenly appear at the head of a Federal cavalry unit, a detachment of horsemen led by an unnamed captain. It is quite clear from Pinkerton's text that Hugh is a civilian; indeed, although Pinkerton refers to him on a number of occasions as Hugh Lawton, Mr. Lawton, and just Lawton or Carrie's husband, nowhere does he call him Captain Lawton, nor does he accord him any military rank whatever. It was just Rowan's misunderstanding of the expression "at their head" that, in the stroke of a pen, conflated Hugh and the cavalry captain, that all of a sudden turned Hugh Lawton from a civilian Pinkerton agent into a Union Army officer, "an enterprising adventurer" indeed. Moreover, it cannot be stressed enough that the Hugh Lawton of this anecdote is as fictional as the anecdote itself. But what is truly odd is not so much that Rowan made a mistake, it's that the hundreds and hundreds of researchers who have written about Hugh Lawton to one degree or another have all relied on Rowan and his derivatives, and not one has ever taken an independent look at this particular chapter of *The Spy of the Rebellion*, where the truth is there for all to see, plain as a pikestaff.

Finally, "The entire party then returned to the Landing, and in the morning my operatives were put across the river, where they reported in due time at headquarters, where they detailed fully the information which they had gained in the rebel capital."[9]

After the adventure, "Mr. and Mrs. Lawton and Scobell soon afterwards returned to Washington, where they were allowed to rest themselves for a time before being again called upon."[10]

Pinkerton goes to inordinate trouble to let us know that this Carrie adventure is set in April 1862. Indeed, he forces it down our throat, again and again. However, and there is no way Pinkerton could be confused here as this information was burned into his memory, that was exactly the very specific time period that Hattie, the other Mrs. Lawton, i.e., "Mrs. Timothy Webster," was serving the first of her many consecutive months in a Confederate prison in Richmond. Hattie, for one, didn't have the luxury, as Carrie did, of resting up for a while before being called on again.

So, since this Carrie episode is a fictional vignette, not connected to the narrative flow of the book's general story, and therefore not dependent on it in any way, and because John Scobell is a made-up character and so not constrained by any timeline, why did Pinkerton choose to set his little story in April 1862, of all possible months the one most likely to cause confusion to the reader and bring down ridicule upon the book? He must have known that would happen. As can be proved over and over in the course of reading *The Spy of the Rebellion*, Hattie and Carrie have to be two different women, so why did Pinkerton feel obliged to use the same last name for both of them? Two Mrs. Lawtons operating in Richmond at exactly the same time, in the same book? We know Pinkerton could be stupid on occasion, but this stupid? We have all seen bad editing, even from major publishing houses, but this bad? Unless Pinkerton was trying to tell us something about this other agent. And was Pinkerton so driven to include her in the book that he was prepared to wreck his credibility as a writer? "Mrs. Carrie Lawton, a female operative on my force." Was he trying, in a clumsy sort of way, to bring a bit of recognition to one of his star operatives, the lady he here calls Carrie Lawton? Not Hattie Lawton, but Carrie Lawton. Could the two women have been related somehow? Sisters? Hence the same last name? Is that what he wanted to convey? Whatever the answer, it has certainly muddied the waters for anyone studying Hattie Lawton.

In the month before Kate Warn died, and because of that, Allan Pinkerton purchased a large lot at Chicago's Graceland Cemetery, for the purpose of interring in it such of his people as did not have a burial plot at the time of their death: "In memory of the employes [sic] of Pinkerton's National Police Agency, December 1867." Lying south of the Pinkerton family lot, this sizable area would become the eternal resting place for several employees and their children buried there over the coming years. Timothy Webster lingered here for a short time in 1871 while relatives fought with Pinkerton over what to do with the martyred detective's skeletal remains. One employee who did remain buried here was Botella Olson, described by the *Brooklyn Eagle* in 1884 as "the Norwegian detective, died May 6, 1862, only 27 years of age." May 6, 1862? Hold on, that's the Civil War? And it's only a week to the day after Tim Webster was hanged by the Confederates in Richmond? Who the deuce is this detective Botella Olson? A brand new name in Pinkertoniana. Never, ever, has he been named in Pinkerton annals. An exciting new discovery. Never has he been mentioned before or since this *Brooklyn Eagle* item. And a Norwegian! Ah, but...[11]

Don't believe a word the newspapers print. Not a word. Not until corroborated. And even then...

Botella Olson was not a man at all, not that the *Eagle* ever said she was. But they obviously thought it was a man, otherwise they would have made something of the fact that everyone called him Betsy. And she didn't die in 1862 at all, which was quite a research disappointment. The *Eagle* got the day and the month right, which has to be to their resounding credit, but the year was actually 1882. And since she was Norwegian, it was Olsen not Olson. Oh, and she was not a detective at all. Botella Olsen, the young and poverty stricken Norwegian domestic who cleaned Pinkerton's Fifth Avenue offices in Chicago, died as the result of a botched abortion.[12]

Allan Pinkerton made it a habit, for several years, of going out to Graceland every New Year's Day, regardless of the weather, to decorate the graves of his relatives and trusted employees, and to make tributes to the departed. He called it Decoration Day. On December 30, 1878, his son, Billy, admitted reporters to his office for a press conference, so they could be briefed on what they would see when they all traipsed out to the cemetery for that year's Decoration Day. After telling them that while artificial flowers had been used up until now, and that this was the first time real flowers, from his father's garden, were being placed on the graves, Billy got down to the business of names. Robert Pinkerton, Allan's older brother, got a scimitar and a basket of flowers laid at his grave. "Kate Warne, an old and trusted attaché, and in 1868 superintendent of a branch of the institution," got a basket of flowers, as did "Kate Brackett, another 'good officer,' as she is now referred to." What's this? Two Pinkerton detectives named Kate? We know who Kate Warn was, but who is this Kate Brackett? The name is repeated in the same article, in a brief list that ends with the words, "These last are all old operatives."[13]

An old operative? Does that mean Civil War? Could it be that Kate Brackett had been one of Pinkerton's spies working undercover in the Confederacy? Kate Brackett has never, ever been mentioned in history. Not a squeak. The 1884 edition of the *Brooklyn Eagle* that published a partial list of those buried in Pinkerton's lot didn't mention her, and if it hadn't been for this Decoration Day article in the Chicago papers of the late 1870s we would never have stumbled across the name in the first place. The 1884 *Brooklyn Eagle* tells us that there was a plain marble slab for each grave, a marker rather than a gravestone, with an inscription chiseled in it. It was very definitely time to go to Graceland Cemetery, by phone and e-mail if not as an actual customer.[14]

No headstone, unfortunately. It's gone now, and, sadly, Graceland does not have a record of what it used to say. However, the good news is what the cemetery does have in its archives. The first, original, recording of her name at the cemetery was Kate Prescott, listed in the log register book under the interment date of February 11, 1869. Eighteen sixty-nine? Lady Luck has very definitely intervened in our investigations. That phrase "old operative" suddenly looks very much as if it might, indeed, imply "Civil War spy." Really, could it be anything else? Could she be the spy Pinkerton writes about in his book, *The Spy of the Rebellion*, the agent he calls Carrie Lawton? The records show that Kate Brackett died of cancer, and that the place of her residence at time of death was St. Louis.[15]

So, now it's off to St. Louis, to the races, to track down a woman who is looking more and more like a Civil War spy: Kate Prescott Brackett, or a combination thereof.

Kitty Brackett and Belle Towler, younger sisters of Kate Warn and Hattie Lawton, were two of the most sensational and news-provoking queens of the St. Louis Tenderloin in the period just after the Civil War. They were colorful and grand, what the French of those days might have called magnifiques, naturally stunning high-class madams with enormous flair and self-confidence, accustomed to applause, who didn't just arrive on a given scene, they exploded upon it, always with the grand gesture, as they stepped gracefully out of their respective and very expensive carriages. Like many stars who were not born with silver spoons in their mouths, Kitty and Belle were philanthropists. They were well aware of what it was like to have to eat with a wooden spoon.

Oscar Fitzerlan Brackett was nowhere near as impressive as his name. He married a very young, too young, Zemanda Katherine Warn (or Samanda Catherine Warn as some records show) in Janesville, Wisconsin, in December 1853, and took her back across the Illinois state line to Rockford, where his family lived. In October 1855 the Bracketts, all of them, left Rockford and headed to recently created Floyd County, Iowa, to St. Charles to be more specific, a town later called Charles City.[16]

Pinkerton's name went on the cover of a lot of books in the 1870s and 80s; one of them was *A Double Life and the Detectives*, published in 1884, the year he died. One of the adventures he writes about in that book is set in May of the year "18– ." They used to do that in those days. The reading public allowed them to get away with being that coy. So, you have no idea of the year, except that it had to have been in the 1860s. "I had in my employ at this time a young widow lady, Mrs. Kate Brelsford." She was French-speaking, and played the piano well. "A female operator, bright, shrewd, lady-like and good looking." We know Pinkerton had only a handful of female operatives at that time, and we know one of them was Kate Warn, and another really has to have been Kate Brackett. So, how many more Kates can there be? We know that in 1863 Kitty Brackett was young and was being described as a widow because she was no longer with a husband. We know she was good looking, bright, and shrewd. Lady-like? Sure. She was a high-class prostitute and almost without doubt a spy. She could be anything she wanted to be. French speaking? One doesn't know. There is certainly no such person in real life as the agent Pinkerton calls Mrs. Kate Brelsford, not with that name, anyway, but there sure is if her name was Mrs. Kate Br———, Kate Br———, Kate Brackett.[17]

Pinkerton tells us that Kate Brelsford had, on more than one occasion previously, been identified with operations that required considerable tact and shrewdness, and that thus far she "had been remarkably successful" in all that she had undertaken. Compare the wording in quotes with that used by Pinkerton in *The Spy of the Rebellion*, when he is writing about Carrie Lawton, who prior to the time of the anecdote in which she stars, had been a most efficient worker and "had been remarkably successful" on her trips into the lines of the enemy. How much more circumstantial evidence do we need to back up our case that Kate Brackett, Kate Brelsford, and Carrie Lawton are all one and the same spy? Well, there will be more, and more.[18]

On October 10, 1864, licensed prostitution was established by martial law in Memphis. Certainly by the end of the month, those two very interesting sisters, Kitty and Belle Warn, had moved there from Chicago, hard on the heels of the new legitimacy, setting up shop at 164 Washington, on the north side of the street. As was quite normal in those days, a "stew" would have a black maid living in. The rest of the human inhabitants were transient, in and out. But, in the particular case of 164 Washington Street, there was one who was a bit more than transient. The Notre Dame school records for September 12, 1865, describe Kitty and Belle's brother George W. Warn as being of Memphis, and he certainly was. Since he was only 14 at that time, it leads to interesting speculations about not only the boy's domestic situation, but also a possible underlying cause for his rather disturbing fate.[19]

In early 1867 Kitty and Belle left Memphis and went up the river to St. Louis, where it didn't take long for the police to get to meet the two new pretty madams at 212 South 5th Street. It didn't take long for the beak to fine them either. St. Louis always did welcome good citizens, especially ones who contributed to the public fund.[20]

By the summer of 1867 Belle had decided to go it alone. She was twenty-four now, and it was the right thing to do. She took up residence at 18 South 8th Street, while Kitty moved over to 1113 Christy Avenue, a large house with seven rooms and with the front parlor opening on the street. There was a side entrance leading into the back parlor, which was the room Kitty chose as her bedroom, and a stairway leading to the upper part of the house. She hired a black cook, of course.[21]

For a few days in mid-August 1867 the two sisters hit the St. Louis headlines together. Belle Towler, "an exquisite nymph, arrayed in a white dress and a snowy Chinese jacket, with a waterfall on the crown of her head, and a bit of a hat hung perpendicularly over her eyebrows," applied to Justice William Keating for the arrest of Lillie Merrell alias Prather, who had made fearful threats against Belle's life and placed her in fear for her bodily safety.

It all started when Lillie's squeeze, a fellow going by the name, or rather the description, of Johnny, decided to wander from Lillie's boarding house at 208 South 10th Street and explore the "superior charms of Belle Towler." And Belle's charms were, in anyone's opinion, of a very high caliber indeed. Lillie grew jealous, naturally, and demanded satisfaction. A duel. Belle refused to comply, and Lillie went in on her muscle, "giving her rival a chug on the back," and throwing stones at her. Kitty Brackett came to the rescue and advanced upon Lillie with a parasol, "a fancy bit of silk and fringe looking more like a butterfly than a sunshade."

The police duly arrested Lillie, who then countered with an assault and battery charge against Kitty Brackett, who, in turn, was also taken into custody. It fell to Justice Keating to be the man to have to sort all this out. His courtroom was "perfumed with lavender, musk, and night cereus, there being no less than four lilies of the valley, who sew not, neither do they spin, in the room, all at the same time. Such an array of frail beauty had seldom been seen in the court." It was all too much for George Martin, first mate of a local steamboat, who got so overheated that he was compelled to leave the courthouse and rush to a public bath house to cool off. Justice Keating's wisdom was legendary, like Solomon's—a $5 fine for Lillie and a $3 fine for Kitty.[22]

Both ladies, Belle and Kitty, continued to get frequent bawdy house mentions in the court page of the press, but then, suddenly, in July and August 1868 you couldn't go anywhere without hearing or reading about Kitty Brackett's diamonds.

"Miss Viola Ellwood has been arrested in St. Louis for stealing $1500 worth of diamonds from Kitty Brackett, keeper of a bagnio."[23]

The day after this Louisville squib was published, Miss Ellwood, a 17-

year-old prostitute, was arraigned before John Jecko, justice of the peace, and acting police justice of the city of St. Louis, on the charge of appropriating the stones from "Kate Brackett, proprietress of a certain house on Christy Avenue." The courtroom was crowded with the demi-monde. Miss Kate was the first witness: "I reside at 1113 Christy Avenue. I am a married lady. My husband's name is O.F. Brackett."[24]

The origins of this story lie in the previous Tuesday. Kitty had been out walking with her sister, Belle Towler. On returning to Belle's house, the two madams had found Miss Ellwood looking for board. Belle didn't want her, so Kitty took her home with her. After Viola raised her veil, Kitty decided she didn't want her either, so young Viola stole Kitty's diamonds. Justice Jecko issued a warrant of commitment for the young lady, and she went to jail to await the action of the grand jury. Detective Sergeant Larry Harrigan, one of St. Louis's less than finest, worked up the case.[25]

In a straight, sober, and legal line, Viola walked after a week behind bars. The statements of Kate Brackett, Laura Pomeroy, one of Miss Kate's girls, and Michael Manning, the livery stable keeper who had driven the defendant in a hack, had not been strong enough evidence, and Viola's "confession" had so obviously been wrung out of her by the Irish cop that it simply couldn't be admitted as evidence against her. The court came to the conclusion that there was only the possibility of Viola having stolen the diamonds. No proof.[26]

But it wasn't all over for the unfortunate Miss Ellwood. The day after she got out of jail, she was back in again. "This fair and frail girl, who got out of trouble about Kitty Brackett's diamonds, and then got in again, has waived all further examination, and gone to jail upon a $1000 bond." We are not privy to the legal chicanery that allowed this to happen to Viola. She got two years, but due to the intercession of the very kind Rev. Mr. Fox and other very kind gents, she was released into their custody for the term of her sentence. But, immediately after she was pardoned by the governor of Missouri on October 5, she split, and was re-arrested while in the company of two other prostitutes, all bound for Memphis.[27]

On February 9, 1869, Kate Brackett died in St. Louis, at 18 South 8th Street, the home of her sister, Mrs. Belle Towler. The death record says she was 29 years and 5 months. Cause of death was uterine cancer, a condition common in, but by no means associated exclusively with, ladies of the night. Famous homeopathic practitioner Thomas Griswold Comstock, the senior attending physician at the Good Samaritan Hospital, was her attending doctor, but despite the fact that the good man was a specialist in women's diseases, he couldn't fix Kitty. All that is sad, of course, but it wasn't particularly uncommon. It's what happened immediately after her death that was out of the ordinary and so secret that only a handful of individuals to this day have ever known about it, and not one of those has ever talked. Until now...[28]

Men came on a train, collected Kitty's body, and took the famous prostitute back to be buried in Graceland Cemetery, in the private lot reserved for Pinkerton employees.[29]

Near the Pacific machine shop, in St. Louis, stood a shanty, if you could call it standing. A family lived in there, if you could call it living. The mother was sick and had been for weeks. One of the children had been an invalid for months, and the others were in a "famishing condition." Day by day what few earthly possessions they'd started out with had now melted away in order to buy food, until finally starvation was staring them in the face. No one bothered to come to their assistance, and hunger and sickness were rapidly doing their evil work. At length a policeman considered it his duty to bring the case to the attention of his chief. Reporters got wind of the story, and one day in the first week of September 1870, the city newspapers were suggesting that here was a chance for unostentatious charity to do a good deed. A day later an elegant carriage stopped in front of the shanty. A richly attired lady got out, and, without any hesitation at all, simply walked into the wretched hovel. A "lady upon whose face beauty had left its impress." A lady clearly used to luxury. "The sight that met the gaze of the lady was calculated to sicken her heart, but she did not shrink from the filthy and emaciated beings that lay like moving skeletons before her, but speaking a few words of comfort to the mother and caressing the wasted cheeks of the starved children, she emptied the contents of her purse into their hands, and without giving her name, or waiting to be thanked for her generosity, she sprang lightly into her carriage, and was borne rapidly away." To the poor sufferers this visit was like a dream, and the beautiful lady appeared to them like an angel from Heaven. "Alas! there was little of the angel left in that gay lady. She was a votary of vice in its most hideous form—a courtezan—a woman of the town—a landlady of a house of bad repute! Yet, was she not more humane than those who turned a deaf ear to the cries of the starving widow and dying orphan?" The next day the carriage returned, and with it came a furniture car loaded with such articles as the sick family needed: A sack of flour, a bundle of tea, sugar, coffee, cakes, crackers, meat, bread, preserves, and other edibles, besides seven pairs of shoes, clean sheets, pillows, towels, soap, and a variety of other articles. "These were deposited in the shanty, and the carriage drove away, while the poor family wept for joy." The family were anxious to know the name of their benefactress, but she was gone. In a short time a physician came in, and the sick ones received medicines. The lady had sent the doctor to attend the family. His bill was to go to her. "He was not to be outdone in generosity by a courtezan, and gave the mother and children the benefit of his skill without charge to anyone. The doctor related the circumstances to us, and said the name of the charitable woman was Belle Towler. Surely some portion of this woman's iniquity will be blotted from the book of remembrance by the tears she shed over that destitute family."[30]

Belle died of serous (*sic*) effusion in the ventricles eight months later on May 2, 1871, in a house on the corner of Market and Walnut, in St. Louis. The record says she was born in the U.S., and that she was 26. Dr. Samuel H. Frazer, of 517 Walnut, was the attending physician. St. Louis undertaker John A. Smithers handled the funeral, but not in the city, rather in Dixon, Illinois, where she was buried with her mother in Oakwood Cemetery. Her tombstone says "Belle Warne." Or does it? Another picture of the tombstone says, "Our Darling Belle. Died May 2, 1871, aged 27 years."[31]

42. Gambling Man

T.J. Smith was a gambling man. Always had been. And why not? His family indulged him. Long-time, big-time wholesale grocers, the gentry of Cincinnati, what with the enormous house at 81 West 8th and everything that went with it. If young Tom wanted to buy a horse every now and then, and race it in the big leagues, then that was all right too. But there was a price to pay for all this freedom, and Smith, being a young man, was prepared to pay it.

The first time Smith made the papers was when he was 25, and it was as a result of something he could hardly have planned: losing some horses in a shipwreck on the Ohio River. Not an auspicious opening leap into the public eye, but a hurdle easily overlooked. It was a far more tolerant world back then, in many ways, especially among that crowd who could afford to be forgiving, at least once or twice.

The following year, while living with his widowed mother, young Smith tried to adjust his vision of the future, set his sights a little lower, and tried to make a go of it all by himself, loosely speaking, by running an oyster depot at 323 Central Avenue. But that was no life for a man like Smith, and so the half-hearted attempt was doomed before it started.[1]

William, his older bother, known to all of the Queen City as Salty Smith, was as tolerant as their old man had been. Salty ran the business, and lived and died every day with his nose clean as a whistle. Well, it would be that clean, pressed to the grindstone as it was.

Despite the fact that his brother generously renamed the firm William C. Smith & Bro., being just a bro wasn't for Young Salty. And then, in the summer of '66, the old man's will was read, eight years after his death. They already knew what it was going to say, but the words, spoken out loud, sealed Smith's fate, and he just up and relocated to St. Louis, where he branched out into more speculative fields, the most notable being in 1868, when he became the second and last husband of the Civil War's most mysterious spy, Hattie Lawton.[2]

For Smith and his trotter Flora Belle, 1872 was a great year. With the important but well-limited participation of trainer Morrell Higbee, Smith had bought the six-year-old chestnut in Canton, Illinois, in the autumn of 1870, for $6,000, which was more than any other man would have paid for her at the time, given her age and that she had never done better than 2:35 over the mile. On July 20, 1872, Flora Belle won the third race at Cleveland, and brought her new owner a prize of $900, not to mention side bets. On August 14, at Utica, this remarkable mare won three desperately contested races for horses that had never been beaten. The purse was a staggering $5000. Two weeks later, on August 29, at Dexter Park, Chicago, she was strongly pushed by W.T. Dixon's Pilot Temple, and only just held him off. But she did hold him off, to win for a purse of $2500, and that's what counts. On September 24, at Cincinnati, she raced for $2000; on October 4 she took $5000 at Indianapolis; and on October 10, at St. Louis's Great Fair, she closed the season with another win for $1000. As the most promising mare in the country, Flora Belle's upcoming 1873 season was looking more than passing good, what with almost certain hot races against the likes of such greats as Goldsmith Maid, Lucy, American Girl, and other trotters of that caliber.

Smith had already refused an offer of $25,000 for her, and told reporters he would be loath to accept $50,000.[3]

By December 1872, Hattie's youngest brother George had been living with the Smiths for a couple of years already. For Christmas she bought him a gold watch and chain for $150, a heavy gewgaw for the young man to stick in his fob pocket and feel the weight of real substance, but it was really just for him to mark time until he died. It was the generally considered opinion among those consulted upon this delicate question that George would profit by working. Labor omnia vincit. Ah, how little those old Romans knew at the best of times. Insert him as noiselessly as possible into a clerk's role with his brother-in-law's company, Thorwegen and Smith, and if that doesn't work, nepotize him to death. The new title alone—"superintendent"—would give him so much self-respect, surely; enough, at any rate, to banish all thoughts of, well.... Just throw money at it. The American way. That last month of 1872, wintry, cold, crisp and even, Hattie paid for George's visits to Dr. Pallen. We don't know which Dr. Pallen it was out of the two of that name practicing in St. Louis: Moses Montrose Pallen, or his son, Montrose Anderson Pallen. It doesn't really matter much which one it was, and it didn't matter then, one supposes. Neither man would have done George much good, at least on the surface; the first was an obstetrician and the second a gynecologist.[4]

The 1873 racing season was drawing near, and the talk of the trotting world was that most valuable mare in America, T.J. Smith's Flora Belle, out of St. Louis, with her mile time now down to 2 minutes 22.5 seconds; 2:21 in private. She had done the quarter in 30 seconds. Flora Belle's stunning emergence on the tracks the previous season now made her every movement the subject of national scrutiny. Then suddenly, in the first week of April, out of the blue, Smith and Hattie went up to Chicago, where T.J. sold Flora Belle to Alex Lewis of Milwaukee, for $25,500.[5]

Early that year, 1873, the Young Salty Smiths, obviously flush with funds, moved into a new house, 2809 Morgan Street, with, less obviously, young George Warn not only still alive, but in tow.[6]

At the end of May, Smith and Hattie, just the two of them, boarded the train for Omaha. Very comfortable, a couple of days and nights if you could afford it, and boy, were they in the money. Then they went westbound through Utah into the Sierra Nevada, and down to San Francisco, arriving in that bustling port in the evening of June 3. But the Smiths had bigger things in mind than a mere trip to the Barbary Coast.[7]

After six days tied up in port, Captain H.Z. Howard gave the order to his new command at noon precisely, on June 16, 1873, and 3881 tons of the Pacific Mail Steamship Company slipped away from the wharf at the corner of First and Brannan streets, cleared San Francisco Harbor, and then eased out into the Pacific, bound for Yokohama and Hong Kong. In addition to the $415,230 in treasure she was carrying, the *Great Republic*, one of the famous paddle steamers of the company's China Line, was also home to 130 Chinese passengers, at least while they were making the crossing. Among the other passengers was Merriman Colbert Harris. He had fought in the Civil War, on the Union side, as a 17-year-old, but the most extraordinary thing about this gentleman was that, a mere ten years later, he was a Methodist bishop, going out to Japan to set up the first Protestant mission in Hokkaido. With him were the Rev. Dr. James Walter Waugh, of the Methodists' India Mission, and the Brothers David S. Houghton and W.A. Spencer, to name but a dozen. Another man on board, one who would achieve a modicum of fame in his particular field, was Edwin Dun, a young livestock expert on loan to the Japanese. Ten'll get you twenty, though, the passenger with the most astonishing past was Mrs. Hattie L. Smith, of St. Louis, making her first tour of the Orient. What with the endless walks and meetings on the promenade deck, and every day fantastic weather and smooth seas, they had all chatted and discoursed and sworn eternal friendship long before Captain Howard pointed out the Midway Islands to them. And by the time they arrived in Yokohama on July 9, after 22 days at sea, they felt as if they had known each other all their lives. But they hadn't really. No one meeting Mrs. T.J. Smith for the first time on that cruise could have had any idea that a mere eleven years earlier she had been a Pinkerton detective, an ex-prostitute, languishing in a Confederate prison in Richmond, and possibly, just possibly, facing the hangman's noose. They couldn't have had an inkling that this pretty, very well-off, and very nice middle-aged lady was, in fact, the Civil War's most mysterious spy. Inscrutable, indeed. Ah, Japan, the Land of the Rising Sun. Forty-eight hours later they were back on the ocean wave, heading for Hong Kong, where they landed on the 18th. For Hattie and T.J., it would be a wonderful round trip that lasted two months and ten days, and was, in truth, a very real way to soak up the flavors of the Far East. On the morning of August 26, one day ahead of schedule, they arrived back in San Francisco from Yokohama, on the same steamer, the *Great Republic*, and in company with the latest scuttlebutt, mail, and newspapers from those exotic parts. Also aboard were 17,090 packages of tea.[8]

The folks back in Smith's home town of Cincinnati remembered their expatriate citizen fondly, you can tell: "Thomas Smith—Young Salty—brother of our well-known wholesale grocer, William C. Smith, on Ninth street near Sycamore, is in St. Louis and getting rich. Salty is as fond of good duds as ever."[9]

43. Warn Castle

They called Denny Hannifin the squatter governor of the Dakota Territory. He was what his fellow Irishmen might have termed a "desperate character." In the fall of 1873, about twenty miles west of Mandan and 26 miles west of the brand new town of Bismarck, this bold boy discovered several veins of lignite. He and his partner, the equally desperate John S. Warn, claimed the vein and organized the first coal company ever formed in Dakota. The novice coal miners traveled westward to their claim under military escort provided by their friend, Lieutenant Colonel George A. Custer, commanding officer of Fort Abraham Lincoln. This is how the expedition was recalled in a 1917 North Dakota newspaper when they were writing an article on Dennis: "In 1873 he, John Warn, Jack Kale and Jesse McCoy, typical frontiersmen, crossed the river, fought a battle with hostile Sioux, on the bluffs now occupied by the city of Mandan, drove the Indians back, and forged on to the Green River, where, near the present site of Dickinson, they took possession of a coal mine, built Fort Hannifin, and held it for two weeks against daily attacks of large bands of Indians, disdaining military aid. John Warn remained entrenched in this outpost seven years, and military authorities have declared it one of the strongest earthworks they ever had known." Seven years is a long time to remain entrenched in an earthworks, even for a worm, but that's what Johnny did. Why not? It was impregnable. His wife couldn't get in. Others may have given the name Fort Hannifin to this architectural oddity, and really large-scale maps may have shown it as Coal Banks, but Little Johnny called it Warn Castle.[1]

Alice divorced her husband on February 19, 1874, but Little Johnny had more pressing things on his mind. He was up in the Dakotas, hunkered down in Warn Castle. Besieged as he was by the murderous Sioux, he couldn't expel the bullets fast enough from his Winchester rifle, let alone get down to Illinois to contest the suit.[2]

44. The James Gang

The Pinkertons very definitely took the law into their own hands when they blew up the notorious outlaw's home, killing and maiming at will. The James boys weren't even there at the time. It was beginning to look as if the aftermath of this episode might include a lawsuit against Allan Pinkerton himself.

On February 16, 1875, at the height of the Pinkertons' famous feud with Frank and Jesse James, a man named George McQueen wrote a guarded letter to a legal eagle he was using out in the town of Liberty, Mo. The lawyer was Major Samuel Hardwicke. Working with Mr. McQueen on this occasion would be, forever, Hardwicke's claim to fame. He knew that even then. He knew it well because McQueen was not the letter writer's real name.

In the cloak and dagger letter, McQueen advises Sam Hardwicke to "Mail in Kansas City or to St. Louis, the inner envelope addressed to D. Robertson, etc., the outer one to Mrs. Hattie Smith, 2809 S. Morgan St., St. Louis."[1]

This letter is all the proof we need to suggest that the famous Civil War spy, Hattie Lawton, had remained a Pinkerton agent, in one form or another, from the time she got out of Castle Thunder at the end of 1862. One must understand that the reason for such an assertion is that McQueen was the maiden name of Allan Pinkerton's mother.

45. Death by Poppy

Trapped in the vortex, beyond any hope of survival, young George plunged ever, ever downward, dragged inexorably through the spiral toward the only place of misery left unexplored: Hell itself. But then, at the last moment, just before he impaled himself upon the Devil's pitchfork, he leveled out. The morphine had kicked in and it was all over. There was no more pain. There was nothing. George W. Warn was dead. He was 24.

John A. Smithers was one of the experienced undertakers in St. Louis. He had handled Belle Towler's funeral a few years earlier. Now, by request of the bereaved, he showed up at the Smith house and took control, as he always did, as he was expected to do, as he was paid to do. Three days later, at 10 o'clock in the morning of July 8, 1875, the cortege set out from 2809 Morgan, bound for Bellefontaine Cemetery and the funeral, $149 worth of it, including six pallbearers, everything paid for by T.J. Smith, gambling man. The half-glass casket alone had set him back $75.[1]

Although George had not left a will or a wife, and both his parents were dead, there was, indeed, an estate from which the Smiths could, in theory, claim their money back: 28 acres in Lee County, Illinois, worth $25 an acre. Seven hundred bucks, up for grabs, and, naturally, each and every living vulture in the Warn family swooped down upon it. The other two like shares, owned by George's minor half sisters Libby and Ella Warn respectively, were not for the taking. Not yet, anyway. But there's always more than one way to skin a cat.

A new man appeared on the Advent calendar just before Christmas, his face smiling through the little flap of the pretty gilt-edged box marked "Probate." John K. Hine was his name, a Lee County man, only twenty-five, and a friend of the Warn family, or at least of some members of the family. At the request of Hattie Smith, and acting on her behalf, Hine requested the Lee County Court to accept him as administrator of young George W. Warn's estate, and that the court did. All this sounds rather benign and run of the mill, but it wasn't at all. There were shenanigans going on behind the scenes. On that same day Mr. Hine became the guardian of Libby and Ella, the two young girls who, at that point of time, owned between them not much more than two milch cows, two heifers, two calves, and a hog—and 56 acres of land right on the Rock River, almost provocatively close to the growing city of Dixon, Illinois. That was land for which men and women might be prepared to play dirty.[2]

Dwight Heaton, the attorney for the girls, wrote to the clerk of the court of Lee County, on January 5, 1876, asking him to issue a summons to Hine demanding to know why he, Hine "should not be removed as guardian on account of his having obtained his appointment by means of false and fraudulent representations, and obtaining his said appointment by illegal means." The request was promulgated that day, and Hine was ordered to appear in the court house at Dixon on January 17, 1876. Also on January 5, Mrs. Diana Childs wrote from Dixon to Hine officially: "I am satisfied and concur in your appointment as guardian of my children, Elizabeth and Ella, and desire that you shall still continue to be their guardian." Of course, this may all be technical courtroom maneuvering, but to the layman it looks as if there might have been some sort of collusion between Diana and her new husband James R. Childs, John K. Hine and his wife, Mr. Laing the third administrator, and T.J. Smith and Mrs. Hattie L. Smith from St. Louis. This seems a rather large cabal, but when one considers that it was no longer 28 acres at stake but three times 28, a seven-way split makes more sense.[3]

By March 1877 things were heating up. The court had allowed $1,119 to the Smiths, but there was no way they could be paid unless the real estate was sold. So, now such a sale became imperative.[4]

T.J. Smith stood on the street for a moment, and stole a glance at his magnificent gold pocket watch. No one noticed this small sign of nervousness, or, indeed, of opulence. He made quite sure of the first; the second was a by-product that couldn't be helped. The big moment was fast approaching on this fine Saturday evening. A night to remember. June 30, 1877. Opening night. It was still difficult to take in the sheer amount of structural change that had been made here, change that Smith himself had not only wrought but supervised into being. The famous old Peck and Swan mansions were gone, and what was there now, dominating the block between Sixth and Seventh, was so new and so startlingly different as transformed by Kirgin & Bro., that you couldn't even tell you were in St. Louis. Not until you got used to it, anyway. 614 Locust. Smith looked across the street for a moment at the creepy statues staring down almost suicidally at him from the roof line of the St. Louis Life Insurance temple, and then, checking the hour again, he turned and walked briskly toward the broad portal that formed the main entrance to the Windsor, described by an impartial press as "one of the finest club houses in the Western country." Within half an hour or so they would be arriving, the great and good of the city. And Smith was the star of the show.[5]

You couldn't penetrate into the interior of the Windsor without going through the bar, and why would you want to? It was the city's newest and swankiest watering hole, supervised by two well-known St. Louis personalities: Tommy Newman, formerly ear-bender of the Laclede Hotel, and Al

45. Death by Poppy   159

Kountz, whom Smith had just persuaded over from keeping the saloon at the Lindell House. Bringing drinks over to your comfortable chair, and whatever food he could find, was that "slick young mulatto," the handsome Bill Casca, a man much in demand as a waiter until his career was cut short on the night of August 16, when he shot his wife in St. Paul's Church.[6]

After struggling manfully through the heady, intoxicating atmosphere of the bar, you would quite naturally swerve across the hall, a little off balance, to your right, and find yourself in the lushly furnished reading room, supplied with all the principal journals, both American and European. Rich paintings hung from the walls, while a life-sized Pandora, statuesque and appropriately cast, greeted you at the entrance. This elegance, this overwhelming completeness, symptomatic of the entire establishment, was something that could, if one wished, be recognized with gasps over and over as one progressed to the gentlemen's club rooms on the second and third floors.[7]

Instead of perambulating around St. Louis under the noonday sun, you could always pick up an elegant brunch at the Windsor between 10:30 and 1:30. This was, of course, a far cry from a full fledged restaurant, and there was indeed a cry for such a thing. A wail. It was definitely something Smith wanted to address, in time. First, though, some much-needed fast money. How could he get that? To what deadly sin could he appeal so quickly and surely? Ah, yes. Human greed. A couple of months into his new tenure, in September, he opened his keno room, with a couple of tables, and another one for faro. In short the tenor of the club changed drastically overnight. It now became a gambling house, and thus a target for police raids. Smith needed protection, and called in A.B. Wakefield, a sinister and wholly unsavory character who claimed to have "power in the Police Board." The deal was that Abe got a percentage of the profits. Alanson Bankson Wakefield had been a three card monte man on the steamboats running down to New Orleans, and was now operating a gambling room in a waterfront bawdy house in St. Louis. Protection obviously wasn't the Keno King's strong suit, as the cops just kept on raiding the Windsor as if Wakefield had never been born. Smith finally threw his hands up in despair and closed the room after only three months. It wasn't long after that, the spring of 1878, that he closed the whole place. That was the end of the Windsor. It had lasted nine months, just long enough for the latest generation of suckers to be conceived, gestated, and delivered.[8]

For a brief while, in 1878 and 1879, before things went bad, Hattie was making the social columns, whether it was a seven-week trip to Indianapolis to visit her very well-off sister-in-law, or a visit to the east, or a soiree she happened to be throwing in St. Louis. In 1880 Hattie made not the society pages but the lost and found column, when her mockingbird flew out of the window. She was offering $5 reward for its return to 2809 Morgan Street. If that was all she lost, then life wouldn't be half bad. But, unfortunately, she was on the point of losing a lot more than her mockingbird. She was poised on the edge of that dreadful abyss that too many humans know only too well.[9]

46. Out on the Old Bozeman Trail

Maggie Rogers, alias Roberta Margaret, aka Bertie, Kate, Kittie. A lot of names for a girl of 18, a milliner, aka prostitute. She and her sister Frances, alias Frankie, aka Frank, blew into town and literally within minutes a justice of the peace had John S. Warn and "Magy Rogers" signing on the dotted line in the world's fastest marriage, in the world's fastest town: Bozeman, Montana. Not even a shotgun in sight, at least not pointed in their direction at that very second. Hey, Baby, what was your name again? Just for the record, the date was November 2, 1878, and, make no mistake, it was just for the record.[1]

The happy union lasted a lot longer than the courtship: 48 days. There were no children. On December 20, John just picked up and left the territory, bound for Bismarck. Meanwhile his new wife, Kitty, went back on the game. Not much choice. On July 7, 1879, Kitty's sister, Frankie, married one of the saloon keepers in Bozeman, George Buttner. It was a festive occasion. Oh happy day! Kittie Warn and Freetricks Fox were the two required witnesses, just as spelled out in their own hand. Imagine a mother calling her baby Freetricks. More out of hope than aspiration, the newlyweds relocated to Virginia City, Montana, for about a year, ranged around that part of the territory for a while, and then, come Lewiston, the bride, glint gone, blush faded, spark extinguished, threw in the towel and headed back to Bozeman, alone. There's no business like the millinery business.[2]

Warnton, in Morton County, Dakota, was established as a post office on August 7, 1879, by the first postmaster and owner of the nearby Coal Banks: John S. Warn. It was located at Johnny's old earthworks, the place he had called Warn Castle. The Keogh stage line crossed the territory at this point, and there was good farming country extending out in every direction. "Warn's duties are light, but he is happy with a government position. The coal bank will be valuable some day, and quite a village may grow up."[3]

It was not just a question of getting the coal out of the ground and to market, it was also getting people to come and settle at Warnton. Some did, some didn't. Johnny's younger half-sister, Libby, tried Warnton for a while, with her family. Their arrival doubled the size of the town, and when they left, soon afterwards, you could hear the surprised gasp of instant shrinkage. Since there weren't many human beings to converse with out there in the wilds of wherever the hell he was, Johnny spent a lot of his time involved with Republican county politics.[4]

At midnight on May 21, 1883, in Bozeman, a doctor came to see Frankie Buttner in her house on Mendenhall Street. She had taken an overdose of morphine, but was still conscious. The doctor left instructions. Early the following morning Frankie took another overdose and died. This surprised the good physician, who must have been overdosing on something himself. Frankie's real name, it seems, wasn't Frankie at all, or even Frances, which, although it might have surprised the doctor, surprised no one who knew anything about milliners or, indeed, any other form of humanity who populated western towns like Bozeman. She was buried as Louise G. Buttner, and her tombstone says she was 21.[5]

In early October 1883, John Warn left his home at Sedalia, west of Bismarck, to go on a hunt. He was still away at 10:30 on the night of Wednesday, November 7, when section foreman Lynch reached the burning house just in time to save the hay and stables. All of John's furniture, as well as the granary, was gone. The total cost, at first estimated at about $2,500, was in fact $500, but that didn't lighten the loss when John got back. With winter fast approaching, and with no possible way to replace the house, that was a loss he sorely felt. What may have been worse, in a way, was that the fire took some valuable relics which had been in his possession for 25 years.[6]

In Bozeman, Montana, the year after the fire in Sedalia, Kitty Warn sued for divorce from John. A summons was issued and the costs of the suit were charged against the husband. Nothing unusual there. The sheriff had scoured the county looking for John, looked under every rock, and couldn't find him. That's because John wasn't under a rock. He wasn't even in the territory. He was 300 miles away in the Dakotas, in the little town of Medora, running J.S. Warn's rather famous Oyster Grotto, and everyone knew it, including, of course, Kitty and the sheriff. Fish, milk, eggs, poultry, game. First-class restaurant, corner of Broadway and 3rd. Very successful, in a Dakota sort of way. Even from as far away as Bozeman, Kitty could just about pick up the faint aroma from the Oyster Grotto's kitchen as it wafted past first one nostril and then the other. Smelled for all the world just like crisp, green lettuce. That July, Kitty got her divorce.[7]

Within a few months Kitty got burned, badly, when she accidentally dropped a lighted match into the folds of her dress. She lingered, under constant medical care, and John came down from Mandan to shed a tear. Kitty died on February 8, 1885, aged twenty-five.[8]

For John, life went on, mine after mine, one item of optimistic press after another until he managed to arrive at 1914.[9] Throughout that year, his 80th, from January onwards he was in receipt of a monthly ten dollars from the Fergus County Poor Fund. They made their last payment to him in December, just when the real Montana cold was starting to settle in.[10]

47. Three Girls Bonded for Eternity

You could tell just by looking at him as he lay there, squealing with pain and indignation, unable to roll over and right himself, that here were the unmistakable signs of a man going belly up. The back taxes alone, the sheer amount he owed on various St. Louis properties, $35,000, was crushing him, a cockroach under a size-12 gumshoe, and it was becoming clearer and clearer that the Morgan Street house, their home for so long, would have to go. In the summer of 1881, while Smith took up temporary residence at the Laclede Hotel, Hattie went to the Illinois farm, where her stepmother and four young half-sisters were living.[1]

In the 1880s, to add to his woes, Smith started to go blind from "a loco-motor disease ataxia," and physicians recommended rest. He and Hattie traveled constantly, trying to find a doctor who could help, but the only thing Smith found at the end of the trail was a huge, unpayable bill, the one item that hadn't fallen through the irreparable hole burned deep into his trouser pocket. In 1885 Hattie deposited her now useless husband at the farm in Lee County and went back to St. Louis.[2]

Reflecting on the content of her curriculum vitae, Hattie was staring right into the face of financial disaster. She didn't have much in the way of past work experience, except, of course, in the fields of prostitution and espionage. There wasn't much call for a Civil War spy these days, and, as for female detectives in general, five months before Allan Pinkerton died on July 1, 1884, his son Billy was interviewed by a reporter from the *Chicago News*: "We do not employ them as a rule. I do not believe in them. In fact, in my experience I have only known two or three that ever amounted to anything. The best one I ever knew was Mrs. Angie M. Warne, who is dead now. She had ideas like a man, and worked them out like a man. Mrs. Warne seemed to reason in a masculine way, and was not afraid to tackle any kind of a case."[3]

That ruled out the Great Game then. But how great or noble does a game have to be in order to be played? Take running a disreputable house, for example. The game, then. This was St. Louis, a city that sported one of the most notorious American tenderloins. Tenderloin means nether regions, and nether regions are as marketable as gold if handled professionally. Hattie was 52 now; it had been a while; quarter of a century, maybe. But that's all right. It's like riding a bicycle. So, without further ado, she set up at 1504 Clark, a little too close for comfort to St. Joseph's Boys' Orphanage, something that would be a bit of a problem before long, what with all those young squirts, with no hand to guide them but their own, spending a good deal of their day not praying in unison but rather planning the trek between the portals of purgatory and the gates of paradise.

Hattie was up and running, back in business, and it hadn't taken long. You don't survive several months as one of Jefferson Davis's house guests without learning how to fend for yourself. A couple of items from the early 1887 lost and founds: "$50 reward. Lost on Saturday, March 5, a well-worn pocketbook containing two $100 bills and two $50 bills. Return to 1504 Clark av., and receive above reward. Mrs Smith." That's a lot of money we're talking about there. And this: "Will party to whom I loaned silk umbrella return same? Mrs. Smith, 1504 Clark av."[4]

By 1888 everyone who could claim a part of George W. Warn's estate was still in there, in person or by proxy, but the expenses were mounting up. Tradesmen had been extending credit, but Hattie, now in good shape financially, was still paying quite a bit out of her own pocket. John Hine, having left George's estate not fully administered, wanted out, and, moreover, asked the court to get a new guardian for the minors. Hine, in fact, died that year, and James B. Charters was named administrator de bonus non, while A.C. Warner was appointed the guardian of the relevant children. The break in the log jam came on March 22, 1888, when T.J. Smith signed a receipt for $247.28 from the new administrator. This receipt was in full satisfaction of Smith's claim against the estate of George W. Warn. Hattie L. Smith did the same for $1,333.77. These two sums were juggled, thrown into the air, parlayed, and played around with; they were added, subtracted, and multiplied by, and Hattie wound up with George's 28-acre estate. At the same time she bought out the interest of her oldest half sister, Libby Miller, who was then living with her husband, B.F., out in Sioux City, Iowa. That left only Ella's 28 acres. It wouldn't be too long before Hattie got that too.[5]

There are few things more simpering, more whimpering than a marriage that's lasted too long, or a long drawn-out probate case coming to an end. Any excitement from outside is welcome. And some excitement did come, rather late in the St. Louis afternoon of May 12, 1888, when a warrant was issued, "charging Hattie Smith" of No. 1054 Clark Avenue, "of keeping a disreputable house within 100 yards of the orphan asylum on the northeast corner of Fifteenth street and Clark avenue."[6]

Mr. Charters wound up his chore as administrator of George Warn's estate on November 23, 1889, and by the second week of 1890 the press was able to report: "Geo. M. Warn settled." It had taken 15 years. The sigh of relief was collective and loud, a balloon deflating.[7]

Some of Hattie's visits to her husband made the Dixon press: "Mrs T.J. Smith, nee Miss Hattie Warne, is up from St. Louis, visiting at her old home near the river west of the city," a May 1, 1891, story reported. It was just over a month later that T.J. Smith committed suicide in his carriage outside the Dixon, Illinois, home of Hattie's half-sister Libby and her husband Frank.

But St. Louis was very definitely where Hattie's real responsibilities lay. At 1324 Spruce Street was a considerable two-story brick building, 30 feet by 145, with 13 rooms and a big yard, a well and cistern, a large hall, and a side entrance. From 1887 it had been run as a rather shady property. Being very convenient to the depot helped, as, of course, it always does, especially after a long train trip. In March 1893 Hattie took over the lease of 1324 Spruce from Nellie Eddy, and soon after moving in was joined there by Vic DeBar, the famous St. Louis madam. The two ladies would remain at this address for five years.[8]

By March 7, 1895, the leading clergy of St. Louis were proposing locating and confining all the prostitutes in one area of town. This "causes just such a commotion among them as did the orders to move from Chestnut street. In order to obtain the views of the demi-monde on the subject, a *Post-Dispatch* reporter called on Lulu Morrison, keeper of a resort on Twenty-third street. She is a bright, well-educated woman, and discussed the subject in a dispassionate manner. Her conversational powers prove that society was the loser when she fell."[9]

One of the greatest of all American writers, Mark Twain, author of *Tom Sawyer*, spent the summer of 1897 at Weggis, in Switzerland. While there he began a number of projects he never finished. Two of these were *Villagers of 1840–3* and *Hellfire Hotchkiss*, the latter forming the first three chapters of a novel. *Villagers* consists of about 8,000 words containing dozens of written sketches and notes on Twain's old neighbors when he was growing up on the Mississippi River, at Hannibal, Missouri. No one really knows what he had in mind when he wrote this particular manuscript. For material he drew on his own memory and an 1884 book about Marion County. In this manuscript, Twain gives false names to certain people, most notably his own family, which he calls Carpenter. The town of Hannibal appears as St. Petersburg.

Young Twain, known back then in those Hannibal days as Sam Clemens, had arrived there from Florida, Missouri, as a four-year-old and the family commenced their new life as lodgers at Pavey's Hotel, near the corner of Main and Hill. Jesse H. Pavey, with no Twain pseudonym to protect the innocent, was a "lazy, vile-tempered old hellion. His wife and daughters did all the work and were atrociously treated." This unattractive human being was a "vicious devil of a Corsican, a common terror in the town," but he was not from the Mediterranean at all, as it turns out. He was from Kentucky. Pavey's youngest daughter, Sue, until the day she died, would tell people her father was a Frenchman. That error even appears on her death certificate. She believed it. Old Man Pavey probably believed it himself. After all, Sue did have a brother named Napoleon.[10]

"Mrs. Mary Sklar or Sklor, 450 N. Spruce St., Nashville, Tenn.: Your daughter, Sarah, died this morning at City Hospital, shall I send remains to you, answer, letter on road to you." That horribly naked prepaid telegraphic message was written and sent by Lulu Morrison from 2117 Chestnut St., St. Louis, on January 21, 1902. Just another dead prostitute. Cause of death: Pubic abscess. One of Mother Morrison's girls. They were starting to drop, as they always did at this time of year. Not like flies, perhaps, but they were dropping.[11]

Lulu herself, come the end of the year, was in dreadfully bad shape, and to her and to Hattie Smith and Sue Pavey it seemed like a good time to think of dying and funerals. It certainly occupied Sue's mind as she made her way out to the cemetery. Bellefontaine was the big one, the grandest cemetery for miles around, and therefore safe to say the next assured stop on the road to paradise. A halfway house for the faithful. Sue purchased Lot No. 8 in Block 196. Number eight was a three-grave public lot; i.e., not a family plot. In other words, it was for three persons. There would be no need for monuments, fancy stones, obelisks, or crypts. This was going to be an unmarked burial place. After all, what could an inscription possibly say? "Here lies famous madam Hattie Smith with her Number One Protégée, Lulu Morrison, and their dressmaker friend, Sue Pavey?" So now, bought and paid for, the hole just lay there, waiting, a monstrous, clay-caked index finger sticking out of it, beckoning randomly, remorselessly, invisible until the time came...[12]

The yawning grave didn't have long to wait. For just a single second on December 5, 1902, as she lay on the operating table in the gloom of Baptist Hospital after a bungled peritonitis operation, Lulu caught a glimpse of the finger, and it was beckoning her. Within seconds she was dead from shock. She was just 30. The death record says she was a housewife. She was buried two days later, the first of the three ladies to be tumbled. Her funeral expenses were paid by William J. Lemp, Jr., the 37-year-old vice-president of the famous St. Louis brewing company. God bless you, Billy.[13]

In March of 1904 Hattie sold the Lee County farm to Louise Gerdes for $5,650. There had been no one living there anyway. It was not and never had been, a working farm; it fell into the category "unproductive." Hattie left her home at 1422 Clark Avenue, St. Louis, and with the money from the farm sale bought 1727 Morgan Street, not far from where she had lived in those good days of the 1870s, the days where the action was. It was at the new Morgan Street house that she would remain for the rest of her life, first with Addie Cheatham, her middle-aged black housekeeper, and then with Sue Pavey.[14]

47. Three Girls Bonded for Eternity

William Frederick August Schultz lived at 3732 Olive Street, St. Louis. On September 5, 1913, he was at home when he was suddenly called over to 1727 Morgan, where Sue Pavey opened the door. A doctor is a doctor, so they say, but Schultz was an ear, nose and throat man. Perhaps Sue should have called in another kind of physician. One who specialized in immortality. Hattie died of arteriosclerosis two days later, at 11 o'clock at night. The death certificate says her right name was Harriet L. Smith, and that she had been born in Germany of German parents. Sue Pavey, the informant for the death certificate, certainly didn't pluck those gems out of thin air, and she had known Hattie a long time. So Lucy Ann Warn, from Southport, New York, a spy to the very end, with false name and false particulars. If Sue didn't know, then it's obvious that Hattie never talked. Her past would remain a secret for another century.[15]

"Harriet L. Smith. Funeral will take place from Arthur J. Donnelly's funeral parlors, twenty-first and Wash streets, to Bellefontaine Cemetery. Due notice of time will be given." That's from the *St. Louis Post-Dispatch*, of September 8, 1913. The following day's issue of the *St. Louis Star and Times* gave the same mention, but they did add that the funeral would take place in the afternoon of Tuesday, the 9th. Online, Bellefontaine's records agree that she was buried on the 9th, but when you speak in person to the staff at the cemetery they insist—insist, I say—that Harriet L. Smith was laid to rest on September 8. The final mystery in a life of mystery.[16]

Appendix A:
The Warn Family

Israel P. Warn, b. 1807, CT, son of Cornelius Warn by his first wife, Eleanor, d. Oct. 9, 1871, Lee Co., IL. Buried Oakwood Cemetery, Lee Co., IL. *M. (i)* Nov. 26, 1828, Erin, Tioga Co., NY., Elizabeth "Betsy" Hurlburt (b. Nov. 30, 1809, CT, d. Sept. 22, 1859, Lee Co., IL, buried Oakwood Cemetery, Lee Co., IL), dau. of Allen Webb Hurlburt and Mahala Brooks. *Issue:*

1. Mahala Ann "Angie" (aka Kate) Warn, b. Oct. 1829, Erin, Tioga Co., NY, d. Jan. 28, 1868, Chicago. Buried Jan. 30, 1868, Graceland Cemetery, Chicago. No issue.

2. Allen B. Warn, b. 1830, Erin, Tioga Co., NY. *M.* Mary Emma (div. Sept. 1871). *Issue:* Franklin B. "Frank" Warn, b. 1856, WI.

3. Lucy Ann Warn, b. March 28, 1833, Southport, Tioga Co., NY, d. Sept. 7, 1913, St. Louis. Buried Sept. 9, 1913, Bellefontaine Cemetery, St. Louis. *M. (i)* Oct. 6, 1853, Magnolia, Rock Co., WI, Fred Barrett (b. Oct. 15, 1829, Dutchess Co., NY, d. Dec. 29, 1920, Los Angeles), son of Abijah Knowlton "A.K." Barrett and his wife Lydia Robinson. No issue. *M. (ii)* 1868, Thomas J. Smith (b. 1835, Cincinnati, OH, d. June 11, 1891, Dixon, IL, buried June 13, 1891, Oakwood Cemetery, Lee Co., IL), son of John W. Smith and Jane. No issue.

4. John S. Warn, b. 1834, Southport, Tioga Co., NY. *M. (i)* Jan. 1860, Lee Co., IL, Alice Andrews (b. Jan. 5, 1846, d. April 18, 1913, Chicago; buried Oakwood Cemetery, Lee Co., IL), dau. of Ives Andrews and Sylvia Bartholome. Div. Feb. 1874. *Issue:* Edward Thompson Warn (b. April 12, 1861, Lee Co., IL, d. April 20, 1932, Danville, IN; *m.* Feb. 15, 1898, Gertrude Estella "Gertie" Warn, his half-aunt by blood; no issue). *M. (ii)* Nov. 2, 1878, Bozeman, MT, Roberta Margaret "Maggie" Rogers (b. 1860, MO, d. Feb. 8, 1885, Bozeman, MT), div. June 27, 1884. No issue. *M. (iii)* Sarah H. Div. March 19, 1896. No issue.

5. Samanda Catherine (also spelled Zemanda Katherine) "Kitty" Warn, b. 1837, Southport, Chemung Co., NY, d. Feb. 9, 1869, St. Louis. Buried Graceland Cemetery, Chicago. *M.* Dec. 1853, Janesville, Rock Co., WI, Oscar Fitzerlan Brackett. No issue.
6. Henry Wallace "Harry" Warn, b. 1840, Chemung Co., NY. Unm.
7. Laura Isabelle "Belle" Warn, b. 1843, Southport, Chemung Co., NY, d. May 2, 1871, St. Louis. Buried Oakwood Cemetery, Lee Co., IL. *M. (i)* Feb. 1859, Dixon, IL, Thomas S. Deyo (b. 1837, MI), son of Solomon Deyo and Elizabeth M. Dubois. No issue. *M. (ii)* Mr. Towler. No issue.
8. Frederick "Freddie" Warn, b. May 22, 1849, Southport, Chemung Co., NY, d. Sept. 19, 1859, Lee Co., IL. Buried Oakwood Cemetery, Lee Co., IL.
9. George W. Warn, b. 1851, Rock Co., WI, d. July 5, 1875, St. Louis. Unm. Buried July 8, 1875, Bellefontaine Cemetery, St. Louis.

M. (ii) July 15, 1860, Palmyra, Lee Co., Ill., Diana Campbell (b. Sept. 24, 1835, Chenango Co., NY, d. Aug. 1902, Lee Co., IL, buried Oakwood Cemetery, Lee Co., IL), eldest child of Alanson B. Campbell and Mary D. Benjamin. *Issue:*

10. Elizabeth M. "Libby" Warn, b. Sept. 6, 1861, Lee Co., IL, d. Aug. 15, 1949, Lewisburg, TN. Buried Aug. 17, 1949, Lone Oak Cemetery, Lewisburg, TN. *M. (i)* 1881, Benjamin Franklin "B.F." Miller (b. April 11, 1858, Palmyra, Lee Co., IL, d. 1905), son of William Mueller and Anna Obrist. *Issue:* 1a. Orville Chester Miller (b. Aug. 25, 1882, Palmyra, Lee Co., IL, d. Aug. 2, 1960, Lewisburg, Tenn; *m.* 1903, Elizabeth Katherina "Lizzie" Otto [b. March 7, 1885, Cook Co., IL, d. April 2, 1936, Sandpoint, Bonner Co., ID], dau. of Adam H. Otto and Maria Heppel; div. 1923; many descendants alive today). 2a. Edna O. Miller (b. March 22, 1889, Sioux City, IA, d. June 23, 1908, St. Louis, unm.; buried Dixon, IL. *M. (ii)* Lewis A. Mallonee (b. 1857, d. May 11, 1929, Point Pleasant, WV; buried Lone Oak Cemetery, Lewisburg, Tenn.), son of James Mallonee. No issue.
11. Ella May Warn, b. Dec. 29, 1863, Lee Co., IL, d. Feb. 23, 1940, Lewisburg, TN. Buried Feb. 25, 1940, Lone Oak Cemetery, Lewisburg, TN. *M.* March 21, 1926, Harold Ellsworth "Hal" Sherman, her late sister's husband. No issue.
12. Lena Belle Warn, b. Aug. 20, 1868, Lee Co., IL, d. Nov. 17, 1925, Brooklyn, NY. Buried Nov. 20, 1925, Fresh Pond, NY. *M.* Nov. 28, 1891, Lee Co., IL, Harold Ellsworth "Hal" Sherman (b. Aug. 6, 1863, IL, d. Dec. 19, 1926, Point Pleasant, WV), son of Lee Sherman and Caroline. No issue.

13. Gertrude Estella "Gertie" Warn, b. April 30, 1871, Lee Co., IL, d. May 26, 1910. Buried Dixon, IL. *M.* Feb. 15, 1898, Edward Thompson Warn, her nephew. No issue.

Appendix B: George Warn at Notre Dame

The costs for a boy attending Notre Dame, as outlined in the institution's catalog for 1864–1865, were as follows:
- Board, bed and bedding, and tuition (Latin and Greek included), per session of five months—$115. No student would be received for a shorter period than one session of five months. So, a student had to be present for at least five months out of every year.
- Washing and mending of linens—$10.
- Doctor's fees and medicine, and attendance in sickness—$2.50.
- Payments were always made in advance, otherwise you didn't get in.
- Each student was expected to arrive with six shirts, four towels, one hat, three pairs of shoes, and one setting of silverware.
- These are the payments made for George W. Warn during his years at South Bend, as recorded by Hattie L. Smith on January 28, 1876, in front of a St. Louis notary public, in her claim against the estate of her late brother, George W. Warn. One must remember, the most likely thing is that these figures represent Hattie's contribution only, and do not reflect in any way any contributions made by her sisters.
- March 1863—$250, for the year's tuition; board; books; etc.
- March 1864—$250, ditto for second year.
- August 1866—$500, ditto to date & for clothing for 4 years.

According to Notre Dame records, the following are the sums paid, always in cash. Since one does not, and never did, send cash through the mail, that means whoever paid did so in person:

October 27, 1864—$120. I.P. Warn is listed as George's father. Mrs. O.F. Brackett from Memphis is listed as his guardian. That year's school catalog, 1864–65, lists the student as George Warn, of Dixon, Ill. The $120 must have been for the $115 basic bed & board, bedding, and tuition, plus the $5 matriculation fee. The most eligible time for entering school was at the beginning of the scholastic sessions, i.e., in September and February, but basically a student could join at any time and be counted from that date. As long as the school got its money. It looks, then, as if George enrolled on or around October 27, 1864.

October 29, 1864—$35. This is only two days after the first cash payment. Whoever made these two payments so close together was staying-over in South Bend for a few days, to make sure everything went off all right with George settling in. Students who spent their summer vacations at the college were charged an additional $35. This may be what the extra $35 was for.

June 22, 1865. Commencement.

September 12, 1865—$143.55. This payment seems to have accompanied his registration record for this, his second year, for that registration was on the same date, September 12: "Warn, Geo. age 14, Memphis, Tenn." See *Notre Dame Student Daybook*, vol. 1, p. 132.

October 17, 1865. Registration record. Money not discussed. "Warn Geo. (Back.)" See *Notre Dame Student Daybook*, vol. 1, p. 160.

November 28, 1865—$134.73. George is at Notre Dame in the 1865–66 catalog. Again I.P. Warn is listed as the father, and Mrs. O.F. Brackett, of Memphis, is his guardian.

May 29, 1866—$106. This was the fifth and last payment, the one that's going to take him through one five-month session. He should be out on his ear by February 1867, due to lack of payment. The grand total paid so far, according to the Notre Dame records, is about $539. But no. He stays on. There must be some accounting records missing from Notre Dame's files.

In the 1866–67 year, George's guardian was still listed in the Notre Dame records as Mrs. O.F. Brackett of Memphis, and his father as I.P. Warn.

May 29, 1867. Money not discussed. Registration record. "Warn, George, age 17—Dixon, Ill." He's back, all right, but again there must be accounting records missing for this second session of 1867. See *Notre Dame Student Daybook*, Vol. 2, page 73.

September 8, 1867. Money not discussed. "Warn, G. (Returned)—age 17. Dixon, Ill." Yet again, there must be accounting records missing. Four days later, on September 12, Robert A. Pinkerton was registered, age 18, Chicago. See *Notre Dame Student Daybook*, Vol. 2, p. 127.

September 9, 1867. George W. Warn, of Chicago, is in the Notre Dame magazine, in the senior class, listed as an additional student.

September 28, 1867. George Warn is cited as one of the best readers in the senior class.

December 14, 1867. George W. Warn is mentioned in the Notre Dame magazine, getting a first in Orthography (Jr.)

The 1867–68 Notre Dame records give Mrs. Belle Fowler [sic] as George's guardian now, and she is at 18 South 8th Street, St. Louis.

March 1868. George leaves Notre Dame.

Hattie's sums of money don't match up with Notre Dame's, and that's because Notre Dame is recording only their tuition fees, and perhaps board as well. Hattie is including in her payments board, books, etc. Another thing: Hattie was almost certainly recording only her contributions, not any made by her sisters.

The main problem is that the years don't agree. But the problem is not a big one because George did go to Notre Dame for four years, and someone paid his way.

Appendix C: H.H.L.

William Henry Herndon was Abraham Lincoln's junior law partner in Springfield, Illinois, before the great man assumed the presidency of the U.S.A. Just after Lincoln was assassinated in 1865, Herndon, who was then 47, began collecting Lincolniana. He called his collection the "Lincoln Record," but nearly all of it pertains to his subject's pre-presidential career. The collection really goes up until February 1861, with the departure from Springfield of the president-elect.[1]

However, all is not lost for our research. There is a little bit of post-departure material in the "Lincoln Record." Herndon says: "Some years before his death [he means 1866, eighteen years before Pinkerton's death in 1884], Mr. Pinkerton furnished me with a large volume of the written reports of his subordinates, and an elaborate account by himself of the conspiracy [he means the Baltimore Plot of 1861] and the means he employed to ferret it out." This "large volume" is now known as Pinkerton's Record Book. One of the written reports to be found in this record book was by Timothy Webster. In it, the agent mentions his fellow operative, H.H.L., and identifies her as a woman. But, better still, another of these written reports was from H.H.L. herself.

By 1866, Herndon, fearing that his offices might be destroyed by fire, determined to have his "Lincoln Record" copied, and so hired a clerk, John G. Springer, then only 22, to transcribe the whole mass of letters and memoranda in his clear, round hand. This mass included that "large volume," Pinkerton's Record Book, which, once it had been copied by Springer, Herndon sent back to the Chicago detective with thanks.

After an autumn of intense work but not altogether faithful transcribing, by December 1, 1866, the job was done. The transcriptions made by Springer were arranged roughly under geographical sub-headings—into topics, if you like—and were sent to Bradford & Johnson, Springfield's best bookbinders, where they were made up into three volumes, "each the size of Webster's Dictionary on legal cap." The binding was "of excellent heavy leather—spring back—strongly done, etc." To sum up, these three professionally bound volumes consist of Springer's transcriptions of Herndon's entire original "Lincoln Record," and a few other documents. Of course, enmeshed in these so-called Springer transcripts was John Springer's manuscript copy of Pinkerton's Record Book, the original of which had gotten sent back to the detective with thanks. No duplicates were made of these three volumes. There existed just that one set, now nicely bound, for Herndon himself.[2]

In 1869 Herndon, who at that moment in his life was in serious financial difficulties, sold the three bound volumes that constituted the Springer transcripts for $4000 to Ward Hill Lamon, who, like Herndon, intended to write a book on Lincoln. On May 13, 1870, Lamon turned the whole lot over to Chauncey Black, his ghost writer, who began collecting the notes into some sort of order, and two years later Lamon's book came out. It was called *The Life of Abraham Lincoln from His Birth to His Inauguration as President.*

Lamon in his 1872 book does not mention Pinkerton by name, merely referring to him as "a private detective," "the detective," or "the chief detective." He holds Pinkerton in the highest scorn, and completely dismisses the Baltimore Plot as the great detective's fabrication, as merely a means to fame and fortune. It is scathing. "Taking with him a couple of other men" to Baltimore, "and a woman, the detective went about his business with the zeal which necessarily marks his peculiar profession." The woman he refers to is Kate Warn. As for the material from Pinkerton's Record Book, Lamon dismisses it thus: "These documents are neither edifying nor useful; they prove nothing but the baseness of the vocation which gave them existence." With that, he doesn't use any of it in his book.

By 1882 Herndon still hadn't written his book. That year Jesse Weik began collecting Lincolniana in Springfield and elsewhere, and in 1885 he and Herndon began their collaboration, in 1889 finally publishing *Herndon's Lincoln: The True Story of a Great Life.* However, the book just about skips over the Baltimore Plot. Herndon died in 1891, and the following year Weik produced a revised version of the book: *Abraham Lincoln: The True Story of a Great Life,* but nothing new was added to the parts about Pinkerton.

It must be remembered that Herndon had returned the original Pinkerton's Record Book to its owner way back in 1866, and from that point on it reposed, with the great detective's other irreplaceable documents, in one of five large and 100-per-cent-guaranteed-fireproof safes made by S.H. Harris

Co., of Chicago. There the Record Book remained, in Pinkerton's office, undisturbed until the Great Chicago Fire of 1871, when it was revealed that Harris's advertising had not been 100-per-cent-accurate. Thus, in a flash, Pinkerton's Record Book ceased to exist in any form whatsoever except one and one alone—the copy made by Springer in 1866 and which now formed part of the Springer transcripts, the three bound volumes which rested in the care of the dangerously unsympathetic Ward Lamon.

Lamon died in 1893 and his daughter, Dorothy Lamon Teillard, acquired the Springer transcripts. She sold them in 1912 to George D. Smith, the New York book dealer, and in January 1914 Henry Huntington acquired them for his library in San Marino, California, for $12,600 (Smith claimed the price was $50,000, but only to garner publicity.) And that is how the Springer transcription, which includes the only surviving copy of Pinkerton's Record Book, was acquired by the Manuscripts Department at the Huntington Library.

In the 1920s Norma Barrett Cuthbert was chief cataloguer of manuscripts at the Huntington. In the Springer transcripts, she found the manuscript copy of Pinkerton's Record Book. But did she? She herself describes this "manuscript, which is actually a copy of a copy of a copy, [and which] has numerous textual peculiarities and discrepancies, which cannot be explained with any assurance of accuracy."[3]

What does this mean, "a copy of a copy of a copy?" That makes three copies. Miss Cuthbert explains it this way: "The very first memoranda, upon which the records were based, presumably were jotted down day by day, more or less on the spot." All right, that would be the first copy, the word "copy" here meaning "version" or "incarnation," there being no implication that anyone was actually replicating it. In other words, by the "very first memoranda" she means those written by the Pinkerton agents in the field, back in the early 1860s. "Later, these reports were copied, apparently quite at random, into the book, and this in turn was copied by Springer." All right, those are the second and third copies right there, the second copy being made by Pinkerton as he made the entries in his book, and the third copy being by Springer.[4]

Cuthbert further explains, unsatisfactorily it must be stated: "Also there were any number of verbal reports which occurred at intervals not always indicated in the manuscript." In order to make better sense out of it, Cuthbert arranged what memos she had in chronological order, but made no other changes to the Springer Manuscript.[5]

Miss Cuthbert worked for years on her book, with the help of people such as Robert Pinkerton II, Allan Pinkerton's great grandson, and it finally came out in 1949, published by the Huntington Library itself. This was the first time the world had ever seen the initials H.H.L. It was the first chance anyone had ever had to match up H.H.L. with the Hattie Lawton of Pinkerton's 1883 book, *The Spy of the Rebellion*.

But it wasn't the first chance anyone had had to match Hattie Lawton up with the initials H.L. Just H.L. Not H.H.L. In July 1947, two years before Miss Cuthbert's book was published, the Lincoln Papers were made public by their owners, the Library of Congress. One of those letters to Lincoln, dated April 21, 1861, is from Pinkerton. The last four pages of this letter comprise his secret cipher, column after column of code words for hundreds of everyday objects, places, and people. And for a handful of his agents as well. One of those agents is H.L., who has the code name Cranberries. For 72 years now that letter has been available, and for the last several of those it's been on line, with a good search engine. The odd thing is, no one ever saw this "H.L." until now.

It will be remembered that in 1869 Herndon, because he was broke, had sold the Springer transcripts to Ward Hill Lamon. On the other hand, he kept the originals of the "Lincoln Record," but not the copies Springer had made of the Pinkerton Record Book, since those had been incorporated into the Springer transcripts and those in turn had been sold to Ward Lamon. It was this original "Lincoln Record," the one kept by Herndon, combined with the material Weik had collected, that in 1891, upon Herndon's death, went to Weik. After Weik's death in 1923, his son sold the entire Herndon-Weik Collection of Lincolniana to G.A. Baker and Co., of New York. Moves to get it given to the Library of Congress began in 1931, and it was finally purchased from Baker by the LOC in 1941. The collection also includes other Lincoln material acquired by the LOC between 1929 and 1982.

Appendix D: Online

There are thousands of websites that mention Kate Warne, Hattie Lawton, Timothy Webster, or Pinkerton. Obviously it would be a chore to list them all, and in the end would there be any point? After all, if for no other reason, the Internet, like a book, is a blank page just waiting there for anyone to lay anything down on it. Just one example, though, for fun...

"The Early Pinkertons" was put on the web in 2007 by Geoff Pinkerton, seemingly a Canadian. A typical conspiracy theory, it takes the form of "the true story" of the founding of the famous Chicago detective agency. While technically not exactly good writing, it is quite gripping, and, because it shows a fair mastery of historical time and place, it is a somewhat convincing narrative.

The author is presented as Margaret Pinkerton Fitchett, the great granddaughter of Allan Pinkerton's mysterious older brother, Robert. For years Miss Fitchett, who did, indeed, remain a proper miss, had been the sole custodian of the nasty truth about Allan and the horrible things he did to Robert, and to Robert's widow and six children. Oh, it's awful! Now Miss Fitchett finally found herself in a position where she could set the record straight, at last she could tell the world how it was not Allan at all who founded the company, but Miss Fitchett's almost unbelievably unsung great grandfather, Robert. It was Robert all the way. Allan did nothing except sponge off his older brother and take all the credit, and, of course, all the money.

Maggie Fitchett's manuscript somehow wound up in Canberra, and for reasons not clear, from there made its way to the state of Washington, and finally from there to Canada and Geoff Pinkerton.

At this point, it begins to cross the reader's mind that this is all a hoax.

After only a few minutes' independent digging anyone can confirm that the heroine was, indeed, a real person. Although she never had the middle name Pinkerton, she was born Margaret Fitchett, in Yorkshire, in 1917, one of eight children of coal hewer Pat Fitchett and his wife, Mary Pinkerton. Mary herself, Maggie's mother, that is, came from a long line of Pinkerton hewers. Pinkerton was a common enough name in the old Lancashire mines. *The Road to Wigan Pier*. Slag heaps. Beneath the coal dust, sallow cheeks and depressed, yellow foreheads. Bloody awful life. The worst. Read Orwell.

In real life, the Chicago Robert Pinkerton, the brother of the famous detective, was born in Glasgow in 1815. Allan was born there four years later. Glasgow is a long walk from Wigan, even above ground. Robert apprenticed as a blacksmith, and Allan as a cooper. In Glasgow, not Wigan. In 1842 both lads emigrated to the U.S.A. and opened up a cooperage in Dundee, Illinois. By the early 1850s, Allan had started his detective agency and Robert was a booking agent for the brand new Galena & Chicago Union Railroad, the first line out of Chicago. He had always lived with Allan, had always been taken care of by his younger brother, but on June 14, 1856, Robert married the widow Sarah Eaves, who for the last seven years had been operating a flourishing little millinery business out of her home on South Clark. At that point Robert moved in with her and opened a news depot on Dearborn, or rather, one was opened for him.[1]

Despite what one may read, this was, at the age of 41, Robert Pinkerton's first and only marriage. The two young Eaves girls, Sarah and Mary, were the closest he ever came to having children, to leading a normal life, but even that didn't last long, the girls fleeing into lousy marriages as soon as they could. In 1883 Billy Pinkerton, in the newspaper article that became known as "Famous Detectives," had this to say about his uncle: "He had also been in the secret service during the unpleasantness and did effective work. He

15. Cumberland, Maryland, May 1862. Back row, from left: H.B. Seybolt, Paul H. Dennis, unidentified provost guard, Allan Pinkerton, provost guard, George H. Bangs, provost guard, John Babcock, Robert Pinkerton (Allan's brother). Front row, from left: Paul Dennis, D.G. McKelvey, Billy Pinkerton, Sam Bridgman. Lying down, from left: William B. Watts, chief wagon master, and Sam Washington, cook. The IDs were made by Allan Pinkerton's son, Robert, and Paul Dennis' name appears twice; which man he is and the identity of the other man are unknown (photograph by James F. Gibson, Library of Congress).

afterward was in charge of one of the watches of the agency and died in 1875." Billy must have been thinking of someone else, or trying to. One gets the distinct feeling, from the awfully faint praise bestowed, that he wouldn't have even mentioned this rather embarrassing relative if he hadn't been giving the interview right there at Graceland Cemetery, one booted foot resting on

Uncle Robert's dead body, so to speak, and if the reporter hadn't asked him point blank to say something, anything, about the man who, aside from this little snippet, never made the press at all, ever in his life. Despite Robert's inclusion in a couple of photographs of several Pinkerton agents and others, taken in Cumberland, Maryland, in May 1862, there is no evidence that he did any work for the U.S. Secret Service. He's just there, it seems, at the edge of the photos, at the pleasure of his younger brother; with that pleasant, rather vacant look on his face, he looks almost normal. He was certainly never an officer of any of his brother's companies, and as for being in charge of one of the agency's watches after the war, there wasn't an "afterward" for Robert, for he died, not in 1875 as Billy had thought, but on November 6, 1863, in Chicago, at the age of 48, and was buried in Dundee Township Cemetery West, in Kane County. On April 6, 1869, he was dug up on his brother's orders and taken to Graceland Cemetery in Chicago. In 1880, Sarah returned to Kane County, and died there on July 14, 1899. She was buried in Dundee, with her first husband, George Eaves.[2]

By the time you get to the end of "The Early Pinkertons," you have long been aware that the whole thing is, indeed, as you had suspected, a hoax. But it's a clever hoax. However, clever as it may be, it is without point, except to hoax, and the taste that's left in your mouth, long after the reading, is one of astonishment and sadness that someone should have gone to so much trouble to learn so much for so little reward. Empty calories.

Chapter Notes

Prologue

1. *Dixon Evening Telegraph*, June 10, 1891, p. 1, "Thomas J. Smith, a Blind Citizen, Shoots Himself on Our Streets," and pp. 1 and 4, "A Sad Suicide"; June 11, 1891, p. 1, no title; June 13, 1891, p. 6, "The Suicide at Rest"; June 16, 1891, p. 1, no title.

Introduction

1. Carl Sandburg, in his *Abraham Lincoln: The War Years*, 502, refers to Timothy Webster as "a pathetic invalid, under the care of Mrs. Carrie Lawton, also a Pinkerton operative." Sandburg's biography of Lincoln won a Pulitzer Prize.
2. *New York Times*, Dec. 17, 1911, p. 42, "Noted Spy's Suicide Ends a Tragic War Drama."
3. Actually, it would be inaccurate to say that *all* modern book historians before Recko dismissed the name Lewis out of hand. Ed Fishel, in his 1996 work, *The Secret War for the Union*, writes "Hattie Lawton (or Lewis)," but obviously very tentatively, and only in an endnote on page 614. He cites no source for this, but it was unquestionably Beymer. It is quite clear that Mr. Fishel was uncomfortable with Beymer's use of the name Lewis, but it is equally evident that he would have been a lot more so if he hadn't somehow included the name Lewis if only parenthetically. That same year, 1996, David D. Ryan called her Hattie Lewis in his book about Elizabeth Van Lew. Like Fishel, Mr. Ryan got the name Lewis from Beymer. However, unlike Fishel, Ryan is a committed Beymerite, and rightly so, at least in this instance. The only book historian between 1996 and Recko in 2013 who mentions the name Lewis is Frances Harding Casstevens; in *George W. Alexander and Castle Thunder* (2004) and *Tales from the North and South* (2007) she tells us that Mrs. Timothy Webster was, in reality, "Hattie H. Lawton, alias Hattie Lewis Lawton, a member of Pinkerton's Female Detective Bureau." Just in case one's heart leaps at the thought that this rather definitive statement might be the product of groundbreaking research, for the origin of the term "Female Detective Bureau" see note 12 of Chapter 2. That should give the reader ample warning.

Chapter 1

1. Lucy Ann's date of birth, March 28, 1833, is from the St. Louis death certificate of Harriet L. Smith, same woman. Her exact place of birth, Southport, New York, is from the 1835 New York state census. Her name, Lucy Ann, is from the 1850 and 1860 censuses, and from her marriage notice in the *Janesville Daily Gazette*, Oct. 15, 1853, p. 2, "Married." She was named

after her aunt on the Hurlburt side. Orin J. Dearborn, Baptist preacher, performed the wedding on Oct. 6, 1853. When the Wisconsin state census was taken, in mid-1855, Fred Barrett had two females living with him. They are unnamed, but one of them really has to be Lucy Ann. If the other one is a daughter, then she didn't survive long. Rock County birth and death records do not exist for that time period, so, given no other places to look, we're reduced to either guessing or not even thinking about it. On Feb. 1, 1859, in Rock County, Fred Barrett would remarry, to the widow Harriet S. Budlong. The 1855 census gives us the fascinating ethnic makeup of Magnolia: One black man in the entire town.

2. *Business Directory of Chicago for October 1, 1856.* Chicago: John Gager & Co., 1856.

3. One of the very first settlers in Chicago was James Kinzie. In 1857 he was living in Clyde, Wisconsin, and came up against a man calling himself Peter G. Roe, but whose real name was Timothy Webster. See Chapter 4.

4. *Chicago Tribune*, Sept. 16, 1856, p. 3, "Prize Fight Between Two Females"; Sept. 17, 1856, p. 3, "The Prize Fight."

5. *Chicago Tribune*, May 30, 1857, p. 1, "The Conspiracy Case"; 1856 Chicago city directory.

6. *Chicago Tribune*, Aug. 24, 1857, p. 2, "Fined at Last."

7. *Chicago Tribune*, Aug. 28, 1857, p. 2, "Cyprians." Peter Snyder, a notorious liquid case, and a regular contributor to Chicago's coffers, had his name spelled Sneider in this news item.

8. *Chicago Tribune*, March 31, 1858, p. 2, "Police Court."

9. *Janesville Daily Gazette*, April 14, 1859, p. 2, "Arrest of Courtezans," from the *Chicago Journal* of April 9, 1859.

Chapter 2

1. Pinkerton, *The Somnambulist and the Detective*, 144 and 145. In everything Pinkerton ever wrote or caused to be written on the hiring of Kate Warn, whenever speaking specifically, he never varies from the early spring of 1855. However, pretty much every modern historian disagrees with Pinkerton, says it was 1856. Some have even come up with an actual date and time of day. It's amazing what researchers can do today with computers.

2. Pinkerton discusses that initial meeting in four places: The lengthy obituary he wrote when Kate died and which was published in the March 5, 1868, issue of the Chicago newspaper the *Republican*, and from there copied in one form or another by most newspapers in the civilized world; his 1874 book, *The Expressman and the Detective*; his 1882 book, *The Somnambulist and the Detective*, which was actually written in 1874–75, with a foreword dated September 1875; and his 1883 book, *The Spy of the Rebellion*. That's it. So any details above and beyond those are the invention of latter day revisionists, in other words fiction. And there's been plenty of that.

3. *Milwaukee Daily Sentinel*, March 15, 1855, p. 3, "City Matters," taken from the *Chicago Daily Times* of March 2, 1855. It was in 1852 that Pinkerton relocated to Chicago. For the next several years he moonlighted as a private detective. The first real manifestation of his own business was the North-Western Police Agency, which he founded in early 1855. But his day job was as a deputy sheriff of Cook County. By 1855 he was gaining a wide reputation both as a deputy and as a private investigator. Even as late as November 1856 he was running for sheriff. You can never be too careful about your security.

4. Pinkerton, *The Expressman and the Detective*, 94.

5. Pinkerton, *The Spy of the Rebellion*, 75.

6. Pinkerton, *The Expressman and the Detective*, 95.

7. The 1861 Chicago city directory lists

her as Kate Warn, widow of George, living at 285 West Adams, which was a Pinkerton house, the same house at which we find "Mrs. Warren" in the 1860 census. It is occasionally demanded by historians—emotionally demanded, actually—how one can possibly know a particular address in a census that doesn't give addresses. The brief answer is "triangulation with city directories," a study of which considerably reduces stress in and greatly improves the manners of those researchers who hitherto had been ignorant of the wonderful opportunities afforded by city directories. Anyway, the way the city directories formatted entries for widows, which was exactly the same way as for divorcees, the word "widow" being used in both cases, would mean that Kate's late or divorced husband's name was George. That could be. The implication in the city directory is that George's last name was Warn. That can't be, since Warn was Kate's maiden name; so we have no idea of George's surname. What makes this line of inquiry less than exciting is that in the 1860 Chicago directory we find, at 283 West Adams (a misprint for 285), Kate Waon [sic], widow of William. Yes, wonderful opportunities.

8. The quotes are from (1) the obit in the *Chicago Republican* of March 5, 1868, and (2) Pinkerton, *The Expressman and the Detective*, 95.

9. *Chicago Republican*, March 5, 1868, Kate Warn's obituary.

10. Pinkerton, *The Expressman and the Detective*, 95.

11. On March 29, 1836, Tioga County, New York, would split into two: Tioga and Chemung. The Warn family, without having to move an inch, now found themselves in Chemung County. The husband of the real Kate Warn, Oscar, out in Iowa, will be discussed further in a later chapter.

12. *Chicago Republican*, March 5, 1868, Kate Warn's obituary. As for the female department, James McKay, author of the book *The Pinkertons*, coined the alternative name Female Detective Bureau. He just made it up. Most historians since then have accepted and regurgitated this term, unaware that it has had currency only since 1996.

13. Pinkerton, *The Somnambulist and the Detective*, 144.

Chapter 3

1. *Chicago Tribune*, Jan. 27, 1854, p. 3, "Recorder's Court"; Jan. 28, 1854, p. 3, "Recorder's Court."

2. The 1860 census for Lee County, Ill.; *Chicago Tribune*, April 8, 1859, p. 1, "The City." The mining country, which was in what was called Kansas Territory back then, wasn't exactly at the mountain known as Pike's Peak; it was 85 miles to the north, close to what would become Denver and Boulder. In 1861 it became part of the new Colorado Territory.

3. *Louisville Daily Courier*, Oct. 23, 1860, p. 4, "From Nebraska"; *Nebraska Advertiser*, Oct. 26, 1860, p. 3, "Thieving." This story was carried by several other papers, including the *Chicago Tribune* of Oct. 23, the *New York Times* of Oct. 24, and the *Janesville Weekly Gazette* of Oct. 26, so plenty of people who knew Allen got to see a little more of his true character, if they hadn't already known it.

4. *Dixon Telegraph*, Jan. 19, 1860, p. 2, c. 5; 1860 census for Lyons City, Iowa.

Chapter 4

1. Those are the opening lines of a deposition taken on July 13, 1857, and used in the case of *Bennett et al. vs Waller et al.*, heard on appeal in the Supreme Court of Illinois, at Ottawa, in LaSalle County, in the April term of 1859. There are one or two spelling mistakes in the published court record, and if they happen to appear in this book in direct quotes from that record, then they have been corrected, since it is the words that

are important in that deposition, not how some clerk arbitrarily spelled them. The case had come from the Cook County Court of Common Pleas, and the deposition related to Timothy Webster's undercover work in Iowa County, Wisconsin, between March and June of that year, 1857, when he was posing as Peter G. Roe, a rich New Yorker there to buy land. Webster's real mission was to get enough information to solve a case that Pinkerton had taken on, a case involving a valuable tract of land in Chicago. The pigeon targeted in Webster's Wisconsin crosshairs was a man named James Kinzie, who, as history would have it, had been one of Chicago's very first settlers. The deposition runs from page 106 to page 177 in Peck, *Reports of Cases Determined in The Supreme Court of the State of Illinois*, Vol. 23. It tells of (1) Tim's mission in Wisconsin, including not only his foray into local politics but also his romantic liaisons while there, most notably with Miss Vandalia Bigelow, whom he was planning to marry on July 4 of that year; (2) Tim's background, including a good account of his very shady participation in the 1857 Tate Gang case in Ohio, in which he used the alias Cook; (3) his attitudes to life in general and to several specific parts of it, and (4) as the court record itself admits, "The following deposition is given at length, as a curious specimen of detective art." It is an astonishingly intimate and detailed seventy pages of biographical material. The odd thing is that, as readily available as this source is, it has never before been used or referred to by anyone writing on or touching on the subject of Timothy Webster.

2. Timothy Webster started off his career in 1835 or 1836, in Manhattan, as an apprentice to his father, a tinsmith. The two of them went back and forth between New York and Princeton, N.J., but it was mainly in the borough of New York that they lived and worked as tinmen, roofing mostly. In 1848 Tim went into New York City politics, as a Democrat in the Eighth Ward, and in the first few months of 1849 he left the tin business to become a policeman. In 1850–51 he went out to California, in the wake of the Gold Rush, and spent three years there. Back in Manhattan by the second half of 1853 he got involved in ward politics again. He became a policeman once more, rising to lieutenant, and it was while in that capacity at the Crystal Palace Exhibition, in 1854, that he met Pinkerton, who offered him a job in Chicago. It wasn't until January 1856 that he made it to the Windy City, and set up home at 148 Clinton Street, but it was as a coffee salesman, a job he held for six months before trying life as a commission agent and then as a moulder. Finally, at the end of the year, he took up Pinkerton's offer, and in 1857 moved his family's base out to the Illinois village of Onarga. For the coffee venture, and his life as a commission agent and as a moulder, see the Chicago city directory for 1856. For his political work see the *New York Herald*, Oct. 24, 1848, p. 2, "The Democratic Primary Election in the Eighth Ward," and Oct. 5, 1853, p. 7, "Twenty-Second Ward in the Field." For his police work see the various New York City directories, as well as Recko, *A Spy for the Union*, 5, 10, 12–21. For his time in California, see *Reports of Cases...*, 106–107; the California state census of 1852, for both San Francisco and Sierra County; the various newspapers that have a letter waiting for Timothy Webster (in San Francisco on May 21, 1851, and April 5, 1852, and in Sacramento on May 7, 1853); and, most important, the *Sacramento Daily Union*, June 28, 1862, p. 1, "Execution of Timothy Webster in Richmond."

3. Peck, *Reports of Cases...*, 119. Cross examination by Mr. Stuart. The Nativist party, or Know-Nothing Party, was very powerful in the United States in the 1850s. Their main hate-target was immigrants. Tim was born in England, in Sussex—a place most American historians call "Sus-

sex County"—and emigrated with his family when he was eight, in 1830. There may be a slight technical excuse for calling him an Englishman, especially if it is done for effect, as it is once or twice in this book, but in real life he was as red, white, and blue as you or me.
4. Peck, *Reports of Cases...*, 144–145.

Chapter 5

1. *Daily Iowa State Democrat*, June 7, 1859, p. 1, "Rascally Attempt to Burn Down the Railroad Bridge."
2. *Davenport Daily Democrat and News*, July 26, 1859, p. 1, "Bridge Report"; Aug. 3, 1859, p. 1, untitled item; Aug. 6, 1859, p. 1, "Removal"; Davenport census for 1860. The hotel was called the New Pennsylvania House to distinguish it from the Old Pennsylvania House, which was located on Second, between Main and Harrison, same family. The new one was ten times bigger.
3. *Davenport Daily Democrat and News*, Aug. 3, 1859, p. 1, untitled item; Aug. 6, 1859, p. 1, "Removal."
4. *Davenport Democrat and Leader*, Jan. 25, 1932, p. 10, "Records of early bridge tender"; *Sacramento Daily Union*, June 28, 1862, p. 1, "Execution of Timothy Webster in Richmond." Why did Tim pick the name Reed? The Sacramento article says Tim spent 1851–54 in California, but it was actually 1850–53. M.M. Reed, fireman, an elected constable of Sacramento, and Tim's brother-in-law, died in 1864, and Fanny married again, in 1877, to lumber merchant William Fitzgerald Frazer. She died on March 24, 1896, aged 65. Bridge Master J.R. Reed's new record book would be taken over by his successors. The same book would be in use in 1866, when the bridge was rebuilt, and would still be *the* log book, in fact, until 1872, when the third incarnation of the bridge came into being. The log then made the trip to the M & M's head office, in Des Moines, and there it gathered dust for sixty years until one day, while they were cleaning up an old lot of papers that had been stored there, the book was discovered among a bunch of decaying documents. L.O. Leonard, special historical research representative for the Rock Island Lines, wrote a newspaper article about the find. He gives some sample entries from the log book of January, February and March of 1860, and tells us that the record was signed by "J.R. Reed, bridge tender." Thanks to Reed's log book, we know, for example, that it rained all day on January 6, 1860. Actually we can also get that from the column "The City," on the front page of the *Davenport Daily Democrat and News* of Jan. 7, 1860, but it is nice to see it in the log book. In fact, on that day in early 1860 the telegraph lines were down owing to the deluge. And that nugget is not from the log book; it's from the paper. Reed's log goes on: "...by the 12th it was 10 below and ice formed so teams could cross on it." But by the 23rd the ice was not safe for teams. However, the ice started moving out at 1:20 in the afternoon of February 27. "The steamboat 'Northerner' came up to Davenport and the ferry began running at 1:30 a.m." The archives of the M & M were eventually purchased by an individual, who in time donated them to a museum in Chicago. The log book should, by all rights, have found its way there along with all the rest of the paper work, but thankfully Mr. Leonard extricated it from the other documents, and, as a result, today the book resides in the Special Collections Department at the library in the University of Iowa, in Iowa City.
5. *Davenport Daily Gazette*, Aug. 6, 1859, p. 1, "Removal."
6. *Davenport Daily Democrat and News*, May 7, 1861, p. 1, "Letter to the Editor."
7. *Chicago Press and Tribune*, Aug. 9, 1860, p. 1, "Important Arrest of Conspirators."
8. *Rock Island Argus*, Aug. 10, 1860, p. 3, untitled item.

9. *Davenport Daily Democrat and News,* Aug. 10, 1860, p. 1, "Another Atrocious Attempt."

10. In the 1860 Davenport census of the New Pennsylvania House, taken on the evening of June 18, we find employee Mary E. Bailey, 22, born In Indiana, and resident guest R. Reed, bridge master, 35, born in Kentucky. We're fortunate to find Tim twice in the 1860 census, the second time being at his home in Onarga, Illinois, on the evening of July 9, with his wife, Charlotte, and the three children. Timothy Webster is listed as 40, born in England. As for his occupation one would fully expect to see "policeman" or something like that. It would be unreasonable to see anything else. But no. Railroad employee. Railroad employee? In a census? Isn't that taking his undercover role too far? Incidentally, prior to the 1880 census, it was not required for a person to be physically present at the address being recorded, the only requirement being that he or she would normally have been there. Whether Tim was physically present at the Onarga address or not the night of the census would seem to be irrelevant to the issue in question.

11. *Davenport Daily Democrat and News,* Jan. 29, 1868, p. 1, "Iowa Martyr." On September 14, 1860, at the Sixth Ward Hickory Club, in Davenport, the following Hickories were elected:
Captain—The President, John R. Reed
1st Lieutenant—Frank Connelly
2nd Lieutenant—James Murphy
3rd Lieutenant—J. Driscoll
Just the boys getting together.
We are told, in the article "Sixth Ward Hickory Club," on page 1 of the Sept. 17, 1860, issue of the *Davenport Daily Democrat and News,* that on the evening of October 7, at the Douglas and Johnson Club Room, a meeting of the Democracy of Davenport Township was due to be held for the purpose of appointing delegates to the Democratic County Convention to be held at the Court House in the city of Davenport the following day. And the meeting was duly held. A committee of five men was appointed to report the names of several gentleman to be delegates, one of whom was "John R. Reed." The latter information is from the *Davenport Daily Democrat and News,* Oct. 8, 1860, p. 1, "Democratic Township Convention."

12. One might read in history books that the people of Davenport were aware that Timothy Webster had a wife and children back in Illinois. That is true, the town was made aware of that, but only after Tim had died. The information was published in an article in the *Davenport Democrat* of May 5, 1862 (see Chapter 33, note 2) in the immediate wake of Tim's execution, and was soon copied by other interested nearby Iowa papers, including for example the *Burlington Hawkeye* of May 10, 1862. It must be stressed here that for the entire time Timothy Webster was a resident of Davenport, from July 31, 1859, to May 2, 1861, no one there had any idea that he had such a family. In fact, everyone thought his name was John Reed.

13. *Davenport Daily Democrat and News,* Feb. 1, 1861, p. 1, "Busy."

Chapter 6

1. Cuthbert, *Lincoln and the Baltimore Plot,* 4; Pinkerton letter to Herndon, Aug. 23, 1866; *Maryland Historical Magazine,* 1950, vols. 45–46, p. 3.

2. Cuthbert, *Lincoln and the Baltimore Plot,* 23.

3. Cuthbert, *Lincoln and the Baltimore Plot,* 23.

4. *Vermont Phoenix,* Jan. 31, 1861, p. 1, "The Chicago Detectives and the Adams Express Robbery," taken from the *Boston Journal.*

5. Steers, *Blood on the Moon,* 18; Egan, *Murder at Ford's Theatre,* 35; *McClure's* magazine, 1894, p. 520; Lincoln letter to Herndon, Aug. 23, 1866. Norma Cuthbert, on page 20 of her book, *Lincoln and the*

Baltimore Plot, proposes that Charles Williams may have been an alias of Pryce Lewis, John Scully, or Samuel Bridgman. Jim Horan, in his 1951 book on Pinkerton, says it was Scully. He brooks no doubt. But don't let Horan's certainty sway you. As for John Seaford, he comes in for a very cursory, almost casual mention by Pinkerton in *The Spy of the Rebellion*, and only there, but no such man ever existed by that name.

6. *Cleveland Morning Herald*, Jan. 20, 1868, p. 1, "Lincoln." For the spelling of the name Hutchinson, see Pinkerton Letter to Herndon, Aug. 23, 1866; however, as can be seen from Tim Webster's deposition in Illinois in 1857, Pinkerton was using the name Hutchieson (*sic*) even back then, in 1857. In the Aug. 23, 1866, letter to Herndon, Pinkerton calls the broker *"Luckett (I think that was his name.)"* It was *The American Magazine*, in 1913, that transformed "Luckett" into "William F. Luckett." The 1860 Baltimore city directory has James H. Luckett, at 44 South Street.

7. Pinkerton letter to Herndon, Aug. 23, 1866. This letter was written at a time when Billy Herndon was gathering Lincolniana to use in his book on the late president. For details of this see Appendix C. Perrymansville, in Harford County, Maryland, is now called Perryman.

8. *The American Magazine*, New York: Phillips Publishing Co., vol. 75, No. 4, Feb. 17, 1913, pp. 17–22.

9. Swett, "The Conspiracies of the Rebellion," 180. Pinkerton, in *The Spy of the Rebellion*, 74, confirms that the lady was Mrs. Warn. She had been in Montgomery working undercover on the Adams Express Company case.

10. Letter to Herndon, Aug. 23, 1866. M.B. was Kate Warn, alias Mrs. Barley, alias Mrs. Cherry, alias "Raisins"; C.D.C.W. seems to have been Charles Williams, who may really have been John Scully; A.T.C. may not be accurate, for as Pinkerton says in this letter, *"If I mistake not..."* But where are T.W. and H.H.L. in this list?

11. Judd letter to Pinkerton, Nov. 3, 1867. Another man on the train with Lincoln was Illinois lawyer Ebenezer Peck, one of the president-elect's friends and supporters. Peck left the train at Indianapolis and returned to Springfield. Peck compiled the book *Reports of Cases...* (see Chapter 4 and the Bibliography).

12. Wilson & Davis, *Herndon's Informants*, 278.

13. M.B. report, Feb. 19, 1861, as seen in Cuthbert. This time Mrs. Warn spells the man's name right. Edwards Sewall Sanford was, at that point of time, 43 years old, and head of the American Telegraph Company.

14. For the routine details of these two or three days, see M.B.'s report of Feb. 19, 1861, in full, in Cuthbert; Judd letter to Pinkerton, Nov. 3, 1867; Wilson & Davis, *Herndon's Informants*, 278 et seq.

15. Washington *Evening Star*, April 12, 1861, p. 2, "The Plot to Assassinate Mr. Lincoln," from the *Albany Evening Journal* of April 10, 1861. The quote offered here is sanctioned by this author as nothing more than a newspaper item; since no informed comment is possible at this time, one hasn't been made. H.H.L.'s only extant report, written on Wednesday, February 20, 1861, could be rather dull reading for 21st-century readers, but because it is one of only a handful of sustained pieces that we have of the lady's writing, it has to be reproduced in full, as it was in Wilson & Davis, *Herndon's Informants*, 305:

We had breakfast at 7.00 a.m., after which we conversed some but nothing was said worthy of note. Just before dinner a stranger came and asked if he could have something to eat. Mr. Taylor said that dinner would soon be ready, and asked him to wait, which the stranger said he would do. At 2.00 p.m., we all sat down to dinner, when the stranger told us that he was a Minister, and was going to preach at a place some six miles from Perrymansville—also that he had lost some money in Philadelphia. After he had finished eating his dinner he told Mr. Taylor that he could not pay him for he had no money, and asked if he (Mr. Taylor) would take a pledge, or wait until he (the stranger) got the money, when he would sent [sic] it—said that his name was "Jones," and that he was from Louisville, Kentucky; that he travelled from place to place preaching &c. Mr. Taylor was very indignant at the way the stranger had managed to get his dinner, and said that was what he called sneaking mean; that the man had not better come to his place again, for he would not fare quite so well if he did. Mr. Taylor went on to say that he believed this man had plenty of money, and reckoned that all he came in the country for, was to have the Slaves rise up against their Masters, and he hoped no more would come. After the 6.30 p.m. Train had passed, Mrs. Taylor's little boy picked up some cards which he brought into the house. Mrs. Taylor remarked that she thought it very strange that they should be thrown off here. I replied to this—that persons got tired of playing sometimes, and would throw them out of the window when they did not want them any more. We had two strangers at supper, and remarks were made about the Preacher who dined with us. During the evening Mr. Taylor came into the house and said that he was going to Havre-de-Grace in the morning to make arrangements about getting his Mother-in-Law to live with him the rest of her life. Nothing more transpired worthy of note—at 9.45 p.m., I went to bed.

16. Wilson & Davis, *Herndon's Informants*, 320–324. For how the secret car moved through Baltimore, see Bryan, *The Great American Myth*, 29.

17. Wilson & Davis, *Herndon's Informants*, 323–324; Washington *Evening Star*, Feb. 25, 1861, p. 4, "Arrivals at the Hotels." There was no *Evening Star* on the 24th, it being a Sunday. It is quite clear from the list that Timothy Webster was one of the presidential party who checked in to the Willard on February 23, and that his name was entered in the hotel register immediately below that of Allan Pinkerton. What this implies can only be guessed at, a good guess, but one thing's for sure: Webster was not on the train. He just met up with his boss at the Willard, that's all. Incidentally, Police Superintendent John A. Kennedy, who had been on the secret train, checked into his apartments at the National Hotel that morning.

18. Washington *Evening Star*, Feb. 25, 1861, p. 4, "Arrivals at the Hotels." That John Pope was one of the army officers detailed to guard the Lincoln party during the inaugural trip is far from "breaking news," but it is a nice story. As for the Scott Guard, there are only a few mentions in history of the organization. "Scott Guard" was a loose, informal term referring to a small company of men invited ad hoc by Winfield Scott, the old hero of the Mexican War and now Commanding General of the United States Army, to guarantee the Lincoln party's safety as it traveled from Springfield, Illinois, to Washington City. Other Scott Guards included Major David Hunter, Captain George Whitfield Hazzard, Colonel Edwin V. "Bullhead" Sumner, and Lieutenant Timothy Webster. Curiously, Major Hunter's wife was the sister of James Kinzie of Chicago, the man who, in Wisconsin in 1857, had been Tim Webster's "mark" when Tim was posing as Peter G. Roe during a sting operation.

19. *Chicago Tribune*, Feb. 27, 1861, p. 1, "Our Washington Letter."

20. Recko, *A Spy for the Union*, 145.

21. Recko, *A Spy for the Union*, 59; *Chicago Tribune*, March 30, 1861, p. 2, "Daring Scheme to Rob the Mail," taken from the *Pittsburgh Gazette*.

Chapter 7

1. *Davenport Daily Democrat and News*, March 12, 1861, p. 1; "Bridge Master's Report"; March 19, 1861, p. 1. "Bridge Master's Report." At week's end, Saturday, March 16, 1861, for the first time since he had left for the east a month and a half earlier, J.R. Reed, rather than his assistant, John H. Thorington, signed off on the weekly bridge report.
2. *Davenport Daily Democrat and News*, March 27, 1861, p. 1, "Sixth Ward Nomination."
3. *Davenport Daily Democrat and News*, April 2, 1861, p. 1, "Nomination Declined."
4. The *Davenport Daily Democrat and News* of April 4, 1861, p. 1, "Sixth Ward Democratic Nomination," tells us that two evenings earlier the Democracy of the 6th Ward got together hurriedly to discuss the situation, and William Renwick was nominated by acclamation to take the place of Mr. Reed. Mr. Renwick went on to win, so everything worked out all right for the party.
5. Pinkerton, *The Spy of the Rebellion*, 112–113.
6. Pinkerton letter to Lincoln, April 21, 1861, The Lincoln Papers, General Correspondence, Library of Congress Manuscript Division. I have taken the wording, spelling, and punctuation from the letter as reproduced in Recko, *A Spy for the Union*, 70–71. There are perhaps 200 code words in this list. Some of the more interesting or amusing are: Washington = Barley; New York = Millet; Richmond = Coffee; Negroes = Sheet lead. Then come ten Pinkerton operatives: J.M.F. = Pears; W.S. = Fruit; G.S. = Apples; A.P. = Plums; T.W. = Peaches; A.C. = Gooseberries; C.W. = Berries; H.L. = Cranberries; M.B. = Raisins; G.H.B. = Hickory Nuts. C.W. is the C.D.C.W. of Pinkerton's August 23, 1866 letter to Herndon; i.e., Charles Williams. A.C. equals Gooseberries, and is the A.T.C. of that letter. This may be Alfred Cridge, but that's far from certain; Norma Cuthbert, in 1949, on page 20 of her book, said A.T.C. was Harry Davies. W.S. surely has to be William H. Scott; J.M.F. may be John Fox; and G.S. remains unknown. The only time I have ever seen Peaches identified with Timothy Webster is in Recko, *A Spy for the Union*, 69.
7. Library of Congress, Lincoln papers; there is a docket among the Lincoln Papers that says: "Package of letters brought by one of Pinkerton's men to Washington in April 1861." Above that in writing is a pencil notation saying "April 23," with a question mark, which, since it is an incertitude written in by a bureaucratic hand other than that of the original writer, can be ignored as nothing more than what it actually is.
8. There are several slightly differing versions of this letter available. This one is from Sears, *The Civil War Papers of George C. McClellan*, 11. Among the Pryce Lewis papers, housed at St. Lawrence University, is a letter written by E.J. Allen to an unknown recipient in New York. The date of the letter is Nov. 8, 1860. Harriet Shoen, the person originally responsible for forming these papers into a collection, wrote this note: "Allan Pinkerton original—'E.J. Allen' used as an alias before the war."
9. *Davenport Democrat and News*, May 3, 1861, p. 1, "Scrimmage"; *Transactions of the Illinois State Historical Society*, 1931, p. 192; *Lincoln Group Papers*, Vol. 1, Lincoln Group of Chicago, 1936, p. 133. For more on the Scott Guard, Chapter 6, note 18.
10. *Davenport Daily Democrat and News*, June 6, 1861, p. 1, "Betrayal, Desertion, Suicide"; 1861 Davenport city directory.
11. *Davenport Daily Democrat and News*, May 3, 1861, p. 1, "Scrimmage"; May 7, 1861, p. 1, "Letter to the Editor."
12. *Davenport Daily Democrat and News*, May 7, 1861, p. 1, "Letter to the Editor."

13. *Davenport Daily Democrat and News*, May 3, 1861, p. 1, "Scrimmage"; May 7, 1861, p. 1, "Letter to the Editor."
14. *Davenport Daily Democrat and News*, May 3, 1861, p. 1, "Scrimmage"; May 7, 1861, p. 1, "Letter to the Editor."
15. Library of Congress, Lincoln papers, Lincoln to Seward, May 2, 1861.
16. *Davenport Daily Democrat and News*, June 6, 1861, p. 1, "Betrayal, Desertion, Suicide." At first glance the paper would seem to be wrong when they say the New Pennsylvania House. Tim had left there earlier in the year, and moved to the Scott House, as can be seen by the 1861 city directory. Mary Ellen Bailey had evidently done the same thing, one way or the other. However, kitchen staff moved from joint to joint, almost on the hop, just as they tend to do today, and wherever Mary Ellen went Tim was sure to go. Was Tim ever married to Mary Ellen? Almost certainly not. As Joe Burgess tells us in his harangue in the *Democrat* of May 7, 1861, Webster would go into the various kitchens where Mary Ellen worked, and tell everyone she was his wife. There would have been no reason for any of her work mates to doubt it. Then she could slip up to his room after work and no one would raise an eyebrow.
17. Muscatine (Iowa) *Weekly Journal*, June 14, 1861, p. 1, "Desertion and Suicide."
18. This is practically word for word from Pinkerton, *The Spy of the Rebellion*, 152. For General Scott, see Chapter 6, note 18.
19. Pinkerton, *The Spy of the Rebellion*, 153. The quote is from Mattie Cook Ellis, thesis, 1917.

Chapter 8

1. Washington *Evening Star*, March 30, 1861, p. 3, "List of Letters"; May 11, 1863, p. 3, "List of Letters."
2. Pinkerton, *Spy of the Rebellion*, p. 141. McClellan formed the Army of the Potomac on Aug. 20, 1861.

3. Pinkerton payrolls, Secret Service Accounts, as written about first by Fishel in his book *Secret War for the Union*, 161. This particular payroll had gone into effect precisely a week earlier, on August 1, the very day this Secret Service became a reality. The first to go on payroll had been Pinkerton himself and Mrs. Warn. Two days later Samuel Bridgman and Pryce Lewis had arrived in the capital, and were also put on the payroll. Timothy Webster and H.H.L., his "new wife," now made five and six. As for Sam Bridgman, according to Billy Pinkerton, in his Oct. 31, 1897, *Inter-Ocean* interview, p. 18, "Plot Is All Right," Sam and Timothy Webster were both working the Crystal Palace exhibition in New York as policemen when they met Allan Pinkerton, who offered them both a job. Billy should have added George Bangs to make it a trio.
4. Washington *Evening Star*, Dec. 11, 1861, p. 3, "A Detective's Squabble." When he set about the task of recreating history, Pinkerton, in his books, letters, public statements, newspaper interviews, and whatever else, would always claim that only a handful of men in the entire country during the Civil War knew that the mysterious E.J. Allen was, in fact, Allan Pinkerton. The truth is, there was never a mystery. Right from the very beginning, everyone knew who Major E.J. Allen was. It's just that no one outside of his organization cared enough to carry that information in their head ad infinitum.

Chapter 9

1. Greenhow, *My Imprisonment*, 61–62. Rose Greenhow claims that Pinkerton was a German Jew, which goes to prove how untrustworthy she must be considered as an historian.
2. Horan & Swiggett, *The Pinkerton Story*, 99. Unfortunately, James McKay, in his 1996 book on Pinkerton, bought into Horan's speculation, and set it in

stone. That has led, of course, to several later historians in turn buying into McKay.

3. Webster's Aug. 23, 1861, report to Pinkerton, as seen in Recko, *A Spy for the Union*, 151. If one is tempted to speculate that Hattie might have been in both cities on the same day, it must be remembered that it was not quite so easy to get from Baltimore to Washington City as it is today, depending on the hour of day, of course.

4. Pryce Lewis "Memoirs," 138–140.

Chapter 10

1. Fishel, *Secret War for the Union*, 91; Pinkerton's Nov. 15, 1861, report to McClellan, as seen in Recko, *A Spy for the Union*, 155. Billy Pinkerton, in his Oct. 31, 1897, interview for the *Inter-Ocean* newspaper, p. 18, "Plot Is All Right," mentions three other Pinkerton agents operating in and out of the South during the Civil War: Hiram B. Jones, George Thiel, and the Irishman Patrick Hade. As for Hade, I think he means Patrick's younger brother, Maurice, born in 1827. George Thiel later became Gus Thiel, head of a private detective agency in St. Louis.

2. *Richmond Daily Dispatch*, Oct. 30, 1861, p. 2, "Maryland Refugees"; Pinkerton's Nov. 15, 1861, report to McClellan, as seen in Recko, *A Spy for the Union*, 158. The Spotswood, spelled with one "t," had opened only as recently as New Year's Day 1861, and was the only first class hotel on Main Street.

3. *Richmond Daily Dispatch*, Oct. 30, 1861, p. 2, "Cold Weather"; Confederate Citizens' File, Citizens, T. Webster. The handwriting of the signature "T. Webster" on the receipt for the hat caps matches exactly that of "Tim Webster" in his August 7, 1861, report to Pinkerton, as seen in Recko, *A Spy for the Union*, 82.

4. Pinkerton's reports to McClellan of Nov. 15, 1861, and Jan. 31, 1862, as seen in Recko, *A Spy for the Union*, 158–159 and 172; Pinkerton, *The Spy of the Rebellion*, 315; Confederate Citizens File, Businesses, Campbell, Wm. & Bro. The "bro" was James J. Campbell, known to all as J.J.

5. Stewart, *Jefferson Davis's Flight from Richmond*, 282–283.

6. Pinkerton, *The Spy of the Rebellion*, 324–325 and 526; Pinkerton's report to McClellan, Nov. 15, 1861, as seen in Recko, *A Spy for the Union*, 155–168.

7. *Richmond Daily Dispatch*, Nov. 18, 1861, p. 4, " Letter List."

Chapter 11

1. Pinkerton, *The Spy of the Rebellion*, 329; *Baltimore Sun*, Oct. 16, 1861, p. 1, "List of Letters"; Oct. 23, 1861, p. 1, "List of Letters." Tim was going by the name of John Hart, at least that's what Pinkerton says. The newspapers in November 1861 would say William Hart. Pinkerton is almost certainly the one to believe in this case, for why would he say John when it was really William? There would be no merit in that. Hart is Hart. And newspapers often got names wrong. Besides, there were letters waiting in the Baltimore post office on October 16 and October 23, for a John Hart, right at the time Tim and Hattie were staying at Miller's Hotel. Agreed, this could be any John Hart, but the name is fairly uncommon. It's not like John Smith. And this John Hart wasn't picking his mail up, that's for sure, otherwise it wouldn't have been advertised in the *Baltimore Sun*. And the most common reason people didn't pick their mail up is that they were out of town at the time. And Tim and Hattie were out of town quite a lot of the time. In the end, it doesn't really matter whether it was John or William; it was Hart. His wife, although the press never actually gave her a first name, would have been called Hattie Hart, and it is easy to see how H.H.L. would have stood for Hattie Hart Lewis. Just responsible speculation, but at least

it makes sense, and it's an original guess, it's not a mere derivation from secondary sources. In a day when the name Timothy was quite unusual in America, it was often "corrected" to Thomas.

2. This whole Miller's Hotel adventure is taken from the *Cincinnati Daily Press*, Nov. 20, 1861, p. 1, "Baltimore. November 20"; *Baltimore Sun*, Nov. 21 1861, p. 1, "Searching a Hotel"; Nov. 22, 1861, p. 1, "The Arrests at Miller's Hotel"; *Baltimore American*, Nov. 22, 1861, "Escape of a State Prisoner"; and also partly from Pinkerton, *The Spy of the Rebellion*, 346–342, but only where that book is corroborated by the newspapers. The *Baltimore American* article made the *Richmond Enquirer* only on Dec. 8, 1861, p. 3, "Maryland Items."

Chapter 12

1. Recko, *A Spy for the Union*, 104; Pinkerton, *The Spy of the Rebellion*, pp. 348 et seq. Pinkerton calls the man Dr. Gurley.

2. To be perfectly fair to John Winder, he had been awarded a lieutenant-colonel's brevet during the Mexican War of 1846–48. Thus he was able to call himself Colonel Winder, even though a brevet brought no increased pay or seniority. However, so far as a substantive rank goes, major was as high as Winder was ever going to get in the U.S. Army.

3. *Richmond Daily Dispatch*, June 26, 1862, p. 2, "Military Appointment."

4. Pfanz, *Richard S. Ewell*, 404; *The Stranger's Guide*, 12.

5. *Richmond Times-Dispatch*, Aug. 23, 1903, Magazine Section, p. 2, "Webster the Spy." The Inglis article, "A Republic's Gratitude," in *Harper's Weekly*, 1911, says: "Once Webster was suspected by his Southern friends, but he brought home a few thousand percussion caps on his next trip, and that act allayed suspicion."

6. Jones, *A Rebel War Clerk's Diary*, Dec. 11, 1861. The secretary mentioned in the diary entry is Judah Benjamin, the Confederate secretary of war.

7. For a much fuller account of how Jones tinkered with his manuscript, see Stewart, *Jefferson Davis's Flight from Richmond*, 282–283. "A pass would be the most pressing thing…" It is by using that deduction that we are able to get a rough fix on when Tim left Washington to begin this second trip.

8. For the definitive biography of William A. Winder, see Singer, *The War Criminal's Son*.

9. This is the first inkling we have that not all was right with Tim's health.

Chapter 13

1. Pinkerton, *The Spy of the Rebellion*, 468–470; Washington *Evening Star*, Dec. 26, 1861, p. 3, "Christmas Day."

2. Pinkerton, *The Spy of the Rebellion*, 469; *Richmond Daily Dispatch*, Dec. 11, 1862, p. 1, "To Be Sent North"; *Richmond Times-Dispatch*, Aug. 23, 1903, Magazine Section, p. 2, "Webster the Spy." It may be that there was another, more tangible compensation for Timothy Webster. The *Dispatch* writes that "he was a trusted secret agent of the Confederate Government and its friends in the North (the secrets of both of whom he sold for a consideration, according to the testimony of Hon. Jno Covode to the Lincoln Government.)" Congressman Covode, who was on the Committee for the Conduct of the War, did mention Tim during a speech in Philadelphia on Oct. 8, 1862, but nowhere in that speech, at least in the published version, did he even imply what the *Dispatch* is saying here, that Tim took money. On page 1 of the semi-weekly *Richmond Enquirer*, Oct. 17, 1862, is an item headed, "What Covode Said About Webster the Spy." This is what he said: I went to Washington to see who it was that was carrying information to the rebels, and we got a man named Webster to carry the rebel mail from Maryland over the Potomac to Richmond; but it was carried through

Washington and assorted by me in the Committee room in the Capitol, and I found who it was in the North that were furnishing information to the rebels, and when we got a large mail, there were a great many who had to go to prison (Laughter and Applause.) After a while the rebels found out Webster's devotion to the Union, and they hung him in Richmond. Many of those who gave information to the rebels were men holding office in Washington—men who had grown rich on the revenue of the Government.

Covode's personal, hands-on involvement in the letter-sorting business has the very loud ring of untruth. He was just a typical braying politician. As for Tim accepting money, if we can take to heart what the Jan. 31, 1861, issue of the *Vermont Phoenix* says in its page 1 article, "The Chicago Detectives and the Adams Express Robbery" (taken from the *Boston Journal*), on the subject of Pinkerton's rules for his employees, and again from the article written on the Pinkerton organization in the Nov. 2, 1867, issue of the *Chicago Republican*, p. 2, "Allan Pinkerton," then such graft would have been unthinkable.

3. Pinkerton, *The Spy of the Rebellion*, 470, 477–479; Pinkerton's report to McClellan of Jan. 31, 1862, as seen in Recko, *A Spy for the Union*, 105. Mr. Recko has Webster accompanied by fellow agent E.H. Stein part of the way. If one is tempted to question the reference to Pinkerton's "phony prudery," or, come to think of it, his fixation on Kate Warn, one need only go as far as a series of billets doux exchanged between the great detective and a certain "Mrs. H.L. Sargant," of Denton, Texas, in the late 1870s. See Pinkerton's National Detective Agency Records, 1853–1899, Letterpress Books and Miscellaneous Reports, Vol. Aug. 5, 1872–Aug. 29, 1875, pp. 152–188 (image numbers do not match page numbers, so begin at image #180, which corresponds to page #152).

4. *Richmond Daily Dispatch*, Aug. 9, 1853, p. 2, "Monument Hotel," and Aug. 10, 1853, p. 2, "Monument Hotel" (the quote is from the latter); *Richmond Daily Dispatch*, Dec. 5, 1854, p. 3, "For Rent—The Monument"; *Richmond Enquirer*, Jan. 5, 1855, p. 4, "Card." On page 140 in the manuscript of the Pryce Lewis "memoirs," the Monument Hotel is referred to as the "Monumental Hotel," just as it is in Pinkerton's book, *The Spy of the Rebellion*, and dismissed as a "second rate house."

5. Pinkerton, *The Spy of the Rebellion*, 496; Beymer, *On Hazardous Service*, 280.

6. Pinkerton, *The Spy of the Rebellion*, 478; Chicago *Daily Inter-Ocean*, Oct. 31, 1897, p. 18, "Plot Is All Right"; *Daily Morning Journal and Courier*, New Haven, Conn., Aug. 23, 1898, p. 7, "War Secret Service." E.H. Stein was a resident agent in Richmond, until April 1862. Billy Pinkerton mentioned other resident agents (as distinct from regular agents), all acting independently of Webster: T.H. O'Sullivan, working in the Ordnance Department; William Angell (also known as Walter Angle), an employee in the Telegraph section of the War Department; and Harry F. Knipe, a clerk in the employ of the Southern Express Company, on South Main Street. Pinkerton liked to play around with names and initials, and gave Harry the code name of "H.J.K." Billy Pinkerton says of Harry Knipe: "He remained there in his Secret Service capacity, until the close of the war," but in other places Billy tells us he got out in the engine room of a flag of truce boat. And we will see, in Chapter 35, how a man who would seem to be Harry Knipe got out in early 1863. Fishel, after studying Pinkerton's payroll accounts, was able to speculate that the agent known only by his initials H.J.K. joined the Secret Service at the very end of 1861. He adds three things about H.J.K., even though he never actually names him. The first is that he

"disappears from the records after five months of payroll entries showing him in Virginia but indicating nothing about his movements or activities." The next is that around April 20, 1862, H.J.K.'s exact status was "unknown, but no reports from him are in McClellan's or Pinkerton's papers; he may have been under detention by Confederate authorities." And finally, "H.J.K. disappears from Pinkerton's payrolls after a May [1862] entry that says his account 'will be rendered as soon as possible after his being released from the rebel lines.'" It's a pity H.J.K. has never been more fully explored by historians because Harry Knipe, the man behind the initials, should never have been a mystery, not since 1883, certainly, when Billy Pinkerton started talking about him in interviews. Ed Fishel, after studying Pinkerton's payroll accounts, was able to speculate that the agent known only by his initials H.J.K. joined the Secret Service at the very end of 1861.
7. Pinkerton, *The Spy of the Rebellion*, 478–479.
8. Pinkerton, *The Spy of the Rebellion*, 479.
9. Pinkerton, *The Spy of the Rebellion*, 479; *Chicago Tribune*, Feb. 2, 1861, p. 1, "Arrest of a Book-Keeper." Chicago city directories, 1858–1861, James Howard.
10. Pinkerton, *The Spy of the Rebellion*, 486–487; Pinkerton's Jan. 31, 1862, report to McClellan, as seen in Recko, *A Spy for the Union*, 172. There were various Thomas W. Goughs in or around Leonardtown. Pinkerton's character is the one born in 1800.
11. Pinkerton's Jan. 31, 1862, report to Pinkerton, as seen in Recko, *A Spy for the Union*, 172.

Chapter 14

1. Pinkerton, *The Spy of the Rebellion*, 488; Beymer, *On Hazardous Service*, 280. One can't help wondering how many overcoats and felt hats Tim Webster normally took with him on a trip, or how Hattie kept such a large hat from falling down in front of her eyes all the time, or how she was even visible under what must have been, for her, a tent rather than an overcoat. This entire story, from the time Tim left Washington to the time he arrived at Richmond, is from *The Spy of the Rebellion*, 488–491; the quote in this paragraph is from Beymer, who was, of course, essentially taking from Pinkerton.
2. Richard Lee Turberville Beale was known as R.L.T.
3. The newspapers only once or twice even hint at an illness, and it's not even really a hint. The best that can really be said of it is, "Is this a hint or isn't it?" Certainly no physiological illness or disease is ever specified in the press. The "old malady," as Pinkerton calls it, first rears its ominous head, in print anyway, at Fredericksburg, on New Year's Day, 1862, at the start of Tim's third trip. A week later the same thing at Abingdon. And for a third short time, again at Fredericksburg. Since these mentions are in the Pinkerton report to McClellan, they are almost certainly genuine. So something was definitely going on with Tim's health. Later Pinkerton identifies the malady as rheumatism. For what it's worth, the Pryce Lewis "memoirs" also say it was rheumatism, and in his 1883 newspaper interview, "Famous Detectives," Billy Pinkerton does say inflammatory rheumatism. Whatever it was, it was undoubtedly overplayed by Pinkerton from time to time, in order to facilitate the reader's acceptance of one or another of his, Pinkerton's, countless lies.
4. Pinkerton, *The Spy of the Rebellion*, 496–497. Although Pinkerton says the last day of January, it is more likely to have been Feb. 1, or even Feb. 2; at least that must have been the date Tim and Hattie arrived in Richmond. As Pinkerton himself says, this was the last time he heard from Tim directly, whatever that means.

Chapter 15

1. Pinkerton, *The Spy of the Rebellion*, 491–492.
2. Pinkerton, *The Spy of the Rebellion*, 492; Pryce Lewis "Memoirs," 118.
3. *National Republican*, May 3, 1862, p. 2, "Spies." Of course, Pinkerton's ineptitude is only one of thousands and thousands of factors that can be said to have caused the war to drag on unnecessarily.
4. Harnett, *Spies for the Blue and Gray*, 101.
5. Pinkerton, *The Spy of the Rebellion*, 495; Pryce Lewis "Memoirs," 117–119; the quote is from Beymer, *On Hazardous Service*, 280. Ed Fishel, on p. 621 of his book, *The Secret War for the Union*, speculates that it was really Tim's health issue that was worrying Pinkerton, not the silence. For an historian who had come on the scene too early to have had access to the Pryce Lewis "memoirs," this was a fairly good speculation, but for one who had never even heard of Billy Pinkerton's newspaper articles of the 1880s and 1890s, it comes across as merely underfed.
6. Pinkerton, *The Spy of the Rebellion*, 495; Pryce Lewis "Memoirs," 121. February 14 is the date given by Pinkerton in *The Spy of the Rebellion*. However, the 14th was a Friday, and according to the Pryce Lewis "memoirs" the two spies left Washington on a Tuesday. Ed Fishel, on p. 621 of his book, *The Secret War for the Union*, has Lewis and Scully leaving Washington on the 18th, not the 14th. Unfortunately, Fishel does not source this piece of information. But we can't dismiss it, because the 18th was a Tuesday, and Fishel had never seen the Pryce Lewis "memoirs." One wonders where he got that. So, in the end, what we have is a difference of opinion on the date, but one is forced to say that the 18th looks better than the 14th, all things considered.
7. The Pryce Lewis "memoirs" tell us that Scully wasn't the first choice for this mission: Charles H. Rosch was. Rosch, a Dane, and one of Pinkerton's great "shadows," refused to go South unless he got insurance for his family. He had a lot of children, and Pinkerton was a Scotsman. With that combination, an insurance policy wasn't going to happen. So, Pryce Lewis could have rebelled, just as Rosch did. Rosch seems not to have suffered by so doing. Another thing, if Lewis was really worried about being spotted in Richmond, then why didn't he insist on a disguise for himself and Scully? A false nose, perhaps; one that glowed in the dark.
8. Pinkerton, *The Spy of the Rebellion*, 496; Pryce Lewis "Memoirs," 121.
9. *Daily Morning Journal and Courier*, New Haven, Conn., Aug. 23, 1898, p. 7, "War Secret Service"; *Daily Richmond Examiner*, April 22, 1862, p. 3, "Court Martial." "Aids" was the spelling used back then, rather than "aides."

Chapter 16

1. E-mail from the St. Lawrence University archivist to the author, June 25, 2018.

Chapter 17

1. Pinkerton, *The Spy of the Rebellion*, 502; Pryce Lewis "Memoirs," 139. The Pryce Lewis "memoirs" say the *Richmond Dispatch*. Pinkerton says the *Enquirer*. The correspondent for the *Memphis Appeal* says the *Enquirer*. The *Richmond Times-Dispatch* of Aug. 23, 1903, p. 2 of the Magazine Section, "Webster the Spy," says the *Enquirer*. If it was the *Enquirer*, or even if it wasn't, the owners of that paper, Nathaniel Tyler, O. Jennings Wise, and W.B. Allegre, were relatively new to the paper, having purchased it only in August of 1860. The paper was the unofficial voice of the Confederate government, yet at the same time it had a reputation of which it was mighty proud, and that was for its honesty in reporting. Mr. Tyler will

make a further and notable appearance in this book. As for the *Richmond Dispatch*, James A. Cowardin founded it in 1850 and was still in control of the paper at the time Lewis and Scully were running amok in Richmond. It was far and away the most popular of the four Richmond dailies, and like the *Enquirer*, enjoyed a high reputation for integrity, although as the war proceeded toward its inevitable conclusion Cowardin's fanaticism for the Lost Cause kept pace.

2. Pinkerton, *The Spy of the Rebellion*, 502; Pryce Lewis "Memoirs," 138–140. In the manuscript of the "memoirs" this location for the bed has been crossed out and replaced with "near the entrance on the right side of the door." A small detail, perhaps, but the amendment was obviously made for a reason. It is unclear what that reason was.

3. Pryce Lewis "Memoirs," 138–140; Beymer, *On Hazardous Service*, 281. This Mr. Pierce will have to remain anonymous, "unfound," at least by this writer. Beymer doesn't name him, merely calls him one of Tim's "stanch Richmond friends," while the Pryce Lewis "memoirs" refer to him as a young man and call him "Mr. Price," but that's just a spelling mistake on the part of the compilers of the "memoirs." At this point in the story those very compilers had *The Spy of the Rebellion* open in front of them, as they did at all times, and they couldn't help noticing that this chapter of Pinkerton's book was unaccountably dull. There was a lot that could be done here to pep it up, and the compilers of the "memoirs" ventured forth on what, for them, proved a hopeless task. The end result is even more boring than Pinkerton's. Worse, the plagiarism, especially in the structure of the story, protrudes like a hernia, and is just as irritating.

4. Pryce Lewis "Memoirs, 141. The editor of the "memoirs" changed "a side window" to "the window." This entire episode, from the time Lewis and Scully hit town until they left Webster's room, was chronicled by Pinkerton in his 1883 book, *The Spy of the Rebellion*, and then, five years later, plagiarized by the author or authors of the Pryce Lewis "memoirs."

5. *Richmond Daily Dispatch*, March 4, 1862, p. 3, "A Proclamation" and "Head-q'rs, Dep't of Henrico"; Pryce Lewis "Memoirs," 144–147. The quote is from Beymer, *On Hazardous Service*, 282. That McCubbin was the next-door boarder to Tim Webster at the Monument Hotel is found in the Pryce Lewis "memoirs" and nowhere else. That doesn't mean it's not true, but it's an awful geographical coincidence if McCubbin had planted himself there without already suspecting Tim. But maybe Winder's policemen did suspect Tim as early as that. The *Richmond Times-Dispatch* of Aug. 23, 1903, Magazine Section, p. 2, "Webster the Spy," says that "maps of the fortifications around Richmond and the approaches there to [sic] were appearing in the Northern papers often enough to arouse the Confederate authorities, as well as to convince them that a traitor was in favor at the War Department." One cannot trust this hopelessly ill-informed article, but nor can one afford to dismiss it with a consequent, "Don't believe anything it says."

Chapter 18

1. *Richmond Daily Dispatch*, Feb. 28, 1862, p. 2, "Fast Day."

2. The Confederate capital moved from Montgomery to Richmond in late May of 1861.

3. Washington, D.C., city directory, 1860; Washington *Evening Star*, Sept. 3, 1861, p. 2, col. 2., no title; Sept. 9, 1861, p. 2, c. 3, no title; *Buffalo Courier*, Sept. 10, 1861, p. 2, no title. There is long-standing precedent to justify the use of the spelling "Eye Street" instead of "I Street."

4. *Richmond Enquirer*, March 4, 1862, p. 4, "Yankee Spies"; *Daily Richmond Examiner*, April 3, 1862, p. 3, "Execution

Under Court Martial"; Pinkerton, *The Spy of the Rebellion*, 506–510. These three sources, the *Enquirer*, the *Examiner*, and Pinkerton, present considerable differences in detail, so one would expect the Pryce Lewis "memoirs" to act as referee, given that Pryce Lewis was actually there. Unfortunately, the "memoirs," in this instance, offer only a sentence-by-sentence, paragraph-by-paragraph copy of Pinkerton. Although some of the words have been changed, as in all cases of plagiarism, it is, nevertheless, a complete and utter fraud, and therefore of no direct value whatsoever. The arrest of Lewis and Scully is also covered, although not in any detail, in the March 3, 1862, issue of the *Richmond Dispatch*, p. 2, "Arrest of Spies," which offers the opinion, and the hope, that the spies would "swing for their turpitude." It is sometimes written that it was Rose Greenhow who identified Lewis and Scully on the streets of Richmond. Billy Pinkerton put that about in his 1883 interview, the interview that became the article known in the country-wide press as "Famous Detectives." However, at the time Lewis and Scully were spotted on the street the notorious Mrs. Greenhow was an inmate of the Old Capitol Prison, in Washington. We are not told which of the two Morton daughters it was who, with her mother, identified the two spies: Mary Eloise, who was then 21, or Charlotte, who was only 13. What Pinkerton doesn't tell us is that in late 1862, and through the spring of 1863, he himself was living at 288 Eye Street as his home away from home. In 1865 the house would be the residence of the famous Major General David Hunter. The building no longer exists.

5. The quote is from the Pryce Lewis "memoirs," 163–168. Recko, *A Spy for the Union*, 125–126; *Richmond Enquirer*, March 4, 1862, p. 3, "More Unionists Arrested" and p. 4, "Yankee Spies"; *Richmond Daily Dispatch*, April 3, 1862, p. 2, "List of Prisoners Confined in Castle Godwin to March 15th, 1862." Later that very day, March 1, Clackner would become an assistant provost marshal, but, technically speaking, at the time he was transporting the men to jail, the office of provost marshal and that of assistant provost marshal had not quite yet come into being in Richmond. Along with Scully in that very first intake of prisoners at Castle Godwin was the politician John Minor Botts, of Henrico County, in there for treason.

6. *Richmond Enquirer*, March 4, 1862, p. 3, "Castle Godwin"; *Richmond Daily Whig*, March 10, 1862, p. 3, "Castle Godwin." The reader can hardly fail to appreciate the self-serving intent behind the newspaper's description of Castle Godwin, and it is just this kind of content that traditionally comes under fire from the slings and arrows of outraged historians of modern times. How dare the Richmond papers describe one of the notorious Confederate prisons as luxury accommodations! Et cetera, et cetera. But just because something is self-serving, does that automatically mean it is wrong? If one doubts the salubriousness of Castle Godwin when compared with that of the Richmond boarding houses quoted, and that's what the paper was talking about, then one has not paid sufficient attention to the novels of Charles Dickens, nor has one been fully awake while watching the movie *Gangs of New York*. George Freeburger, aged 29, a cooper by trade, was appointed to the office on March 1, 1862. Tom Bradford, keeper of Bradford's Hotel, on Franklin Street, was a man of irrepressible spirits, as any drunk could tell you.

7. *Richmond Daily Dispatch*, March 3, 1862, p. 2, "Proclamation"; *Richmond Enquirer*, March 5, 1862, p. 2, "Closing of the Bar Rooms."

8. *Richmond Enquirer*, March 4, 1862, p. 2, "Proclamation," and p. 3, "The Armed Police" and "Provost Marshal"; *Daily Richmond Examiner*, March 2, 1862, p. 3, "The City Government Under Martial

Law," which gives a complete list of the 24 detectives under McCubbin, including George W. Clackner, Philip Cashmyer, and Theodore Woodall, a notorious Baltimore thug. Rocketts was a suburb of Richmond, named for Robert Rocketts, an 18th-century ferryman there.
9. *Richmond Daily Dispatch*, March 8, 1862, p. 3, "Martial Law"; April 24, 1862, p. 2, "Assistant Provost Marshal." One often reads, even in works or statements by people who knew better, that John H. Winder was the provost marshal of Richmond, but he was never provost anything. His only official title, from October 21, 1861, until May 5, 1864, was Commandant of the Department of Henrico.
10. *Richmond Enquirer*, March 4, 1862, p. 3, "Suspension of Judicial Proceedings" and "Heavy Rain." The Mayor's Court was the only court not threatened by martial law.
11. *Richmond Daily Dispatch*, March 3, 1861, p. 2, "Proclamation of Martial Law."

Chapter 19

1. *Richmond Enquirer*, March 4, 1862, p. 4, "Yankee Spies." As with any government, the bigwigs in Richmond were not the Southern people. Not even close. This was proved once and for all when, pretty much to a man, they fled the capital on the night of April 2, 1865, rats deserting a sinking ship, leaving their subjects to take the rap the following morning when the Yankee army entered Richmond, black troops first. That the Confederacy lasted longer than a year is thanks not to Jefferson Davis and his cabinet, in their gray morning suits, but to the real boys in gray, the ones in uniform, officers and men.
2. Pinkerton, *The Spy of the Rebellion*, 531. *The Spy of the Rebellion* doesn't say how Hattie learned of the arrest, but Beymer does, on page 284 of his book, *On Hazardous Service*, and Beymer was interviewing Billy Pinkerton, son of the founder. It was from the newspaper. If that's true, and it sounds right, then it does, in fact, place that moment at the morning of March 4, when Hattie opened her copy of the *Enquirer*.
3. Pinkerton, *The Spy of the Rebellion*, 531–533. The letter, ostensibly written by "a good rebel, a citizen of Baltimore" (Pryce Lewis "Memoirs," 118), warned Webster not to come north via Leonardtown, because the Yankee spycatchers were lying in wait for him. Of course, it hadn't been a rebel who wrote it, it had been Pinkerton. That is if the letter ever existed.

Chapter 20

1. Pinkerton, *The Spy of the Rebellion*, 533.
2. Pinkerton, *The Spy of the Rebellion*, 533–534.
3. Pinkerton, *The Spy of the Rebellion*, 534.
4. *Richmond Daily Dispatch*, March 8, 1862, p. 3, "Martial Law."

Chapter 21

1. *Daily Richmond Examiner*, April 3, 1862, p. 3, "Execution Under Court Martial"; April 5, 1862, p. 3, "City Intelligence"; Pinkerton, *The Spy of the Rebellion*, pp. 534–539. Pinkerton, well aware that Timothy Webster's widow, Charlotte, and her one remaining child would be reading *The Spy of the Rebellion* avidly, could not possibly have written the truth, that Tim and Hattie moved into the Taylor house. Instead he came up with William Campbell's house, with its family environment, Willi, Wilhelmina, and toddler Heini, the quintessential Teutonic manger scene complete with alpenhorns, lederhosen, and group yodeling. Much more palatable, if faintly demented.
2. *Richmond Daily Dispatch*, Sept. 5, 1862, p. 1, "Occupied."

3. *Richmond Daily Dispatch*, March 26, 1862, p. 2, "Meeting of Richmond Ladies"; March 27, 1862, p. 1, "Suggestions about Gunboats"; April 1, 1862, p. 2, "The Ladies' Defence Association"; April 5, 1862, p. 2, "The Ladies' Gunboat Association." During the Civil War the word "defence" was still usually spelled that way but "defense," long in use, was gaining ground, although not in the South.

Chapter 22

1. Pinkerton, *The Spy of the Rebellion*, 525; Beymer, *On Hazardous Service*, 284–285; Pryce Lewis "Memoirs," p. 219–221.
2. Beymer, *On Hazardous Service*, 284; Pinkerton, *The Spy of the Rebellion*, 534–535. According to the Pryce Lewis "memoirs," page 219, Pryce Lewis did not know of Scully's court-martial until he himself went for his.
3. Pinkerton, *The Spy of the Rebellion*, 535–536.
4. Recko, *A Spy for the Union*, 125.

Chapter 23

1. *Richmond Daily Dispatch*, March 20, 1862, p. 2, "Exodus from the County Jail."
2. Pryce Lewis "Memoirs," 211–212, 217–219, 224; *Richmond Daily Dispatch*, April 10, 1862, p. 2, "Castle Godwin."
3. Pryce Lewis "Memoirs," 224.
4. Pryce Lewis "Memoirs," 224–225.
5. Pryce Lewis "Memoirs," 225. There is a problem with this part of the narrative as written in the Pryce Lewis "memoirs." Again, it is obvious from both the structure and the wording that they are plagiarizing Pinkerton's *The Spy of the Rebellion*, and that book is the only source we have that names a specific charge against Lewis and Scully. The newspapers, for example, only say "spying." Of course, it may be that Pinkerton and the Pryce Lewis "memoirs" are right. Maybe the two spies really did lurk within the fortifications of Richmond.

6. Pryce Lewis "Memoirs," 225–226; *Daily Richmond Examiner*, April 3, 1862, p. 3, "Execution Under Court Martial." The *Richmond Examiner* confirms that the two ladies "appeared as witnesses against" Lewis and Scully. ¶ Only a month earlier, on the 21st of February, General Winder, "the blundering old man," had celebrated his 62nd birthday. At the other end of the age spectrum William Chase Morton was 16, and his brother Howard was 14.
7. William H. Scott was the Pinkerton agent who ran Pinkerton's headquarters in Washington. ¶ In the first quote in this paragraph, an editing hand changed the word "Lewis" to the word "me," which, considering it is meant to be Lewis dictating to Major David Cronin, was an appropriate redaction.
8. Pryce Lewis "Memoirs," 226.
9. Pryce Lewis "Memoirs," 227.
10. Pryce Lewis "Memoirs," 225, 228. Whoever wrote the original manuscript of the "memoirs," and it probably was Pryce Lewis dictating to Major Cronin, said that the trial lasted "four days." Another hand subsequently edited this to "three or four days."

Chapter 24

1. Pinkerton, *The Spy of the Rebellion*, 327; Pryce Lewis "Memoirs," 232. After leaving Richmond in 1863, Frederick John Cridland became full consul at Mobile, and remained at his post until 1886. He finished his career at Charleston in 1890, returned to England, and in 1899, at the age of 74, perhaps just to prove that he was more than the "fussy little man" scholars have portrayed him as, married a woman 45 years his junior. He died at his London home in 1905.
2. *Richmond Daily Dispatch*, April 5, 1862, p. 2, "The Condemned Spies."
3. Pinkerton, *The Spy of the Rebellion*, 526.
4. Beymer, *On Hazardous Service*, 285.

5. Pinkerton, *The Spy of the Rebellion*, 526.

6. Pinkerton, *The Spy of the Rebellion*, 526. Here, and in a few other places, Pinkerton, being a well-known atheist, uses "God" in a blasphemous way. As this will offend many readers, I have tried to take the sting out of this practice by rendering the word with a dash instead of a vowel. Following the generally accepted Victorian convention, I have done something similar with certain other words that might cause such shock and dismay. For those readers who are not privileged to suffer from these sensibilities, I trust the dashes will not make it too difficu-t to decipher the words.

7. Pinkerton, *The Spy of the Rebellion*, 526.

8. Pinkerton, *The Spy of the Rebellion*, 526.

9. Pryce Lewis "Memoirs," 236–237. Obviously fearing a lawsuit from the Pinkertons should this manuscript ever get published, the editor of the Pryce Lewis "memoirs," or, possibly, Pryce Lewis himself, crossed through the words "downright outrageous lying," and replaced them with "lack of judgment or worse."

10. Billy Pinkerton, in his 1883 interview, which formed the basis for the widespread press article, "Famous Detectives," tells us that Father McMullen was actually a Winder detective posing as a priest so that he could get information from Scully's confession. It's a fun story, and although there is no truth to it, Father McMullen undoubtedly encouraged Scully to confess all to General Winder as the only chance he had of getting off with his life. And it may well be that the priest was right.

11. *Daily Richmond Examiner*, April 22, 1862, p. 3, "Court Martial"; *Richmond Enquirer*, May 2, 1862, p. 1, "The Execution of Webster, the Federal Spy." The quotes in this paragraph are both from the *Examiner*. ¶ One must be very careful when it comes to the Pryce Lewis "memoirs." These "memoirs," which are untrustworthy at the best of times, deteriorate into a rather sickening self-exculpation when they tell of the betrayal of Tim Webster. "It was all Scully's fault." ¶ The quote about the Devil is an updated rendering of the line in *Canterbury Tales*, Squire's Tale, 602. Shakespeare refers twice to this old saying, once in *Comedy of Errors* and again in *The Tempest*.

Chapter 25

1. Pinkerton, *The Spy of the Rebellion*, 536.

2. Pinkerton, *The Spy of the Rebellion*, 536; *Daily Richmond Examiner*, April 3, 1862, p. 3, "Execution Under Court Martial."

3. Pinkerton, *The Spy of the Rebellion*, 536.

4. *The Spy of the Rebellion* is our only source for all this. There is no other potential source. We can expect no corroboration from the already highly suspicious Pryce Lewis "memoirs," since Lewis and Scully were not privy to any of what happened.

5. The name Cashmyer: One also sees it spelled Cashmeyer, Cashmyre, and Cashmire. He himself spelled it Cashmyer. ¶ The *Daily Richmond Examiner*, April 5, 1862, p. 3, "Execution Under Court Martial," has this: "Timothy Webster and his wife, boarders at Mrs. Taylor's on 4th street, between Clay and Leigh, were on [sic] yesterday arrested on the charge of being Lincoln spies." See the same paper, April 23, 1862, p. 3, "City Intelligence," which tells us that Tim and Hattie, at the time of their arrest, were living at a "respectable boarding house." And finally the article "Webster the Spy," on page 2 of the Magazine Section, *Richmond Times-Dispatch*, Aug. 23, 1903, which says that "Webster was arrested at his boarding house on Fourth Street, between Clay and Leigh." ¶ We don't know

why Tim and Hattie moved from the hotel to the boarding house. Given the way the world turns, it is just possible that it was at the urging of General Winder.

6. Pryce Lewis "Memoirs," 247. Again, it is clear from this that Pryce Lewis was plagiarizing Pinkerton's *The Spy of the Rebellion*, and doing it so hard that either his eyes or his mathematics deceived him as he counted the number of persons getting out of the carriage.

7. Pinkerton, *The Spy of the Rebellion*, 537–540. On page 540 of the book, Pinkerton describes Tim at the time of his capture as "wasted by disease, weakened by his long and painful illness."

8. *Southern Lady, Yankee Spy*, pp. 73 and 75; *Richmond Daily Dispatch*, April 3, 1862, p. 2, "List of Prisoners Confined in Castle Godwin to March 15th, 1862"; May 1, 1862, p. 2, "Released"; May 21, 1862, p. 2, "Castle Godwin"; *Richmond Daily Whig*, March 10, 1862, p. 3, "Castle Godwin"; Pinkerton, *The Spy of the Rebellion*, 540.

9. *Richmond Daily Dispatch*, April 3, 1862, p. 2, "List of Prisoners Confined in Castle Godwin to March 15th, 1862." Hattie's brother, Harry, enlisted on Sept. 1, 1861, and served in Co. G of the 10th Illinois Infantry.

Chapter 26

1. *Daily Richmond Examiner*, April 3, 1862, p. 3, "Execution Under Court Martial"; *Richmond Daily Whig*, April 4, 1862, p. 3, "Conviction of Two Spies"; *Richmond Daily Dispatch*, April 5, 1862, p. 2, "The Condemned Spies."

2. The *Richmond Daily Dispatch* published this under the heading "Arrests," on page 2 of their April 4, 1862, issue: "A man named Webster and his wife, natives of Kentucky, but acting in the interest of Lincoln, were arrested yesterday, and put in Castle Godwin, on suspicion of being spies." The same paper, on page 2 of their April 10 issue, under the heading "Castle Godwin," confirmed that "Tim Webster, Mrs. Webster, Kentucky, spies" were committed to Castle Godwin on April 3.

3. *Richmond Daily Whig*, April 4, 1862, p. 3, "Conviction of Two Spies." A note of caution to the reader: The Pryce Lewis "memoirs" tell of this two-week respite on page 251 of the manuscript. The typescript of the "memoirs," which differs greatly from the manuscript, has the same story on pages 124–126.

4. *Richmond Daily Dispatch*, April 5, 1862, p. 2, "The Condemned Spies."

5. *Richmond Enquirer*, as reproduced in the *Memphis Daily Appeal*, April 11, 1862, p. 1, "To Be Hung."

6. *Memphis Daily Appeal*, April 10, 1862, p. 2, "Letter from the Confederate Capital." The *Appeal* left Memphis on June 5, 1862. It was the prudent thing to do, for the advancing Union army would be arriving in town the following day. The paper set up shop in Grenada, Miss., and recommenced publishing on June 9. Although we don't see any pen name in the *Appeal*'s columns concerning Webster, this correspondent generally went by "Dixie." It was always thought that "Dixie" was John Barton, but J. Cutler Andrews, in *South Reports the War*, page x, has found out that it was really the famous poet and newsman, John Reuben Thompson.

7. *Memphis Daily Appeal*, April 10, 1862, p. 2, "Letter from the Confederate Capital." As for how the underground railroad worked, there is another version, on page 93 of Volume 1 of *A Rebel War Clerk's Diary*, by John B. Jones.

8. *Daily Richmond Examiner*, April 28, 1862, p. 3, "The Spy."

9. *Daily Richmond Examiner*, April 28, 1862, p. 3, "The Spy."

10. *Richmond Daily Dispatch*, April 30, 1862, p. 2, "Trial, Sentence, and Execution of Timothy Webster as a Spy."

11. *Richmond Enquirer*, May 2, 1862, p. 1, "The Execution of Webster, the Federal Spy."

12. Obviously OCH is a man.
13. *Western Democrat*, May 6, 1862, p. 3, "A Spy Hung"; *Richmond Times-Dispatch*, Aug, 23, 1903, Magazine Section, p. 2, "Webster the Spy."
14. *Richmond Daily Dispatch*, Dec. 11, 1862, p. 1, "To Be Sent North."
15. *Daily Richmond Examiner*, April 28, 1862, p. 3, "The Spy"; *Richmond Enquirer*, May 2, 1862, p. 1, "The Execution of Webster, the Federal Spy."
16. There is nothing in the *Rebel War Clerk's Diary* entry of April 6 that couldn't have been taken from the newspapers of April 4 and 5, so it's hard to determine the value, and even the meaning, of what he wrote for those two days. Part of the problem is his byzantine wording, something usually resorted to when a person is prevaricating. It certainly feels as if it's been written after the event: "Two spies (Lincoln's detective police) have been arrested here, tried by court-martial, and condemned to be hung. There is an awful silence among the Baltimore detectives, which bodes no harm to the condemned. They will not be executed, though guilty." As for the clerk's diary entry for April 10, that definitely seems spurious, or, as one should correctly say, "added after the war was over": "The condemned spies have implicated Webster, the letter-carrier, who has had so many passports. He will hang, probably. General Winder himself, and his policemen, wrote home by him. I don't believe him any more guilty than many who used to write by him; and I mean to tell the Judge Advocate so, if they give me an opportunity." It's just that the rebel war clerk's attitude toward Webster here seems far too self-servingly benign when one remembers what he said about him in his entry of December 11, 1861.
17. *Richmond Daily Dispatch*, April 5, 1862, p. 2, "The Condemned Spies"; *Daily Richmond Examiner*, April 22, 1862, p. 3, "Court Martial."

Chapter 27

1. Pinkerton, *The Spy of the Rebellion*, 540; *Daily Richmond Examiner*, April 22, 1862, p. 3, "Court Martial"; *Richmond Daily Dispatch*, Nov. 28, 1855, p. 2, "Law Notice"; April 30, 1862, p. 2, "Trial, Sentence, and Execution of Timothy Webster as a Spy"; *Richmond Enquirer*, May 2, 1862, p. 1, "The Execution of Webster, the Federal Spy." On page 540 of *The Spy of the Rebellion*, Pinkerton says, "The trial of Webster was ordered for an early day." And that was as it should have been, in conformity with the American ideal of a fair and speedy trial. But then Pinkerton complains, whines almost, that Tim's trial came too soon, "with a haste that was inhuman." According to Pinkerton, General Winder was afraid Tim was going to die on him there and then. ¶ Beymer, on pages 286–287 of his book, *On Hazardous Service*, insists that the "trial of Timothy Webster, civilian spy, was immediately begun by a civil court," but that subsequently it became a court-martial, a military trial. But he doesn't say why this happened, and the reason he doesn't is because it didn't. ¶ The *Dispatch* and the *Examiner*, both of April 22, have this: "For some time past the court martial being held in McDaniel's Jail have been engaged in the investigation of the case of one Timothy Webster, who is charged with being a spy," which seems to indicate that the court-martial came to Tim's bedside and stayed there until the end of the trial. Pinkerton says, "The court was convened. Owing to Webster's weakened condition their sessions were held in the jail." By "jail" he means Castle Godwin, which, at that time, was a prison, even though persons might be incarcerated there without a formal conviction. Pinkerton adds that because Tim bore himself so manfully throughout the trial, "his physical health perceptibly improved, so much so that the tribunal removed their sittings to the courthouse,

and Webster was able to be in daily attendance."

2. *Daily Richmond Examiner*, April 22, 1862, p. 3, "Court Martial"; *Richmond Daily Dispatch*, Nov. 28, 1855, p. 2, "Law Notice," and April 30, 1862, p. 2, "Trial, Sentence, and Execution of Timothy Webster as a Spy"; *Richmond Enquirer*, May 2, 1862, p. 1, "The Execution of Webster, the Federal Spy."

3. Pryce Lewis "Memoirs," 269.

4. Pryce Lewis "Memoirs," 269. The editor of the "memoirs" changed "Webster sat by me on the opposite side of a long table" to "Webster and I sat on opposite sides of a long table," but otherwise let this inane passage stand. ¶ Incidentally, Pinkerton, on page 111 of *The Spy of the Rebellion*, wrote that Webster had gray eyes. That's an important little point for plagiarism spotters.

5. Pryce Lewis's role in the trial of Timothy Webster is related in his "memoirs," 268-70.

6. *Richmond Enquirer*, May 2, 1862, p. 1, "The Execution of Webster, the Federal Spy"; *Semi-Weekly Raleigh Register*, May 3, 1862, p. 2, "A Spy Hung"; *Richmond Daily Dispatch*, April 30, 1862, p. 2, "Trial, Sentence, and Execution of Timothy Webster as a Spy." The *Dispatch* says, of Tim: "He also said he could make several parties in the War Department 'shake in their jackets' by his revelations, but he made none up to his last hour."

7. *Semi-Weekly Raleigh Register*, May 3, 1862, p. 2, "A Spy Hung."

8. The quote is from the *Richmond Enquirer*, May 2, 1862, p. 1, "The Execution of Webster, the Federal Spy."

9. Pinkerton, *The Spy of the Rebellion*, 540; Beymer, *On Hazardous Service*, 286-287; *Daily Richmond Examiner*, April 22, 1862, p. 3, "Court Martial"; *Richmond Daily Dispatch*, April 30, 1862, p. 2, "Trial, Sentence, and Execution of Timothy Webster as a Spy"; *Richmond Enquirer*, May 2, 1862, p. 1, "The Execution of Webster, the Federal Spy."

10. Pinkerton, *The Spy of the Rebellion*, 540; Beymer, *On Hazardous Service*, 276-287; *Daily Richmond Examiner*, April 22, 1862, p. 3, "Court Martial"; *Richmond Daily Dispatch*, April 22, 1862, p. 2, "Trial Concluded"; April 28, 1862, p. 2, "Condemned to be Hung"; April 30, 1862, p. 2, "Trial, Sentence, and Execution of Timothy Webster as a Spy"; *Richmond Enquirer*, April 15, 1862, p. 1, "Spy Caught"; April 29, 1862, p. 3, "The Federal Spies"; May 2, 1862, p. 1, "The Execution of Webster, the Federal Spy"; *Richmond Daily Whig*, April 8, 1862, p. 3, "City Items." The spy they caught at Falmouth was Andrew Murray, whom they booked into Castle Godwin as from the 15th of April. See the *Richmond Daily Dispatch* of April 16, 1862, p. 2, "Arrest of a Spy," and April 22, 1862, p. 2, "Inmates of Castle Godwin." There is no suggestion, and no reason to believe, that Murray was a Pinkerton man.

11. Pinkerton, *The Spy of the Rebellion*, 548-549. Most historians who have written about Hattie Lawton claim, without citing any sources other than their predecessors in the field, that she had a trial and that she was sentenced to a year, or even to a year and a day, in Castle Thunder. But these scholars, along with their scholarly pronouncements, are rendered unscholarly the moment they have Hattie being sentenced to a non-existent prison. Regardless of the prison she was in, she was there without trial, and the proof of that will appear from time to time in the course of Chapter 33.

12. *Daily Richmond Examiner*, April 23, 1862, p. 2, "The Spies."

13. *Memphis Daily Appeal*, May 7, 1862, p. 1, "Letter from Richmond."

14. Jones, *A Rebel War Clerk's Diary*, April 24, 1862; *Richmond Daily Dispatch*, April 28, 1862, p. 2, "Condemned to be Hung." As for the rebel war clerk being so at variance with the truth, it must be said, not in his defense by any means, but by way of explanation, that he never made

any bones about the fact that he tinkered with his diary after the war, using two main tools: Old newspapers and his memory. He must not be dealt with too harshly for what he did, for that is how all Southern diaries were written in those days, at least those that were published. The fact is, though, that this process renders such a diary untrustworthy.

Chapter 28

1. Fishel, *The Secret War for the Union*, 100 and 148. Two of the agents who got out of Richmond were E.H. Stein and his wife. The following is the first biographical material ever published on this remarkable couple. Enoch Henry Stein, the agent of the red beard, was born on Aug. 3, 1823, in Prague. He came to the U.S.A. at the age of twenty, married, and had three children. Billy Pinkerton, in 1897, said of Stein, "Before the war he had been a sporting man, and spent much time traveling about playing cards." E.H. Stein's second wife was Fannie Susan Cary, born in Wilkes-Barre, Pa., on March 10, 1834. The two of them were the first Secret Service agents into the South. Following Tim Webster's arrest, and with death sentences being talked about with abandon, the game had turned out to be a lot more dangerous than the Steins had bargained for, and they saw little reason to hang around. They'd had enough of spying. Stein made it back to Pinkerton's tent on April 20, while Fannie took another route out of Richmond. After they left the spying game they went to Chicago, where they started the hugely successful City of Paris Dollar Store, with everything selling for a dollar. Stein died of cholera in New York on August 13, 1871. Fannie married twice more and died in New Orleans on her 90th birthday. As for Fannie, or "Mrs. E.H. Stein," as she was known, Pinkerton immortalized her as Mrs. E.H. Baker in Chapter 26 of his *The Spy of the Rebellion*.
¶ After Stein and all the others got out in April 1862, the only Pinkertons left in Richmond were Hattie Lawton, Tim Webster, and Lewis and Scully, all in prison in Richmond, and at least three resident operatives, still at liberty, deep undercover, unsuspected: William Angell, T.H. O'Sullivan, and Harry Knipe.

2. Pryce Lewis "Memoirs," 270.
3. Pryce Lewis "Memoirs," 270. The editor of the "memoirs" changed Scully's reaction to "made no reply."
4. Pryce Lewis "Memoirs," 270. Mercifully, the editor of the "memoirs" deleted this small, rather self-serving paragraph.
5. Pinkerton, *The Spy of the Rebellion*, 549.
6. Pinkerton, *The Spy of the Rebellion*, 549.
7. Pinkerton, *The Spy of the Rebellion*, 549–550. This story, about Hattie going to Varina Davis, is so unlikely it's almost a joke. Is it something Hattie told Pinkerton? Or did Pinkerton just make it up? The story has appeared in many books, but they are all derivative of Pinkerton. There is no corroboration beyond the fact that Lee was in Richmond that week, and that's no big deal, as Lee was in Richmond most days during that period of his career.

Chapter 29

1. Pinkerton, *The Spy of the Rebellion*, 550.
2. When his time came, in February 1865, in Philip Cashmyer's tent at Florence, South Carolina, Winder cheated the hangman by dropping dead. It was Hattie's curse.
3. This anecdote of General Winder's visit to Tim's cell is told only in Pinkerton, *The Spy of the Rebellion*, 550–552. Pinkerton took the idea, much of this dialogue, and parts of the scene itself from "The Execution of Timothy Webster, the Spy," published on page 2 of the April 30, 1862, issue of the *Daily Richmond Examiner*.

Where Pinkerton has Hattie begging the evil general to think of Tim's family, this is really Pinkerton thinking of Tim's real wife, Charlotte, who, in 1883, would be reading the book out there in Onarga, 85 miles south of Chicago on the Illinois Central RR. In reality, General Winder would have caught that little slip, and said something like, "Oooh, I thought you *were* his family, Mrs. Webster." Winder's reflection upon Webster's weak knees is my speculation.

4. Pinkerton, *The Spy of the Rebellion*, 554.

5. *Daily Richmond Examiner*, April 29, 1863, p. 3, "Timothy Webster, the Spy"; *Richmond Daily Dispatch*, April 30, 1862, p. 2, "Trial, Sentence, and Execution of Timothy Webster as a Spy." The *Examiner* suggests that the grounds for such an appeal might have been the incompetency of Lewis and Scully as witnesses.

6. Pinkerton, *The Spy of the Rebellion*, 554.

7. *Richmond Daily Dispatch*, April 30, 1862, p. 2, "Trial, Sentence, and Execution of Timothy Webster as a Spy."

Chapter 30

1. Captain George W. Alexander was one of Winder's Baltimore clique.

2. *Richmond Daily Dispatch*, Sept. 17, 1879, p. 3, "White Sulphur Springs."

3. The quote is from the *Daily Richmond Examiner*, April 30, 1862, p. 2, "The Execution of Timothy Webster, the Spy." On page 551 of *The Spy of the Rebellion*, Pinkerton has Tim saying, "I wish to die like a man." On page 556, as they are leading him away, Tim tells Hattie, "I will be brave, and die like a man." Even more to the point, on page 552, Hattie herself says, "he will die like a man."

Chapter 31

1. R & F RR = Richmond & Fredericksburg Railroad.

2. *Richmond Daily Dispatch*, Oct. 30, 1860, p. 1, "Camp Lee"; Oct. 31, 1860, p. 1, "The Encampment."

3. *Richmond Daily Dispatch*, Oct. 30, 1860, p. 1, "Camp Lee"; Oct. 31, 1860, p. 1, "The Encampment."

4. Recko, *A Spy for the Union*, 130; *Daily Richmond Examiner*, April 30, 1862, p. 2, "The Execution of Timothy Webster, the Spy"; *Richmond Enquirer*, May 6, 1862, p. 4, "To the Editors of the Enquirer." Regarding Woodbridge's slaves, the reader is recommended to glance at the *Richmond Daily Dispatch*, Sept. 26, 1862, p. 2, "Proceedings in the Courts."

5. *Daily Richmond Examiner*, April 30, 1862, p. 2, "The Execution of Timothy Webster, the Spy." Modern historians will tell you that the papers lied when they said Tim cried on his way to the gallows, but that's only wishful thinking on the part of the historians. They would much rather have had him die like a man.

6. *Daily Richmond Examiner*, April 30, 1862, p. 2, "The Execution of Timothy Webster, the Spy"; Pinkerton, *The Spy of the Rebellion*, 550–552.

7. *Daily Richmond Examiner*, April 30, 1862, p. 2, "The Execution of Timothy Webster, the Spy."

8. *Daily Richmond Examiner*, April 30, 1862, p. 2, "The Execution of Timothy Webster, the Spy"; Recko, *A Spy for the Union*, 130.

9. Recko, *A Spy for the Union*, 130; *Richmond Daily Whig*, April 30, 1862, p. 3, "Hanging of a Spy"; *Daily Richmond Examiner*, April 30, 1862, p. 2, "The Execution of Timothy Webster, the Spy"; Lowell (Mass.) *Daily Citizen and News*, May 6, 1862, p. 2, c. 3, no title.

10. *Richmond Daily Dispatch*, May 1, 1862, p. 2, "Released." However, when we come to two later issues of the same paper—May 21, 1862, p. 2, "Castle Godwin," and June 6, 1862, p. 2, "To Go Home"—we know something is not quite right with this story.

11. *Richmond Sentinel*, Nov. 11, 1864,

p. 1, "Death of a Detective"; *Daily Richmond Examiner*, Nov. 11, 1864, p. 2, "A Birth and Death in One Family"; *Richmond Daily Whig*, Nov. 11, 1864, p. 2, "An Old Public Functionary Departed."

Chapter 32

1. Ryan, *A Yankee Spy in Richmond*, 45. It is a matter of historical fact, not opinion, that Miss Van Lew was a Richmond lady who spied for the Union for about 18 months, between the end of 1863 and the close of the war. Up to that time she had been engaged in trying to improve the lives of Federal prisoners. One presumes Hattie was one of these. This remarkable lady, Miss Van Lew, died in September 1900, but just before she did, she told her nieces about a journal she had written, and exactly where she had buried it in her back yard. Now, this is where the "historical fact" becomes a little hard to swallow. The nieces dug up the paperwork, but most of it was missing. What we have left is fragments that represent various periods during the war. In typical 19th-century Southern fashion, this is not a diary as we know it today. The entries were unquestionably written later than the dates to which they belong. For example, 1865 events are discussed in an entry purporting to be 1862. The executor of Miss Van Lew's estate was a man named John P. Reynolds.

2. Pinkerton, *The Spy of the Rebellion*, 560. The article "Webster the Spy," on page 2 of the Magazine Section of the *Richmond Times-Dispatch* of Aug. 23, 1903, says that Tim's grave in Richmond was located "on the north side, near one of the city cemeteries."

3. *Richmond Daily Dispatch*, May 3, 1871, p. 1, "Webster, the United States Spy."

Chapter 33

1. *Rock Island Argus*, May 2, 1862, p. 2, c. 7, no title.

2. *Davenport Daily Democrat and News*, May 5, 1862, p. 1, "Hung as a Spy." For more on this article and how it has been misused in history, see Chapter 5, note 12.

3. *Davenport Daily Gazette*, May 6, 1862, p. 1, "The Ex-Bridge Tender."

4. *Daily National Intelligencer*, May 7, 1862, p. 3, "Execution of a Spy"; *Chicago Tribune*, May 7, 1862, p. 3 and 6, "Very Late from the South." Ironically, on that very day, May 7, the *Chicago Tribune*, not knowing that Timothy Webster had been a Pinkerton man, reproduced one of the big *Richmond Dispatch* articles on him.

5. *Davenport Daily Democrat and News*, May 12, 1862, p. 1, "That Spy."

6. *Richmond Daily Dispatch*, May 21, 1862, p. 2, "Castle Godwin." Warden Freeburger was, indeed, known as Georgie, whereas Captain George W. Alexander, to name but one, very definitely wasn't. Frederick Shaffer was known, in print as elsewhere, as Fred.

7. *Richmond Daily Dispatch*, May 1, 1862, p. 2, "Released"; June 6, 1862, p. 2, "To Go Home."

8. *Chicago Tribune*, July 31, 1862, p. 4, "Personal."

9. *Richmond Enquirer*, Aug. 12, 1862, p. 3, "Castle Thunder"; Casstevens, *George W. Alexander and Castle Thunder*, 48; Buhk, *True Crime in the Civil War*, 14; Pickenpaugh, *Captives in Blue*, 39; Speer, *Portals of Hell*, 93–95; Field, *Silent Witness*, 283; Pryce Lewis "memoirs," 273, 277. The new prison was named Castle Thunder before Aug. 12, 1862, but not long before. The first published mention of the name is in the *Richmond Enquirer* of that date, p. 3, "Castle Thunder."

10. *Richmond Daily Dispatch*, Aug. 19, 1862, p. 1, "Removed Downtown; Oct. 25, 1862, p. 2, "Prison Items"; Union Provost Marshals' File, 4114, Frances Abel. According to her own account, in the Turner-Baker Papers, under Abells, she was born in New York as Frances Tuttle, and had been married to a William H.

Abells, who had been killed at First Manassas. ¶ It is claimed in the Pryce Lewis "memoirs," page 272, that Lewis and Scully were transferred from Castle Godwin to Castle Thunder on August 6. This seems too early, but the "memoirs" do say that the two spies were among the first to be removed there. *Richmond Daily Dispatch*, Aug. 6, 1862, p. 1, "New Lodgings"; *Baltimore Sun*, Sept. 22, 1863, p. 4.

11. *Evidence Taken Before the Committee of the House of Representatives, Appointed to Enquire into the Treatment of Prisoners at Castle Thunder*, 27–28; Casstevens, *George W. Alexander and Castle Thunder*, 79–82.

12. *Richmond Enquirer*, Sept. 5, 1862, p. 2, "The Notorious Rucker" and "A Wholesale Order." It hadn't taken long for General Winder's enforcement of martial law in Richmond to have a salutary effect on the city. As early as March 17 the *Dispatch* was able to state without the shadow of a doubt that most of the pickpockets, thieves, rowdies, loafers, and so forth had been driven out of the city and beyond the pale. Unfortunately they had now become predators out there in the surrounding counties. What did this do for the Richmond streets? It left them clear for "the disorderlies," as well as for the typically enormous number of practitioners of the old but unsung and very public art of genital exposure.

13. Letter from S.S. Baxter, agent appointed by Confederate Secretary of War Randolph, Nov. 13, 1862, to Randolph, found in *War of the Rebellion (Official Records)*, Series II, Vol. IV, 943.

14. *Richmond Daily Dispatch*, Oct. 11, 1862, p. 2, "Visit to a Confederate Prison"; Curtis, "The 'Old Capitol' and Its Keeper," p. 225.

15. Pryce Lewis "Memoirs," 279–281. The editor of the "memoirs" changed "get us released" to "succeed." ¶ Wood wound up making himself obnoxious to the Confederates generally. The Oct. 31, 1862, issue of the *Richmond Enquirer* complained that he been in the South too long and that it was time for him to leave. ¶ As for the article in the paper, the one the "memoirs" mention, it's true. It was in the form of a letter written by Stanton to Col. Ludlow on the 27th, disavowing Wood. The *Alexandria Gazette* also covered this event, on page 1 of their Nov. 1, 1862, issue, "Difficulty with Mr. Wood," and Nov. 3, 1862, p. 4, c. 1, no title. The following day Wood was on the flag of truce boat, but, unfortunately the anecdote about the leap from the dock onto the boat is a crock of fertilizer, so the question everyone was dying to ask—did Wood make the leap on horseback or not?—is moot. On Nov. 2, Wood was back in Washington, without a last batch of prisoners he had been expected to bring with him. His mission had been a dismal and well-noted failure.

16. *War of the Rebellion (Official Record)*, Series 2, Volume 4, p. 917.

17. *War of the Rebellion (Official Record)*, Series 2, Volume 4, p. 917.

18. *Richmond Daily Dispatch*, Nov. 6, 1862, p. 1, "Released on Parole."

19. Ryan, *A Yankee Spy in Richmond*, 45.

Chapter 34

1. *North American and United States Gazette*, Dec. 11, 1862, p. 2, "From Fortress Monroe"; *Daily South Carolinian*, Dec. 16, 1862, p. 3, "Flag of Truce."

2. *Richmond Daily Dispatch*, Dec. 12, 1862, p. 1, "Going Away"; *Washington Evening Star*, Dec. 13, 1862, p. 2, "From Fortress Monroe"; *Daily South Carolinian*, Dec. 16, 1862, p. 3, "Flag of Truce"; *A Rebel War Clerk's Diary*, Dec. 11, 1862. As we see, above, this is what the rebel war clerk wrote in his "diary" for Dec. 11, 1862: "Scully and Lewis, condemned to die as spies, have been pardoned by the President, and are to be sent North." Note that he writes Scully and Lewis, not Lewis and Scully. That's very unusual. To say "Scully and Lewis" is almost like saying "Hardy

and Laurel." The *Alexandria Gazette*, which was a Yankee paper, of course, wrote this in their issue of Dec. 16, 1862: "Scully and Lewis, who have been confined in Castle Thunder, under sentence of death as spies, in co-partnership with Webster, who was hung, have been pardoned and are to be sent North."

3. *Richmond Daily Whig*, Dec. 12, 1862, p. 1, no title; *Richmond Daily Dispatch*, Dec. 12, 1862, p. 1, "Going Away." The name Sarah needs to be gone into here, to a point. The newspapers often got people's first names wrong, and this may well have been one of those occasions. Probably was. Moreover, there was a Miss Sarah Webster living in Richmond at the time, a native of the city, in fact. But there is still the chance that Sarah was the name Hattie was giving out: Sarah Webster. See Chapter 1 for reasons why Sarah would be an important name to consider.

4. *Richmond Daily Dispatch*, Oct. 15, 1861, p. 1, "Cranberries."

5. *Richmond Enquirer*, Dec. 13, 1862, p. 2, "Female prisoners sent off"; *Richmond Daily Dispatch*, Dec. 13, 1862, p. 3, "Prison items." As we can see from the text, the papers are confused about Miss Underwood's first name. Is it Maria or Belle? The *Richmond Daily Dispatch* of July 28, 1862, p. 1, "Local Matters," also refers to her as Maria, but Casstevens, in her book on Castle Thunder, calls her Margaret Underwood, of Washington, D.C.

6. So, where did this myth of the "four Federals" start? Ed Fishel, on page 254 of his seminal and influential 1996 book, *The Secret War for the Union*, has this: "Hattie Lawton, still carried on the records as Mrs. Timothy Webster, was one of a party of four federals exchanged for Belle Boyd, Dec. 13, 1862." This is going to sound hard to believe but Mrs. Casstevens, in her book on the women of Castle Thunder, states, on page 82, that Mrs. Webster was "exchanged for a Union soldier." One might need to think about that for a minute or two before the implications sink in.

7. *New York Times*, Dec. 16, 1862, p. 1, "Release of 270 National Prisoners"; *Boston Daily Advertiser*, Dec. 16, 1862, p. 2, c. 1, no title; *Bangor Daily Whig & Courier*, Dec. 16, 1862, p. 2, c. 5, no title; *North American and United States Gazette*, Dec. 16, 1862, p. 1, "From Fortress Monroe and the South."

8. *Richmond Daily Dispatch*, Jan. 26, 1867, p. 1, "Castle Thunder"; May 3, 1871, p. 1, "Webster, the United States Spy"; *Richmond Times-Dispatch*, Feb. 3, 1907, p. 10, "Castle Thunder." The 1867 newspaper is conflating two Websters: Captain Timothy Webster and Captain A.C. Webster. The latter, who had nothing whatever to do with the Pinkertons, was hanged in Richmond in 1863, for violating his parole. His wife was never in Richmond. By 1871 the same *Dispatch* was remembering the great Pinkerton spy as Jas. Webster, and that, after his conviction he had been sent to Castle Thunder to await his execution. "While there he openly acknowledged his mission." They go into much more detail about his jump, which wasn't his jump at all, but A.C. Webster's. As for the 1907 paper, a reader had written in asking for information about Castle Thunder. The paper's expert replied that "Captain Alexander was in charge of it at the time Miss Van Lew and Webster were held as suspects or spies." Timothy Webster was never in Castle Thunder, and Miss Van Lew was never held as a suspect in any prison. The paper goes on: "A well known druggist informs us that he witnessed the hanging of the notorious Webster, which took place in the yard of the prison about 10 o'clock of the morning. One Caphart was the hangman."

9. This paragraph is, as one can readily see, guesswork, but it is based, to a significant extent, on the case of Lewis and Scully, who would, the following year, trace that very path to Washington. Four

days elapsed between the time Lewis and Scully were released from Dixie on Sept. 26, 1863, and the moment they were given a pass in Annapolis by Major Chamberlain on Sept. 30.

10. *New York Herald*, Nov. 29, 1862, p. 4, "Justice to Major Allen"; Thomas Eckert papers, 264. When Lewis and Scully got out in 1863 and arrived in Washington, they were similarly at a loss as to what to do next. It was different for them in that Pinkerton no longer had a presence in the capital, but there existed in their arrival an eerie coincidence: The Pryce Lewis "memoirs," page 308, have Lewis saying, "I didn't know where to go." ¶ Pinkerton was sending not only goods to Lewis and Scully but money too.

11. Thomas Eckert papers, 267. It was this telegraphic message, and this alone, that proved that the H.H.L. from the old Baltimore Plot days of early 1861 was, in fact, Mrs. Timothy Webster, the woman Pinkerton named Hattie Lawton. Before this, no historian had ever offered any proof; only guesswork. Correct guesswork, as it turns out, but still guesswork.

12. Thomas Eckert papers, 267. If anyone can be called Pinkerton's Number Three man it is Francis Warner, ranking behind Pinkerton himself and George Bangs. Frank was born on Jan. 26, 1819, in Massachusetts, and came to Illinois when he was 22. In the 1850s he found himself sheriff of LaSalle County, and from there was launched his Pinkerton career. He stayed with the firm after the war, as a superintendent, and died on March 2, 1902.

Chapter 35

1. There are clues and there are leads. The clues might include letters waiting in various post offices and as advertised by the papers. Chicago, for example, has several letters, many indeed, over the next few years, waiting for Miss or Mrs. Hattie Warren, Harriet Warren, Harriet Webster, Hattie Lewis, and there's one, on May 23, 1864, for Mrs. Hattie Warn. This really sounds like our woman. After all, how many Mrs. Hattie Warns can there be? In 1864? Especially in Chicago? The answer is only one, surely. Famous last words.

2. Pinkerton letter to Lincoln, June 5, 1863, The Lincoln Papers, Library of Congress. Notice how Pinkerton blames McClellan for what happened to Tim Webster and Hattie Lawton, not to mention to Lewis and Scully. As to the identity of the fourth agent mentioned by Pinkerton, the one who had recently escaped from Richmond, we can't quite be sure, because Pinkerton doesn't tell us. But, if one were pressed, one would have to say it's Harry Knipe.

3. Notre Dame records; Lee County, Illinois, probate, George W. Warn, 1875..

4. Notre Dame records. March 1863 was only a few months after Hattie made it out of Dixie.

5. Notre Dame records. In February 1859, in Dixon, Illinois, per the *Dixon Telegraph* of Feb. 24, 1859, p. 4, c. 5, "Lora B. Warn." For Lora B. read Laura Isabelle, Belle to her friends. Belle Warn, the youngest of George Warn's full sisters, was then 15, almost 16. She married Thomas Solomon Deyo, a local lad of 19. The new Deyo couple went where everyone went in those days, to Iowa. They took Mrs. Deyo, the widowed mother, with them, along with Tom's younger brother Charles. By August of the following year, and probably a lot earlier than that, they were still out there, everyone that is except Belle. She was living with her sister, Kitty, in Chicago. Belle was 16 now, and had a job. Same job Kitty had. Belle became Mrs. Belle Towler, but it has not been possible for this author to find Mr. Towler, if there ever was, indeed, such a man.

Chapter 36

1. *Society of Montana Pioneers*, 72.
2. *Society of Montana Pioneers*, 72;

Grant, *A Guide to Historic Virginia City*, 7 et seq.
3. Grant, *A Guide to Historic Virginia City*, 7 et seq.; *Bad Lands Cow Boy*, June 4, 1885, p. 1, "The Lost Cabin Gold Mine."
4. *Bad Lands Cow Boy*, June 4, 1885, p. 1, "The Lost Cabin Gold Mine."
5. *Bad Lands Cow Boy*, June 4, 1885, p. 1, "The Lost Cabin Gold Mine."
6. *Bad Lands Cow Boy*, June 4, 1885, p. 1, "The Lost Cabin Gold Mine." The diary of Abram Voorhees (see Bibliography, under Documents), is an uncanny corroboration of John Warn's story.
7. *St. Louis Globe-Democrat*, Dec. 23, 1883, p. 2, "The Lost Cabin Mine Found."
8. *Bad Lands Cow Boy*, Medora, D.T., June 4, 1885, p. 1, "The Lost Cabin Gold Mine." Johnny lived in Medora in the 1880s.
9. *Bad Lands Cow Boy*, Medora, D.T., July 2, 1885, p. 1, "The Lost Cabin Gold Mine."
10. *Montana Post*, Feb. 18, 1865, p. 3, "New County." The *Montana Post* was published in Virginia City.

Chapter 37

1. Civil War Draft Registration Records, 1863–1865, RG 110, Records of the Provost Marshal General's Bureau (Civil War), NARA, RG 110; Databases of Illinois Veterans.
2. *Dixon Telegraph*, April 3, 1872, p. 1, "Personal"; 1870 census, Wyoming, Allen Warn.
3. *Ottawa Free Trader*, Aug. 12, 1871, p. 5, "State of Illinois."

Chapter 38

1. Notre Dame Archives, telegraph from Allan Pinkerton to George W. Warn, Jan. 25, 1868.
2. Notre Dame Archives, telegraph from Allan Pinkerton to George W. Warn, Jan. 25, 1868; *Chicago Tribune*, Jan. 29, 1868, p. 1, "Died."
3. *Chicago Republican*, Nov. 2, 1867, p. 2, "Allan Pinkerton"; Graceland Cemetery records. The *Republican* became the *Inter-Ocean* in 1872.
4. This death notice is from page 1 of the *Chicago Tribune* of Jan. 29, 1868, and was reproduced the following day by the *Chicago Republican*, who added that Kate died in the morning of the 28th. On Jan. 29, the death of "Kate Warn" was registered in Cook County.
5. The original, handwritten, entry in the Graceland Cemetery logbook, dated Jan. 30, 1868, says "Angie M. Warren." Warren and Warn can sound identical. One often sees "Warren" in the press and even in the censuses. Indeed, Angie M. Warren was also the name on the cemetery's burial card. However, her name on the grave locator card is Kate Warn, which is also the name on the tombstone Allan Pinkerton put up for her. Her grave is slightly to the right and rear of Pinkerton's marker, placed there when he himself came to be buried in Lot 558, Section C, sixteen years later.
6. *Brooklyn Daily Eagle*, Aug. 31, 1884, p. 9, "A Detective's Resting Place," reproduced from the *Chicago Herald*.
7. *Brooklyn Daily Eagle*, Aug. 31, 1884, p. 9, "A Detective's Resting Place"; Mrs. Warn's tombstone; March 1959 letter to do with the wording on the tombstone, held by Graceland Cemetery.
8. This notice appeared on Feb. 1, 1868, in both the *Chicago Tribune* (page 4) and the *Chicago Republican*. Exactly a week later, on February 7, the *Republican* published a list of wills proved, including "Warn, Angie M." Unfortunately, the place where Chicago wills were lodged went up in the 1871 Chicago fire. Today there are only a few pre-fire wills extant in the Archives Department of the Clerk of the Circuit Court of Cook County. Angie's is not one of them. However, we do know one or two things about the will: She left the family farm, of 89 acres, to her three

youngest siblings (at that time), George, Libby, and Ella. And there is this item, from the *Chicago Republican* of Oct. 1, 1868: "Estate of Angie N. Warn [sic.] Claim of Enoch H. Stein for $48. Allowed."

9. Eckert, Pinkerton, 370. In the 1863 Washington city directory one finds "Allen, E.J., U.S.A., 181 Pa av, h. 288 I north." That's work at 181 Pennsylvania Avenue, and home 288 Eye.

10. *Daily Inter-Ocean*, May 31, 1896, p. 1, "At Graceland."

Chapter 39

1. The above story of Julia Hubbell was put together largely from the Chicago city directories, the U.S. censuses, and probate records.

2. Illinois probate papers, Hubbell, Julia.

Chapter 40

1. E-mails from museum employee to the author, July 12, 2017, and July 28 and 29, 2017. Most of the sources today will tell you that the museum acquired the image in 1924. But the museum itself says 1927.

2. *Chicago Tribune*, May 7, 2015, "Kate Hannigan on Kate Warne," by Debbie Carlson. Mrs. Hannigan is a novelist. My own guess is that it is she who discovered this item and brought it to the attention of the world.

3. E-mail from museum employee to the author, July 12, 2017.

Chapter 41

1. George Curtis, who is fictional, is based largely on Timothy Webster. The name comes from one of Pinkerton's friends, George Ticknor Curtis. Mrs. E.H. Baker was really Mrs. E.H. Stein, as we have seen in Chapter 28, note 1.

2. Pinkerton, *The Spy of the Rebellion*, xxv, xxvii, xxxi.

3. Pinkerton, *The Spy of the Rebellion*, 367.

4. Pinkerton, *The Spy of the Rebellion*, 367.

5. Pinkerton, *The Spy of the Rebellion*, 370. Pinkerton's wording here leaves no doubt that John Scobell was not an operative. Mind you, he was not a real person either. But, just in case one reads in secondary sources that John Scobell was a Pinkerton operative…

6. Pinkerton, *The Spy of the Rebellion*, 382.

7. Pinkerton, *The Spy of the Rebellion*, 381.

8. Pinkerton, *The Spy of the Rebellion*, 381 et seq.

9. Pinkerton, *The Spy of the Rebellion*, 392.

10. Pinkerton, *The Spy of the Rebellion*, 393.

11. *Brooklyn Daily Eagle*, Aug. 31 1884, p. 9, "A Detective's Resting Place." George Bangs brought Timothy Webster back to Chicago and Pinkerton buried him there, at Graceland. A short time later, Tom Robinson, Webster's son-in-law, asked Pinkerton if the dead man's remains could be removed to Onarga, Illinois. Pinkerton said no. So Tom came back with a revolver and threatened the detective chief. Pinkerton told him to get out, and then, a short while later, sensing that it meant more to Tim's daughter than it did to himself, called on Robinson and told him to go ahead. So, Tim was disinterred and removed to Onarga, where he was finally laid to rest on May 18, 1871. See the *Chicago Tribune*, June 14, 1871, p. 2, "The Northwest." On the little headstone above his grave read the words: "Timothy Webster—I died for my country." See the *National Tribune*, Washington, D.C., Dec. 5, 1901, p. 3, "Died for His Country," taken from the *Eastern Illinois Register*, published in Paxton, Ill.

12. *Brooklyn Daily Eagle*, Aug. 31, 1884,

p. 9, "A Detective's Resting Place; *Daily Inter-Ocean*, May 8, 1882, p. 1, "A Life Sacrifice." Find-a-Grave, the online site, has Botella Olson's birthplace as Norway, and her death date as May 6, 1862, aged 26–27, just as the *Brooklyn Eagle* did. The Cook County death index of 1882 has her as Olsen, which would be the correct spelling if she was of Norwegian extraction, which she was.

13. *Brooklyn Daily Eagle*, Aug. 31, 1884, p. 9, "A Detective's Resting Place"; *Chicago Tribune*, Dec. 31, 1878, p. 8, "General News"; *Daily Inter-Ocean*, Dec. 31, 1878, p. 1, "Tributes to the Departed," and Dec. 27, 1879, p. 1, "Pinkerton's Kindness."

14. *Brooklyn Daily Eagle*, Aug. 31, 1884, p. 9, "A Detective's Resting Place"; Graceland Cemetery records.

15. The handwritten cemetery lot card shows her as Kate Prescott Bracket (one "t"), and a copy of this card was subsequently typed, and finally recopied in 1966. The original card was probably discarded with the original typed one. She is also listed as Kate Prescott on the grave locator card. Unfortunately, the name Prescott, one t or two, leads us absolutely nowhere. When you look at the name as a compositor might, it looks suspiciously like Brackett.

16. Zemanda's marriage to O.F. Brackett is from the book *Brackett Genealogy*. Unlike her sister Lucy Ann's marriage to Fred Barrett, this event does not seem to have been recorded by the state of Wisconsin, nor is it mentioned in the Janesville newspaper. There can be no doubt about the marriage, it's just that the *Brackett Genealogy* book seems to be wrong in the details. In the 1856 Iowa state census, for St. Charles, we find Oscar F. Brackett, stone cutter and a member of the state militia, aged 25, and Samanda B. Brackett, 19. There are no children. As it would eventually turn out, O.F. Brackett was much more at home in the hills of Dakota with the likes of Little Johnny Warn than he was with any one of his three wives. You should see what he did to them. Franklin Priest once told a good story in his local paper, the *Decatur Daily Republican* (Illinois) of Aug. 27, 1873: "A human being in form, six feet high, stout built, with black chin whiskers, about 40 years of age, weight about 200 pounds, registered his name at the Priest House, as O.F. Brackett, from Toledo, Ohio. Aug. 11, 1873. He reported himself as having charge of the masonry work on the Wabash road. He was taken sick and lay at the hotel very sick for eight days, receiving all the attention and cure a good nurse could give him night and day with the best of medical attention. All at once he disappeared, forgetting to pay his hotel bill, for medicine paid for by the hotel and wash bills, also other bills about the city. Newspapers will confer a favor on hotels by 'passing him round' F. Priest, Prop., Priest's Hotel."

17. Pinkerton, *A Double Life and the Detectives*, 278, 294 et seq. One of the featured players in the Kate Brelsford anecdote is the Merchants' Union Express Company. That company was founded in 1866, so the story must be set that year or afterwards. You'd think so, anyway, but since it is Pinkerton we are reading, let's try not to allow ourselves to be carried away by mere trifles such as the truth.

18. Pinkerton, *A Double Life and the Detectives*, 294 et seq. Here's another piece of circumstantial evidence presented with the view to demonstrating that Carrie Lawton and Kate Brackett were one and the same woman. Pinkerton does describe Carrie as about 25 years of age. Kitty Brackett was 25. As a matter of comparison, Hattie Lawton was 29. There is a difference, usually quite a substantial difference, one that, as a natural swordsman, Pinkerton would have been keenly aware of. Something else: Pinkerton's rather detailed description of Carrie's eyes is very redolent of the way he describes Kate Warn's eyes.

19. The 1865 census for Memphis's Second Ward named only one person per

household, in this case Miss Belle Warren, no occupation. Including Belle, there were two white females and a colored female, aged between 18 and 45. The city directory for that year has, at 164 Washington, Katharine Brackett, boarding house. On October 27, 1864, Mrs. O. F. Brackett, of Memphis, is listed in the Notre Dame records as George Warn's guardian. Same thing for the school's catalogues for 1864–1865, 1865–1866, and 1866–1867. However, for George's last year at Notre Dame, 1867–1868, Mrs. Belle Towler, of St. Louis, is mentioned. By that time the sisters had relocated.

20. The ladies were still in Memphis in late 1866, as proved by the Notre Dame school records of 1866–67. The St. Louis item concerning the bawdy house comes from the *Daily Missouri Republican* of Feb. 26, 1867, p. 3, "Police Court," in which Kitty is named as Katie Bracket. In addition to that, the St. Louis city directory for 1867 has Mrs. Oscar F. Brackett's residence as 212 South 5th Street, while Belle is not mentioned that year, either in Memphis or St. Louis. ¶ One supposes, almost hopes, that Kitty and her miserable husband were divorced legally, but Mrs. O.F. Brackett was too catchy a name to let go of, even though from November 25, 1866, over in Galena, Illinois, one Lottie Hardt was now sporting that very same name on a more current carte de visite. ¶ Ed Fishel was researching the Pinkerton account books when he found a Civil War spy listed only as O.F.A., an agent who seems to have been operating in September 1862. See *The Secret War for the Union*, 634. Knowing how Pinkerton liked to play around with names and, especially, initials, could O.F.A. be O.F.B.? In other words, Mrs. O.F. Brackett. That is to say, Kate Brackett. Well, of course it could. More evidence that Kate Brackett was Carrie Lawton. When something's wrong, you've got a real research fight on your hands. When it's right, the evidence just keeps coming in.

21. Notre Dame school records, 1867–68; St. Louis city directory, 1868; *Missouri Daily Republican*, July 28, 1868, p. 3, "A Heavy Robbery."

22. *Missouri Daily Democrat*, Aug. 16, 1867, "Female Broil" and "Cross Fire"; Aug. 17, 1867, "Fracas Among the Fancy."

23. *Louisville Daily Democrat*, July 26, 1868, p. 1, "Items of News Condensed."

24. *Daily Missouri Republican*, July 28, 1868, p. 3, "Heavy Robbery"; Aug. 6, 1868, p. 3, "A Habeas Corpus Case."

25. *Daily Missouri Republican*, July 28, 1868, p. 3, "A Heavy Robbery"; Aug. 6, 1868, p. 3, "A Habeas Corpus Case."

26. *Daily Missouri Republican*, Aug. 6, 1868, p. 3, "A Habeas Corpus Case."

27. *Daily Missouri Republican*, Aug. 9, 1868, p. 3, "Viola Ellwood," and Oct. 8, 1868, p. 2, "Pardoned and Re-arrested."

28. Missouri Death Records, 1850–1931; St. Louis, Missouri, Death Records, 1850–1902.

29. The St. Louis census, taken on July 11, 1870, may not have been very diplomatic when it came to the "what do you do for a living?" column, but it was certainly informative: Bell Towler, whore, 26, born in New York, personal estate of $7000. She was clearly more than a whore. At this house alone she was running sixteen girls altogether, most of them between the ages of 18 and 23, and all listed in the census as "whores." Some sported surnames that would have foxed even the wiliest genealogist: Jennie Engineer and Hattie Roller being the most amusing. The disreputable house next door was run by whoremaster Newt Anderson and his wife Jennie. This is where the very well-known Cyprian Belle Clifford lived, along with Maggie May and Nellie Turner.

30. *Missouri Daily Democrat*, Sept. 13, 1870.

31. Missouri Death Records, 1850–1931; St. Louis, Missouri, Death Records, 1850–1902. It took quite a while, March 23, 1875, before Belle's estate was finally

settled. See Missouri Wills and Probate Records, 1766–1988.

Chapter 42

1. *Cincinnati Daily Press*, July 28, 1860, p. 2, "Particulars of the Sinking of the Steamer, S.P. Hibberd"; Cincinnati city directory, 1861; Ohio probate cases, John W. Smith, Cincinnati, 1866.

2. Cincinnati city directory, 1866, 1867; *Dixon Evening Telegraph*, June 13, 1891, p. 6, "The Suicide at Rest"; George Warn's probate papers, Lee County, Illinois, 1875. In May 1870, Hattie's brother, George, even at the age of 19 a doomed soul, went to live with the Smiths and their two servants, at 15 South Sixth Street, St. Louis. The reason one doesn't find George in the 1870 census for St. Louis is that he was visiting his older brother John in Dixon, Illinois. By 1872, he, Hattie and T.J. Smith had moved to 811 Washington Avenue, St. Louis.

3. *Inland Monthly Magazine*, Vol. 2, No. 1, Sept. 1872, p. 506; *Chicago Tribune*, Aug. 30, 1872, p. 6, "Flora Belle"; *Chicago Tribune*, Sept. 1, 1872, p. 8, "The Winners"; *Missouri Republican*, April 8, 1873, p. 8, "Flora Belle."

4. St. Louis city directory, 1873; George Warn's probate papers, Lee County, Illinois, 1875. William Henry Thorwegen was a German, born in 1837. He had been in America since he was six. He was a steamboat captain and a very well-heeled businessman of St. Louis. Captain Thorwegen and Edward Dix had formed a company, Thorwegen & Dix, to run the St. Louis Saloon and Billiard Hall, at 24–28 South Fourth Street, at the corner of Walnut. In December of 1870 T.J. Smith bought out Mr. Dix, and the company name changed to Thorwegen & Smith.

5. *Milwaukee Daily Sentinel*, April 12, 1873, p. 2, "A Fast Trotter for Chicago." Alex Lewis was merely the purchasing agent. He was working for Charles M. Reed, the millionaire of Erie, Pennsylvania. ¶ Just after selling Flora Belle, Smith was in the market for another great trotter. He probably would have purchased the Kansas wonder, Smuggler, if that animal had made a better showing during his sales pitch.

6. St. Louis city directories, 1872 and 1873. "Mrs. H.L. Smith, 2809 Morgan St., St. Louis, Mo." is the address to which Pinkerton sent three letters in 1873: The first on May 9, in response to one Hattie sent him two days earlier, and then two in September. In the May letter he talks about Hattie's stepmother, Mrs. Diana Warn, and the Dixon property in Lee County, Illinois; in the second one he mentions Hattie's recent visit to Chicago, when he missed her by virtue of his being away in Onarga, Ill., and her long voyage on the steamer *Great Republic*; and in the last he refers to Hattie's young half-sister Libby. Aside from that, there is nothing of much interest in these letters, which are to be found mis-categorized (as usual) on pages 377–380 and 408–412, under the heading 1875–1883, in Pinkerton's National Detective Agency Records, 1853–1899, Letterpress Books and Miscellaneous Reports, held by the Library of Congress. The one good thing about these letters, though, is that they prove, not only by some of the wording in them but by their very existence, that Pinkerton and Hattie were in at least fairly regular contact over the years.

7. Hattie's brother, Henry Wallace Warn, a miner, lived on the west side of Gilbert, between Bryant and Brannan. He hadn't been shot by Annie Scott's brother after all.

8. San Francisco *Daily Evening Bulletin*, June 21, 1873, p. 1, "Finance and Trade"; *New York Herald*, June 25, 1873, p. 10, "American Ports." The *Great Republic* had just been pulled off the San Francisco to Panama route and was now back to plying the seas to and from China. She would leave San Francisco on the 16th of each month, while her sister steamer, the

Japan, would leave on the 1st. This *Great Republic* should not be confused with a Mississippi River steamer with the same name, and operating at the same time. This steamboat ran between St. Louis and New Orleans, under the command of Capt. W.H. Thorwegen, the business partner of Hattie's husband, T.J. Smith. Just a coincidence.

9. *Cincinnati Enquirer*, Feb. 1, 1875, p. 8, no title.

Chapter 43

1. *Grand Forks Herald*, Sept. 17, 1917, p. 2, "Governor of Squatters Is Seriously Ill." There is some confusion about the exact location of Fort Hannifin, aka Coal Banks aka Warn Castle. Hopefully the *Bismarck Tribune*, April 5, 1879, p. 1, "Extension Excursionists," will relieve that confusion, if not dispel it entirely. ¶ Hannifin had lived in Amboy, in Lee County, Ill., at the same time as Johnny Warn's brother Allen. It is next to impossible that John and Denny didn't know each other from those days.

2. *Dixon Telegraph*, March 10, 1881, p. 4, c. 4; *St. Paul Daily Globe*, Feb. 16, 1889, p. 8, "Scalps were in Demand." Alice would marry again, on February 23, 1881, to John G. Rohn, in Chicago.

Chapter 44

1. Pinkerton Collection, Library of Congress, transcription of letters in letterpress copybooks, the originals of which are no longer extant. The Pinkerton collection itself was donated to the Library of Congress by Robert A. Pinkerton in 1956, and by Pinkerton, Inc., in 2000. Additional material was acquired in 1972 and 2000. One of these copies was reproduced by the late Ted Yeatman in his book *Frank and Jesse James*, 351. The man mentioned in Kansas City was Pinkerton operative Dave Robertson, a Scotsman who had joined the agency in 1868, very soon after immigrating to the U.S.A. Dave would later be one of the witnesses to Pinkerton's will.

Chapter 45

1. St. Louis city directories, 1872–1875; *St. Louis Republican*, July 8, 1875; George W. Warn probate papers, Lee County, Illinois, 1875.

2. Hine and his wife Cynthia, and well-known grain and seed man George D. Laing, a Scotsman, were duly placed on a two hundred dollar bond to assure this administration.

3. On January 28, 1876, in St. Louis, Hattie Smith and her husband Thomas J. Smith appeared before a notary, John R. Boas, a resident of that city, but also a commissioner for the state of Illinois, to swear that they were owed $1,945 and $149 respectively by the dead man's estate. T.J.'s part of the debt was George's funeral expenses in 1875. A thousand dollars of Hattie's debt went back to the 1860s when she paid for George's schooling at Notre Dame. The bulk of the remainder was George's board and lodging with the Smiths, at $20 a month, which he had never paid. She was claiming precisely three years' worth—$720. ¶ On January 25, 1877, John K. Hine was still guardian ad litem for Libby and Ella Warn, although, by now, Libby was spending more and more time with Hattie Smith in St. Louis. Hine says, "The children and their mother, who is the widow of Israel P. Warn, live on the place. There is therefore no rental, or at all events no rents received, all being used in their support from day to day, and this has been the situation ever since the father's death some years ago. A lot of household furniture in the dwelling house is occupied by their mother and themselves, and of the probable value of $35." There were also five cows, valued at $125 total. ¶ Certainly by February of 1877, Lena Belle Warn, then a

minor, was living with her "aunt," Hattie L. Smith, in St. Louis. Hattie's relationship to the youngest four children of Israel P. Warn, i.e., those by his second wife, Diana Campbell, is confused in these probate documents by the fact that Hattie was so much older than her four half-sisters, Libby, Ella, Gertie, and Lena. She was born in March 1833, and in New York state, whereas the four young girls were born thirty years or more later and in Illinois.

4. George Warn's probate papers, Illinois, 1875. On April 16, 1877, in Dixon, Solomon H. Bethea was appointed guardian ad litem for the four youngest Warn girls. At that point John K. Hine was still George W. Warn's administrator and was trying to sell the land.

5. *St. Louis Globe-Democrat*, June 30, 1877, p. 8, "The Windsor Club"; July 1, 1877, p. 5, "The Windsor."

6. *St. Louis Globe-Democrat*, June 30, 1877, p. 8, "The Windsor Club"; July 1, 1877, p. 5, "The Windsor"; Aug. 17, 1877, p. 8, "Bill Casca's Crime."

7. *St. Louis Globe-Democrat*, June 30, 1877, p. 8, "The Windsor Club."

8. *St. Louis Globe-Democrat*, June 30, 1877, p. 8, "The Windsor Club"; Feb. 19, 1879, p. 5, "Sickened Statesmen"; Oct. 29, 1879, p. 3, "The Wakefield Case"; Rammelkamp, *Pulitzer's Post Dispatch*, 75. Wakefield lingered on this planet until 1907, when he died in an insane asylum in Kansas.

9. *St. Louis Globe-Democrat*, March 10, 1878, p. 6, "St. Louis Society Notes"; *St. Louis Globe-Democrat*, Sept. 8, 1878, p. 3, "St. Louis Society Notes"; *St. Louis Post-Dispatch*, Jan. 4, 1879, p. 8, no title; *St. Louis Republic*, April 6, 1903, p. 6, "To-Day in St. Louis," citing from their columns of April 7, 1878; *St. Louis Globe-Democrat*, June 1, 1880, p. 8, "Lost and Found." One has to say that T.J. Smith had three interesting sisters, or, more correctly, perhaps, two brothers-in-law of considerable achievement. Eliza Jane married Pittsburgh industrialist Alex King and died in 1859. King then married her sister, Sadie, by whom he had three children, one of whom married Richard Mellon. The third of T.J.'s sisters, Mary Ann, married James Dickson, who owned, among many other things, the Indianapolis Opera House. The Smiths and their collateral branches were not short of cash. ¶ Hattie was certainly experienced at hosting memorable parties, such as the one on March 6, 1878: A "pleasant little entertainment was given to Miss Libbie Warne ... by her aunt, Mrs. T.J. Smith, 2809 Morgan street." There was dancing, and there were other amusements too, and then, toward midnight a delicious supper was served. Miss Lena Smith (*sic*), Libby's sister, was there. On April 6, "Mrs. T.J. Smith of No. 2809 Morgan street gave a reception. Among those who assisted her in receiving were Mmes Morrisse, Lewis, Roper, McConnell, Boner, Simpson, Morrison, Sims, Miss Cowen and Miss Libbie Warne." A few months later, on September 6, again at the Morgan Street house, Hattie threw a brilliant surprise 17th birthday party for "her sister, Libbie Warne."

Chapter 46

1. Montana County Marriage Records, 1865–1993, John S. Warn; Montana County Marriages, 1865–1997, John S. Warn; Montana County Divorce Records, 1865–1950, Gallatin Co., April 12, 1884, Roberta M. Warn, plaintiff, Case #768.

2. *Green Bay Press-Gazette*, July 3, 1879, p. 4, "Information Wanted"; Montana County Marriage Records, 1865–1993, George Buttner.

3. *Bismarck Tribune*, Sept. 5, 1879, p. 1, "Place Named Warnton."

4. *Bismarck Tribune*, Nov. 26, 1880, p. 1, "Purely Personal." That last sentence in the paragraph: Something similar could have been said if Johnny had been a Democrat, and, of course, it would have been.

5. *Bozeman Weekly Chronicle*, May 23, 1883, p. 3, "One More Unfortunate."

6. *Bismarck Tribune*, Nov. 16, 1883, p. 5, "Fire at Cedelia."
7. *Bad Lands Cow Boy*, Dec. 11, 1884, p. 1, c. 2.
8. *Bozeman Weekly Chronicle,* Feb. 11, 1885, p. 3, no title; as well as her estate probate records of that year.
9. *Bad Lands Cow Boy*, June 25, 1885, p. 1, "The Lost Cabin Gold Mines"; July 2, 1885, p. 1, "The Lost Cabin Gold Mines"; *Daily Yellowstone Journal*, Oct. 1, 1890, p. 3, "Accommodations at Old Town"; *Fergus County Argus*, Sept. 22, 1892, "List of Letters," and Sept. 7, 1893, p. 2, "Court Proceedings"; *Anaconda Standard*, Nov. 30, 1893, p. 5, "They Will Give Thanks." In 1885 John Warn left the Dakotas for Miles City, Montana, where he intended to get together a group to go looking for the Lost Cabin Mine. But things fell through, and he opened up the Commercial Hotel in Glendive, Montana. In 1890 he moved to Miles City where he opened up another restaurant. He got married again, to a woman named Sarah, but that lasted five minutes, six if you include the bitter recriminations. She tried for a divorce in 1893, but for technical reasons couldn't get one until 1896, by which time Johnny was living at Pleasant Valley Ranch in Maiden, Fergus County, Montana, with his son, E.T., who was just getting over a long-term career in the U.S. Army. E.T. wound up going into business, inventing useful things, and marrying his aunt, Gertie Warn, which, on the surface anyway, seems a pretty odd thing to do. E.T. died in 1932 in an old soldiers' home.
10. *Fergus County Democrat*, Dec. 31, 1914, p. 15, "Poor Fund"; April 22, 1915, p. 9, "Poor Fund." The really strange thing about the three Warn brothers is not so much that they were all miners but that we don't have a clue, not even a rough idea, of when or where any of them died. John in Montana and the Dakotas, Allen in Indian Territory, and Harry in California. Maybe. That's only where they were last spotted. As far as newspaper death notices are concerned, government death records, wills, anything else that could reasonably lead us home on even just one of them, the total and complete nothingness is such as to suggest that they might still be alive.

Chapter 47

1. *St. Louis Globe-Democrat*, July 30, 1880, p. 8, "Tax Sale Deferred"; St. Louis city directories, 1881, 1882.
2. *Dixon Evening Telegraph*, June 13, 1891, p. 6, "The Suicide at Rest."
3. *St. Louis Post-Dispatch*, Jan. 28, 1884, p. 7, "Women as Detectives?" taken from the *Chicago News*.
4. *St. Louis Post-Dispatch*, March 9, 10, 11, 12, 1887, p. 6, "Lost and Found"; July 25 and 26, 1887, p. 6, "Lost and Found."
5. *Dixon Evening Telegraph*, July 6, 1899. In this issue of the *Dixon Telegraph* is a list of Lee County landowners. The Warn family farm was still in the name of Angie Warn. It comprised two bits of land in Section 1, Township 2, with a total acreage of 83.89 acres. It was the first parcel of land in Palmyra Township on the northern side of the river, as you come down the river going west from the town of Dixon. The 1900 plat map of the same township has the same stretch of land in the name of Hattie L. Smith. Ergo, Hattie must have acquired it in 1899 or 1900. However, not so fast. So many times, especially with official lists, data remain the same long after they have changed in real life. The county doesn't care who owns a piece of land as long as the taxes are paid. Their records are, consequently, sometimes out of date by decades. Hattie had certainly acquired two-thirds of the farm by the end of George Warn's probate, in 1889, and it may be that 1899 or 1900 is when Ella's third finally fell into Hattie's hands. We simply don't know when Hattie acquired that final third. In any event, she would hold on to it, all of it, until there was no longer any need to do so.

6. *St. Louis Post-Dispatch*, May 13, 1888, p. 5, "A Warrant."

7. George Warn's probate papers, Lee County, Ill., 1875; *Dixon Evening Telegraph*, Jan. 9, 1890, p. 4, "Probate Court."

8. *Dixon Evening Telegraph*, May 1, 1891, p. 1, no title; *St. Louis Globe-Democrat*, March 2, 1887, p. 9, "The Civil Courts"; *St Louis Post-Dispatch*, March 20, 1898, p. 35, "S"; St. Louis city directories between 1890 and 1902. Indeed, Nellie Eddy, described by the press in 1895, after she had left Spruce, as the keeper of an immoral house, would make the press on a number of occasions for trying to gas herself.

9. *St. Louis Post-Dispatch*, March 7, 1895, p. 6, no title. The 1896 city directory has Lulu Morrison at 2223 Chestnut, while the 1897 and 1898 editions have her at No. 2327. In 1899 she was listed at 818 N 23d, and in 1900 at 2117 Chestnut. The 1900 census for 2117 Chestnut Street has her as head of household, age 27, single, born Aug. 1872, Missouri. Her parents, the census says, were also born in Missouri. Her occupation is uncompromisingly given as "prost house," a rented house, as it turns out. In fact, the owner was trying to sell it at that very moment. Most of the houses in this area were houses of ill-fame. Lulu had three girls, boarders: May Price, 23, Margaret Johnson, 21, and Mabel Smith, 18.

10. Both quotes are from Twain, the first from *Villagers of 1840*–3, and the second from *Jane Lampton Clements*. ¶ The next to youngest of the Pavey daughters, Rebecca Frances, born in 1836, would become the model for Twain's classic character Becky Thatcher. Fanny, as she was known in real life, married three times, her last husband being a St. Louis attorney named John R. Boas. One of Mr. Boas's clients in the 1870s and 1880s was Mrs. Hattie L. Smith, alias Hattie Lawton, the most mysterious spy of the Civil War. ¶ Susan Mildred Pavey was born on the last day of 1843. She married wagon maker Samuel T. McMellon in Boonville, Mo., on April 14, 1859, but the marriage didn't last long. For a brief while there had been a daughter, also named Susan.

11. Burdick, *Cases on Torts*, 344; St. Louis death records, Bessie Hight, 1902, Nashville censuses and city directories. Only the year before in her too-short lifetime, Sarah had been a clerk on Union Street, in Nashville, Tennessee. Then, one day, she made the fateful move to St. Louis and became Bessie Hight, one of Lulu Morrison's "children." Now she was dead. It had all been in her stars. Sagittarius. Just a month earlier, on December 2, Sarah had turned 20. It must have made her wonder, in her dying moments, if the escape from the pogroms and the knouts of the Cossacks had all been worth it? The effort. Maybe for her parents, with the saloon and the grocery store in Nashville. Maybe. The American dream for them. The American nightmare for her.

12. St. Louis city directories between 1897 and 1905. Susan M. Pavey is on the Bellefontaine Cemetery records as being the actual purchaser of the lot. In other words, it is in her name. But that's not to say the other two didn't chip in. They probably did; they almost certainly did, since this lot was for these three specific ladies and no one else. The cemetery record office couldn't say when the lot was purchased, but it had to be 1902. No other year would make sense, given Lulu's age. It had to have been before December of that year because that's when it was first used. That's when Lulu was buried.

13. *St. Louis Post-Dispatch*, Dec. 16, 1908, p. 1, "Lavender Displeasing," and p. 2, "Lemp Accuses Wife," Feb. 10, 1909, p. 2, "Continued from Page One," Feb. 15, 1909, p. 2, "Lavender Displeased Wm. J. Lemp"; *Washington Times*, Feb. 11, 1909, p. 1, "Attitude of Lemp Undergoes Change." In the 1909 divorce case of William J. Lemp, Jr., before the Missouri Supreme Court, his long-term affair with Lulu was dredged up and dragged out in public.

She is described as "Miss Lulu Morrison, the keeper of a house of prostitution in St. Louis." Lemp protested that it was only at the solicitation of his brother, Louis, that he paid her funeral expenses, as an act of charity to a poor, unfortunate woman, and not because he had any regard for her whatsoever. Lemp claimed he last spoke to Lulu in June 1899, before his engagement to Lillian.

14. *Dixon Evening Telegraph*, March 22, 1904, p. 2, no title; George W. Warn's probate papers, Lee County, Illinois, 1875–89; 1910 St. Louis census; Adelaide Walker Cheatham was then 54.

15. The information on Dr. Schultz was gathered first of all from Hattie's death certificate, which, because he was the attending physician, gives his name and address. From there it was on to the city directories, censuses, his 1967 death certificate, and very basic and limited lists of doctors. ¶ Mr. Donnelly, the undertaker, got the information from the death certificate and gave it to the cemetery and the newspapers. ¶ The other Mrs. Timothy Webster, some would say the real Mrs. Webster, Charlotte Sprouls, had already died, on Dec. 1, 1907, in Santa Clara, Calif., aged 90.

16. *St. Louis Post-Dispatch*, Sept. 8, 1913, p. 14, "Deaths," March 26, 1916, p. 45, "Deaths." Sue Pavey, the third of the three ladies, was buried on March 27, 1916. Then the grave was sealed. The story of Hattie Lawton was finally over.

Appendix C

1. *Lincoln's Herndon: A Biography*, 171 et seq.
2. Hertz, *The Hidden Lincoln*, 51.
3. Cuthbert, *Lincoln and the Baltimore Plot*, 22.
4. Cuthbert, *Lincoln and the Baltimore Plot*, 22.
5. Cuthbert, *Lincoln and the Baltimore Plot*, 22.

Appendix D

1. Sarah Thurgood was born on Feb. 4, 1811, in Bishops Stortford, Herts, daughter of a grocer. In 1838, on the Isle of Thanet, in Kent, she married George Eaves, a whitesmith, and they moved in with her parents. George came over first, as was the custom, on the *Margaret Evans*, arriving in New York on Oct. 21, 1847, and setting up in Chicago as a machinist. Sarah and the two girls followed nine months later, on the same ship, arriving in New York on June 20, 1848. George died in 1853. ¶ As for Allan Pinkerton and his brother Robert, and where they came from, who their parents were, and so forth, so much rubbish has been written about all that. There is a one-stop shop that gives all the information you'll ever need: The 1841 Glasgow census. William Pinkerton, 70, weaver; Isabella Pinkerton, 55; Robert Pinkerton, 25, blacksmith; Allan Pinkerton, 20, cooper.

2. Every source, outside of official documents, that addresses Robert Pinkerton's death, and this includes, rather embarrassingly, Miss Fitchett, gives September 6, 1868, which is the botched date inscribed on his tombstone. He actually died on November 6, 1863, as can be confirmed by the Cook County death records. All the Chicago city directories after 1863 show no Robert, and, what's more, they list Sarah as his widow. The 1865 Illinois state census tells the same story. All that evidence should be persuasive enough to enable one to withstand the peer pressure of all those erroneous secondary sources. Robert Pinkerton inspired no lamentations of any sort in the *Chicago Tribune*, not because no one cared, but for the simple reason that no one knew he had ever existed.

Bibliography

Primary Sources

DOCUMENTS

Censuses. U.S. censuses, 1790 through 1940, and various state censuses, primarily 1855, 1858, and 1865.
City directories, primarily for Chicago, St. Louis, New York, Richmond.
Confederate Citizens File. The Confederate Papers Relating to Citizens or Business Firms, 1861–1865. NARA M346. This file was created years after the war by the Confederate Archives Division of the U.S. Adjutant General's Office, in order to help assess the great number of Southern claims pouring into Washington as soon as the war ended.
Ellis, Mattie Cook. "The Secret Service Division of the United States from 1860 to 1910." Submitted as a thesis by Miss Cook for her M.A. degree at the University of Wisconsin, 1917.
Lincoln Papers, General Correspondence, Library of Congress, Manuscript Division.
Pinkerton, William A. & Pinkerton, Robert A. "Timothy Webster: Spy of the Rebellion." A broadsheet, no more, issued by the Pinkertons in Nov. 1906.
Samuel Felton Papers, Box 1, Folder 12, at the Historical Society of Pennsylvania, Philadelphia. Has accounts submitted to Samuel Felton, Sr., by Allan Pinkerton. Pinkerton lists his operatives not by name or initials, but by number (1 is Pinkerton himself, 2 is Kate Warn, 3 is Tim Webster and H.H.L., 5 is Scully and Sam Bridgman). This code was broken by Jane Singer and Dr. James O. Hall in the early 2000s.
Secret Service Accounts, NARA, Record Group 110, Entry 95. Fishel cites them as "Pinkerton payrolls, S.S. accts." The S.S. accounts constitute a bulky record of disbursements for the Secret Service made by John Potts, chief clerk of the War Department from the beginning of the war until 1870. This was the fund from which Pinkerton's employees (and Lafayette Baker's too) were paid. Record Group 110, Entry 106, is the Monthly Statement of the Account of Detective Allan Pinkerton, April 1862 to January 1863, arranged chronologically. In these, H.H.L. is listed at $6 a day, but only in the month of April. One can draw virtually no conclusions from any of this.
Thomas T. Eckert Papers, Huntington Library, San Marino, Calif.
Turner-Baker Papers. More properly called Case Files of Investigations by Levi C. Turner and Lafayette C. Baker, 1861–1866. NARA M797, RG94. Records of the Adjutant General's Office, 1780s–1917, in the National Archives.
Union Provost Marshals' File of Papers Relating to Individual Civilians. NARA, M345
Voorhees, Abram H. *Overland Journey from Michigan to Montana.* 1864. Diary. Beinecke Rare Book and Manuscript Library, Yale University.

Billy Pinkerton Newspaper Articles

St. Louis Globe-Democrat, Oct. 15, 1883. This article called "Famous Detectives" originated in the *Chicago Times*, whose reporter was given an interview by Billy Pinkerton in front of the graves at Graceland Cemetery.
Inter Ocean (Chicago), Oct. 31, 1897, p. 18, "Plot Is All Right."
Daily Morning Journal and Courier, New Haven, Aug. 23, 1898, p. 7, "War Secret Service," taken from the *Chicago Evening Post*.

Secondary Sources

Sources marked with an asterisk (*) are used with caution as the author considers them to contain speculative or fictionalized elements, or to be based in part on unreliable sources.

Books

Agnew, Jeremy. *Crime, Justice and Retribution in the American West, 1850–1900*. Jefferson, NC: McFarland, 2017.
*Ames, John. *The Real Deadwood*. New York: Chamberlain Bros., 2004.
Andrews, J. Cutler. *South Reports the Civil War*. Princeton, NJ: Princeton University Press, 1970.
*Bearce, Stephanie. *Top Secret Files. The Civil War*. Waco, TX: Prufrock Press, 2015.
*Beymer, William Gilmore. *On Hazardous Service: Scouts and Spies of the North and South*. New York: Harper & Bros, 1912. The last chapter, pages 259–287, consists of a word for word reproduction of the article "Timothy Webster," written by Beymer two years earlier. The book was re-published in 2003 by the University of Nebraska Press, as *Scouts and Spies of the Civil War*.
Blackman, Ann. *Wild Rose: The True Story of a Civil War Spy*. New York: Random House, 2005.
*Bonansinga, Jay. *Pinkerton's War: The Civil War's Greatest Spy and the Birth of the U.S. Secret Service*. Guilford, CT: Lyons Press, 2012.
Brackett, Herbert I. *Brackett Genealogy*. Washington, D.C.: Herbert I. Brackett, 1907.
*Brasher, Glenn David. *The Peninsula Campaign & The Necessity of Emancipation: African Americans and the Fight for Freedom*. Chapel Hill, NC: University of North Carolina Press, 2012.
Brooks, Patricia. *Where the Bodies Are: Final Visits to the Rich, Famous, Interesting*. Boston: Globe Pequot Press, 2002.
Bryan, George S. *The Great American Myth: The True Story of Lincoln's Murder*. New York: Carrick & Evans, 1940.
*Bryan, George Sands. *The Spy in America*. New York: J.B. Lippincott Company, 1943.
Buhk, Tobin T. *True Crime in the Civil War: Cases of Murder, Treason, Counterfeiting, Massacre, Plunder & Abuse*. Mechanicsburg, PA.: Stackpole Books, 2012.
Burdick, Francis M. *Cases on Torts*, 3rd ed. Albany, NY: Banks & Co, 1909.
*Byrne, Gary J., with Schmidt, Grant M. *Secrets of the Secret Service: The History and Uncertain Future of the U.S. Secret Service*. New York: Hachette, 2018.
*Casstevens, Frances H. *George W. Alexander and Castle Thunder*. Jefferson, NC: McFarland, 2004.
*Crowdy, Terry. *The Enemy Within: A History of Espionage*. Oxford: Osprey, 2006.
Cuthbert, Norma Barrett. *Lincoln and the Baltimore Plot, 1861, from Pinkerton Records and Related Papers*. San Marino, CA: Huntington Library Publications, 1949.
Donald, David Herbert. *Lincoln's Herndon: A Biography*. New York: Knopf, 1948.
*Draz, Daniel W.; Starrett, Paul; Turner, Tom; Hayward, Vince. *Introduction to Professional Investigations: Concepts and Strategies for Investigators in the Private Sector*. San Clemente: LawTech Publishing Group, 2009.

Egan, Brendan H., Jr. *Murder at Ford's Theatre: Chronicle of an Assassination.* Bloomington, IN: Xlibris Corporation: 2007.
*Eggleston, Larry G. *Women in the Civil War.* Jefferson, NC: McFarland, 2013.
*Enss, Chris. *The Pinks: The First Women Detectives, Operatives, and Spies with the Pinkerton National Detective Agency.* Billings, MT: TwoDot, 2017.
Evidence Taken Before the Committee of the House of Representatives, Appointed to Enquire into the Treatment of Prisoners at Castle Thunder. Richmond: Confederate House of Representatives Committee, 1863.
Field, Ron. *Silent Witness: The Civil War Through Photography and Its Photographers.* Oxford: Osprey Publishing, 2017.
Fishel, Edwin C. *The Secret War for the Union: The Untold Story of Military Intelligence in the Civil War.* Boston: Houghton Mifflin, 1996.
*Foster, G. Allen. *Eyes and Ears of the Civil War.* New York: Criterion, 1964. This is the *Ebony* magazine article, in book form.
Gill, Martin, editor. *The Handbook of Security,* 2nd ed. Basingstoke: Palgrave Macmillan, 2014.
Goff, Patricia Dissmeyer. *Timothy Webster: The Story of the Civil War Spy and His Family.* Onarga, IL: Goff Publications, 2000.
Grant, Marilyn. *A Guide to Historic Virginia City.* Helena, MT: Montana Historical Society Press, 1998.
*Green, Carl R. & Sanford, William Reynolds. *Allan Pinkerton.* Springfield, NJ: Enslow Publishers, 1992.
*Greenhow, Mrs. *My Imprisonment, and the First Year of Abolition Rule at Washington.* London: Richard Bentley, 1863.
*Harnett, Thomas Kane. *Spies for the Blue and Gray.* Garden City, NY: Hanover House, 1954.
Hertz, Emanuel, ed. *The Hidden Lincoln: From the Letters and Papers of William H. Herndon.* New York: Viking Press, 1938.
History of Lee County. Chicago: H.H. Hill & Co., 1881.
*Horan, James David. *The Pinkertons: The Detective Dynasty That Made History.* New York: Crown, 1967.
*____ & Swiggett, Howard. *The Pinkerton Story.* New York: Putnam, 1951.
*James, Marquis. *They Had Their Hour.* Indianapolis: Bobbs-Merrill, 1934. This comes from an article Mr. James had written in *American Legion Monthly,* vol. 10, No. 2 (Feb. 1931).
*Jeffreys-Jones, Rhodri. *Cloak and Dollar: A History of American Secret Intelligence.* New Haven, CT: Yale University Press, 2002.
Johnson, Jeffrey A., ed. *Reforming America: A Thematic Encyclopedia and Document Collection of the Progressive Era.* Santa Barbara, CA: ABC-Clio, 2017.
*Jones, Wilmer L., Ph.D. *Behind Enemy Lines: Civil War Spies, Raiders and Guerrillas.* Dallas: Taylor Publishing, 2001.
*Karsten, Peter, ed. *Encyclopedia of War and American Society,* Volume 1. Thousand Oaks, CA, London, Delhi: Sage Publications, & New York: MTM, 2005.
*Kelly, C. Brian, with Smyer, Ingrid. *Best Little Stories from the Civil War.* Naperville, IL: Sourcebooks, 2010.
Labaw, George Warne. *A Genealogy of the Warne Family.* New York: Frank Allaben Genealogical Company, 1911.
Lamon, Ward Hill. *The Life of Abraham Lincoln from His Birth to His Inauguration as President.* Boston: James R. Osgood & Co., 1872. Ghost written by Chauncey F. Black.
*Lavine, Sigmund A. *Allan Pinkerton: America's First Private Eye.* New York: Dodd, Mead, 1963.
Mansch, Larry D. *Abraham Lincoln, President-Elect: The Four Critical Months from Election to Inauguration.* Jefferson, N.C.: McFarland, 2005.
*Markle, Donald E. *Spies and Spymasters of the Civil War.* New York: Hippocrene, 1994.
*McKay, James. *Allan Pinkerton: The Eye Who Never Slept.* Edinburgh: Mainstream, 1996. Published in U.S.A. in 1997 by John Wiley & Sons, of New York, as *Allan Pinkerton: The First Private Eye.*

*McPherson, James M. *The Negro's Civil War: How American Blacks Felt and Acted During the War for the Union.* New York: Ballantine, 1991.
*Morn, Frank. *The Eye that Never Sleeps: A History of the Pinkerton National Detective Agency.* Bloomington: Indiana University Press, 1982.
*Mortimer, Gavin. *Double Death: The True Story of Pryce Lewis, the Civil War's Most Daring Spy.* New York: Walker & Co., 2010.
Moss, Marissa. *Kate Warne, Pinkerton Detective.* Berkeley, CA: Creston Books, 2017. Juvenile.
*Nash, Jay Robert. *Spies: A Narrative Encyclopedia of Dirty Deeds and Double Dealing from Biblical Times to Today.* New York: M. Evans & Co., 1997.
*O'Hara, Paul S. *Inventing the Pinkertons: or, Spies, Sleuths, Mercenaries, and Thugs. Being a Story of the Nation's Most Famous (and Infamous) Detective Agency.* Baltimore: Johns Hopkins University Press, 2016.
Orrmont, Arthur. *Master Detective Allan Pinkerton.* New York City: Julian Messner Books, 1965.
Peck, Ebenezer. *Reports of Cases Determined in the Supreme Court of Illinois at April Term, 1859, November Term, 1859, and January Term, 1860.* Vol. XXIII. Chicago: D.B. Cooke & Co., 1860. *Bennett and Stow vs Waller.*
Pfanz, Donald C. *Richard S. Ewell: A Soldier's Life.* Chapel Hill, NC: University of North Carolina Press, 1998.
Pickenpaugh, Roger. *Captives in Blue: The Civil War Prisons of the Confederacy.* Tuscaloosa: University of Alabama Press, 2013.
*Pinkerton, Allan. *The Expressman and the Detective.* Chicago: W.B. Keen, Cooke & Co., 1874.
*_____. *The Spy of the Rebellion.* Hartford, CT.: M.A. Winter & Hatch, 1883.
Portrait and Biographical Album of Rock County, Wisconsin. Chicago: Acme Press, 1889.
*Potter, John Mason. *Thirteen Desperate Days.* New York: Ivan Obolensky, Inc., & Toronto: George J. McLeod, 1964.
*Quarles, Benjamin. *The Negro in the Civil War.* Boston: Little, Brown, 1953.
Rammelkamp, Julian S. *Pulitzer's Post Dispatch 1878–1883.* New Jersey: Princeton University Press, 1967.
Ramsland, Katherine. *Beating the Devil's Game: A History of Forensic Science and Criminal Investigation.* New York: Berkley Publishing Group, 2007.
*Rappaport, Doreen. *No More! Stories and Songs of Slave Resistance.* Cambridge, MA: Candlewick Press, 2002.
Recko, Corey. *A Spy for the Union: The Life and Execution of Timothy Webster.* Jefferson, NC: McFarland, 2013.
Ross, Ishbel. *Rebel Rose: The Life of Rose O'Neal Greenhow.* New York: Harper & Brothers, 1954.
*Roth, Mitchel P. *Historical Dictionary of Law Enforcement.* Westport, CT: Greenwood, 2001.
*Rowan, Richard Wilmer. *The Pinkertons: A Detective Dynasty.* London: Hurst & Blackett, 1931.
*_____. *The Story of the Secret Service.* New York: Literary Guild of America, 1937.
*Ryan, David D., ed. *A Yankee Spy in Richmond: The Civil War Diary of "Crazy Bet" Van Lew.* Mechanicsburg, PA: Stackpole, 2001.
Rzepka, Charles J. *Detective Fiction.* Cambridge, England: Polity Press, 2005.
*Sandburg, Carl. *Abraham Lincoln.* New York: C. Scribner's Sons, 1940. Volume 3, p. 502.
Sanders, James U., ed. *Society of Montana Pioneers,* Vol. 1, 1899.
Sears, Stephen W. *George B. McClellan: The Young Napoleon.* New York: Ticknor & Fields, 1988.
Singer, Jane. *The War Criminal's Son: The Civil War Saga of William A. Winder.* Lincoln, NE: Potomac Books, 2019.
*Snodgrass, Mary Ellen. *The Civil War Era and Reconstruction: An Encyclopedia of Social, Political, Cultural and Economic History.* New York: Routledge, 2015.
Speer, Lonnie. *Portals to Hell: Military Prisons of the Civil War.* Mechanicsburg, Pa.: Stackpole Books, 1997.
*Stashower, Daniel. *The Hour of Peril: The Secret Plot to Murder Lincoln Before the Civil War.* New York: Minotaur, 2014.
Stewart, John. *Jefferson Davis's Flight from Richmond.* Jefferson, NC: McFarland, 2015.

The Stranger's Guide and Official Directory for the City of Richmond. Richmond, Va.: Geo. P. Evans, 1863.
*Sulick, Michael J. *Spying in America: Espionage from the Revolutionary War to the Dawn of the Cold War.* Washington, D.C.: Georgetown University Press, 2012.
*Sullivan, Larry E. *The Encyclopedia of Law Enforcement.* Thousand Oaks, CA: Sage, 2004.
*Sutherland, Jonathan D. *African Americans at War: An Encyclopedia,* Volume 1. Santa Barbara, CA: ABC-Clio, 2004.
Timmer, Doug A., & Eitzen, D. Stanley. *Crime in the Streets and Crime in the Suites: Perspectives on Crime and Criminal Justice.* Boston: Allyn and Bacon, 1989.
*Varon, Elizabeth. *Southern Lady, Yankee Spy.* New York: Oxford University Press, 2003.
*Wagner, Heather Lehr. *Spies in the Civil War.* New York: Chelsea House, 2009.
*Walbridge, Mike. *African American Heroes of the Civil War.* Portland, ME: J. Weston Walch, 2000.
*Ward, Harry M. *Public Executions in Richmond, Virginia.* Jefferson, NC: McFarland, 2012.
*Wheelan, Joseph. *Libby Prison Breakout.* Philadelphia: PublicAffairs, 2010.
*Williams, David Ricardo. *Call in Pinkerton's: American Detectives at Work for Canada.* Toronto: Dundurn Press, 1998.
Wilson, Douglas L., & Davis, Rodney O. *Herndon's Informants: Letters, Interviews, and Statements about Abraham Lincoln.* Urbana and Chicago: University of Illinois Press, 1998.
*Winkler, H. Donald. *Stealing Secrets: How a Few Daring Women Deceived Generals, Impacted Battles, and Altered the Course of the Civil War.* Naperville, IL: Cumberland House, 2010.
*Wright, John D. *The Routledge Encyclopedia of Civil War Era Biographies.* New York: Routledge, 2013.
*Writers Program. *The Negro in Virginia.* New York: Hastings House, 1940.
Yeatman, Ted P. *Frank and Jesse James: The Story Behind the Legend.* Nashville: Cumberland House Books, 2000.

Magazine Articles

Beymer, William Gilmore. "Timothy Webster: Spy." *Harper's* Magazine, Oct. 1910, Vol. 121, pp. 761–772. This article would, two years later, go to form the final chapter of Beymer's 1912 book, *On Hazardous Service.*
Bourke, Charles Francis. "The Story of the Pinkertons." *Leslie's Monthly Magazine,* vol. 59, No. 6, April 1905, pp. 616–625.
Bryan, George S. "Famous Spies in American History." *The Mentor,* Vol. 9, No. 8, Sept. 1, 1921, pp. 11–12.
*Bzovy, Margaret. "Kate Warne: First Female Pinkerton Detective." *American Western Magazine,* January, 2004.
*Chance, Sue. "Allan Pinkerton: A Psychobiographical Sketch." *American Imago,* Vol. 42, No. 2, pp. 131–142.
Davis, Curtis Carroll. "The 'Old Capitol' and Its Keeper: How William P. Wood Ran a Civil War Prison." *Records of the Columbia Historical Society, Washington, D.C.* Historical Society of Washington, 1989, Vol. 52, pp. 206–234.
Dawson, Brenda. "Kate Warne—First Woman Detective?" *Chambers' Journal,* March 1956, pp. 4–5.
*Foster, G. Allen. "John Scobell—Union Spy in Civil War." *Ebony,* Dec. 1963, pp. 135–145. Rerun Oct. 1978, pp. 73–81.
Inglis, William. "A Republic's Gratitude: What Pryce Lewis Did for the United States Government and How the United States Government Rewarded Him." New York: *Harper's Weekly,* Dec. 30, 1911, Vol. LV, No. 2871, p. 24.
Levy, Lynn. "Kate Warne, PI: The First Female Private Investigator had a Baltimore Connection." *PI Magazine,* Feb. 2005, pp. 28–29.
Moffett, Cleveland. "How Allan Pinkerton Thwarted the First Plot to Assassinate Lincoln." *McClure's* Magazine, 1894, p. 520–529.

Pinkerton, Allan. "Allan Pinkerton's Unpublished Story of the First Attempt on the Life of Abraham Lincoln." *American Magazine*, vol. 75, Dec. 1912–June 1913, pp. 17–22. This has an abridged version of the Aug. 23 1866, letter from Pinkerton to Herndon, telling of the Baltimore Plot.
Rhoades, Priscilla. "The Women of Castle Thunder." *Kudzu Monthly*, 2, No. 8, August, 2002. *Kudzu Monthly* was an e-zine, an electronic magazine, and does not seem to be any longer represented on the Internet. Consequently I have been unable to find this article, but I have seen some of its contents in works by other people.
*Rowan, Richard Wilmer. "Lincoln's Sister." *American Weekly*, Feb. 11, 1951, p. 4 et seq.
Sabine, David B. "Pinkerton's Operative—Timothy Webster." *Civil War Times Illustrated*, vol. 12, No. 5, August 1973, pp. 32–38.
Swett, Leonard. "The Conspiracies of the Rebellion." *The North American Review*, vol. 144, No. 2, Feb. 1887, pp. 179–189.

Newspapers

Albany Evening Journal 1861 (NY)
Alexandria Gazette 1862 (VA)
Anaconda Standard 1893 (MT)
Bad Lands Cow Boy 1884–85 (ND)
Baltimore American 1861 (MD)
Baltimore Sun 1861–63 (MD)
Bangor Daily Whig and Courier 1862 (ME)
Bismarck Tribune 1879–83 (ND)
Boston Daily Advertiser 1862 (MA)
Boston Journal 1861 (MA)
Bozeman Weekly Chronicle 1883–85 (MT)
Brooklyn Daily Eagle 1884 (NY)
Burlington Hawkeye 1862 (IA)
Chicago Daily Inter-Ocean 1878–96 (IL)
Chicago Daily Times 1855 (IL)
Chicago Republican 1867–68 (IL)
Chicago Tribune 1854–2015 (IL)
Cincinnati Daily Press 1860–61 (OH)
Cincinnati Enquirer 1875 (OH)
Cleveland Morning Herald 1868 (OH)
Daily Iowa State Democrat 1859 (IA)
Daily Missouri Republican 1867–68 (MO)
Daily National Intelligencer 1862 (DC)
Daily South Carolinian 1862 (SC)
Daily Yellowstone Journal 1890 (MT)
Davenport Daily Democrat and News 1859–62 (IA)
Davenport Daily Gazette 1859–62 (IA)
Davenport Democrat and Leader 1932 (IA)
Dixon Evening Telegraph 1890–1904 (IL)
Dixon Telegraph 1860–81 (IL)
Evening Star 1861–62 (DC)
Fergus County Argus 1892 (MT)
Fergus County Democrat 1914 (MT)
Grand Forks Herald 1917 (ND)
Green Bay Press-Gazette (WI)
Janesville Daily Gazette 1859 (WI)
Janesville Weekly Gazette 1860 (WI)
Louisville Daily Courier 1860 (KY)

Louisville Daily Democrat 1868 (KY)
Lowell Daily Citizen and News 1862 (MA)
Memphis Appeal 1862 (TN)
Milwaukee Daily Sentinel 1855–73 (WI)
Missouri Daily Democrat 1867–70 (MO)
Missouri Republican 1873 (MO)
Montana Post 1865 (MT)
Muscatine Weekly Journal 1861 (IA)
National Republican 1862 (DC)
National Tribune 1901 (DC)
Nebraska Advertiser 1860 (NE)
New Haven Daily Morning Journal and Courier 1898 (CT)
New York Herald 1848–73 (NY)
New York Times 1860–1911 (NY)
North American and United States Gazette 1862 (PA)
Ottawa Free Trader 1871 (IL)
Pittsburgh Gazette 1861 (PA)
Richmond Dispatch 1853–79 (VA)
Richmond Enquirer 1855–61 (VA)
Richmond Examiner 1862–64 (VA)
Richmond Sentinel 1864 (VA)
Richmond Times-Dispatch 1903–07 (VA)
Richmond Whig 1862–64 (VA)
Rock Island Argus 1860–62 (IL)
Sacramento Daily Union 1862 (CA)
St. Louis Globe-Democrat 1877–87 (MO)
St. Louis Post-Dispatch 1884–1908 (MO)
St. Louis Republic 1903 (MO)
St. Louis Republican 1875 (MO)
St. Louis Star and Times 1913 (MO)
St. Paul Daily Globe 1889 (MN)
San Francisco Daily Evening Bulletin 1873 (CA)
Semi-Weekly Raleigh Register 1862 (NC)
Vermont Phoenix 1861 (VT)
Washington Times 1909–13 (DC)
Western Democrat 1862 (Charlotte, NC)

Index

Abel, Frank 120
Abraham Lincoln: The True Story of a Great Life 174
Adelaide (mail boat) 125
Alexander, Captain 108, 114, 118–120, 122, 127
Allen, A.R. 46
Allen, E.J. 38, 42, 46, 107, 129, 137; *see also* Pinkerton, Allan
Allen, Kate 137; *see also* Warn, Mahala Ann "Kate"
American Girl (horse) 152
The American Magazine 35
Anderson, John Reid 127
Anderson, Sally 127
Archer, Col. William 72
The Arrest of Tim and Hattie 88
assassination plots 32–33, 36–39, 41, 173
Ayres, Bert 3

Babcock, John 139, 178
Bad Lands Cow Boy 133
Bailey, Mary Ellen 31, 39, 42–44, 86
Baker, Mrs. E.H. 141
Baker, G.A. 176
Baker, Lafayette 120
Baltimore American 92
Bangs, George H. 34, 42, 115, 178
Barley, Mrs. *see* Warn, Mahala Ann "Kate"
Barnes, T.D. 30
Barrett, Fred 13
Beale, Joseph Boggs 8
Beale, Major 60
Bellefontaine Cemetery 157, 166–167
Benjamin, Secretary Judah 66, 77, 94–95, 99
Bernstein, Arnie 136
Beymer, William Gilmore 7–8, 55, 58, 66, 70–71, 80, 84
Bissell, Mr. 30
Black, Chauncey 174
Bossieux, Lt. Louis Juste 126
Boyd, Belle 127

Brackett, Kate 145–150; *see also* Lawton, Carrie; Prescott, Kate
Brackett, Oscar Fitzerlan 146, 149, 171–172
Brelsford, Mrs. Kate 146–147; *see also* Lawton, Carrie
Bridgman, Sam 178
Brooklyn Daily Eagle 136, 144–145
Brooks, Roxana 14
Brown, Dr. G.W.I. 3
Brownville, Nebraska 23
Bryant, Mr. 138
Burgess, Joseph 29, 43–44
Buttner, George 160
Buttner, Louise G. "Frankie" 161; *see also* Rogers, Frances

Campbell, William 48–49, 57, 78, 88, 100
Caphart, John 112–113
Carfrae, Joan (Mrs. Allan Pinkerton) 17
Casca, Bill 159
Cashmyer, Philip 82, 87–89, 122
Castle Godwin 10, 73, 82–83, 88–90, 98, 101, 113, 118–120, 123–124, 126–127
Castle Thunder 113, 120–122, 127–128, 156
Central Hotel 3
Chadwick, Mr. 30
Charters, James B. 164
Cheatham, Addie 166
Cherry, Mrs. (alias Raisins) *see* Warn, Mahala Ann "Kate"
Chicago Daily Inter-Ocean 56, 66, 137
Chicago Daily Times 18
Chicago Evening News 66, 163
The Chicago History Museum 139
Chicago Times 118
Chicago Tribune 15, 29–30, 38
Childs, Mrs. Diana 158
Childs, James R. 158
Clackner, George W. 73, 82–83
Clayton, Minnie 16
Clemens, Samuel *see* Twain, Mark
code names 41–42

Index

Coffey, Billy 3
Comstock, Thomas Griswold 149
"The Conspiracies of the Rebellion" 36
"Conspiracy Case" 15
Corby, the Rev. William 135
Cordell, Jenny 16
Cridland, F.J. 83
Cronin, David 67, 70
Crump, William Wood 80, 98
Curtis, George 141
Custer, Lt. Col. George A. 155
Cuthbert, Norma 8, 35, 175–176

Daily National Intelligencer 117
Davenport Daily Gazette 117
Davenport Democrat 30–31, 40, 44, 116–117
Davies, Harry W. 34
Davis, Jefferson 10, 71, 74–75, 95, 100, 104, 118–119, 122–123, 163
Davis, Varina (Mrs. Jefferson Davis) 103–104
DeBar, Vic 165
Dennis, Paul H. 34, 178
detective agency formation 18
Dingman, Mrs. 16
Dix, General 50
Dixon, W.T. 152
Dixon, Illinois 1
Donnelly, Arthur J. 167
A Double Life and the Detectives 146
Duffy, Caroline 16
Dun, Edwin 154

Earl, John 50
"The Early Pinkertons" 176, 179
Eaves, George 178
Eckert, Thomas 8, 136
Eddy, Nellie 165
Ellwood, Miss Viola 148–149
escape 50
Evening Telegraph 1
The Expressman and the Detective 18, 20

"Famous Detectives" 65, 177
Felton, Samuel Morse 33–34
Fisher, Mary 15
Fitchett, Margaret Pinkerton 177
Flora Belle (horse) 152–153
Ford, Michael 15
Fowler, Mrs. Belle 172
Fox, Freetricks 160
Fox, the Rev. Mr. 149
Frazer, Dr. Samuel H. 151
Freeburger, George A. 74, 102, 112, 118

Gerdes, Louise 166
Gilman, Charlotte 120
Gilmer, John Harmer 80, 100
Glenwood, Emma (alias Canada Maria) 16
Godwin, Capt. Archibald C. 75
Goldsmith Maid (horse) 152

Gough, Washington 57
Graceland Cemetery 135–137, 144–145, 150, 178–179
Graham, Stutterin' Dave 140
Greanor, Capt. John H. 128
Great Republic (steamer) 154
Greenhow, Rose 46–47
Gurney, Seth 27–29

Halyburton, Judge J.D. 100
Hamlin, Hannibal 39, 41
Hannifin, Denny 155
Hansen, Lucy 13, 15
Hardwicke, Maj. Samuel 156
Harnett, Thomas Kane 64
Harper's Magazine 7, 66
Harrigan, Det. Sgt. Larry 149
Harris, Merriman Colbert 154
Harris, S.H. 174–175
Hart, John (William?) 50; *see also* Webster, Tim
Hart, Mrs. 50; *see also* Lawton, Hattie
Hayden, Frances 138
Heaton, Dwight 157
Hellfire Hotchkiss 165
Herndon, James C. 51
Herndon, William 35, 173–174, 176
Herndon's Lincoln: The True Story of a Great Life 174
Hicks hat caps 48
Higbee, Morrell 152
Hill, General 90
Hine, John K. 157–158, 164
Hoge, the Rev. Moses D. 111–112
The Hoofs and Guns of the Storm: Chicago's Civil War Connections 136
Horan, Jim 8, 47
Houghton, David S. 154
Howard, Capt. H.Z. 154
Howard, James 56–57
Howard, Kate 15, 16
Hoyt, Emma 15
Hubbell, George E. 43
Hubbell, George W.L. 138
Hubbell, Julia Ann 137–138
Hubbell, Melvin 138
Huntington, Henry 175
Hurlburt, Allen 132–133
Hutchinson, John H. 34–35; *see also* Pinkerton, Allan
Hutton, Mrs. 54

imprisonment 9–10

James, Frank 156
James, Jesse 156
Jameson, Mrs. Frances D. 125–127
Jamieson, Mrs. Francis F. 120
Jecko, John 149
Jones, Hiram B. 34

Index

Jones, John Beauchamp 49, 53, 125
Judd, N.B. 36–38

Kale, Jack 155
Keating, Justice William 148
Kennedy, John A. 38
Kentucky Joe (alias Josephine Davis) 16
Kinsella, John 34
Knipe, Harry 65
Kountz, Al 158–159

Ladies' Gunboat Association 79
Ladies' National Defense Association 79
Laing, Mr. 158
Lamon, Ward Hill 37–38, 174–176
Lawton, Carrie 6–7, 140–144, 146–147
Lawton, Hattie (Lucy Hansen; Harriet Lewis; Hattie Lewis; Sarah Simmons; Mrs. Hattie L. Smith; Lucy Ann Warn; Mrs. Timothy Webster) 5–11, 33–35, 37, 39, 42, 45–47, 50, 55–61, 64–65, 71–73, 76–79, 81, 86–91, 95, 101, 104–109, 111, 113–115, 117–120, 123–124, 126–131, 140, 142–144, 146, 152–153, 156, 173–176
Lawton, Hugh 142–143
Lee, Gen. Robert E. 104
Lemp, William J., Jr. 166
Lewis, Alex 153
Lewis, Harriet 13
Lewis, Hattie 7–10, 13, 15–16, 45, 47, 55–56, 65, 70; *see also* Lawton, Hattie
Lewis, Pryce 7–8, 46–47, 64–74, 76–78, 80–86, 88–91, 93–100, 102, 112, 120, 122, 125, 128–129
The Life of Abraham Lincoln from His Birth to His Inauguration as President 174
Lincoln, Abraham 32–33, 36–39, 41–42, 44–45, 82, 91, 121, 129, 134, 141, 173, 176
Lincoln, Mary Todd 38
Lincoln, R.T. 38
Lincoln and the Baltimore Plot 8
"Lincoln Record" 173–176
Lost Cabin Mine 132–133
Luckett, James H. 34
Lucy (horse) 152
Ludlow, Col. William H. 121

Manning, Michael 149
Martin, George 148
Maynard, Capt. John C. 75
McClellan, Gen. George 42, 44–46, 49, 53, 56–57, 62–64, 105, 142
McClure's 34
McCoy, Jesse 155
McCubbin, Capt. Samuel, Jr. 71, 75, 77, 82, 109–110
McGee brothers 50
McGill, John 83, 85
McKay, James 8
McKelvey, D.G. 178

McMullen, Augustine L. 85
McQueen, George 11, 156; *see also* Pinkerton, Allan
Melodeon Hall 15
Memphis Appeal 92, 97, 101
Merrell, Lillie (alias Prather) 148
Metamora (steamboat) 125
Miles, Ellen 15
Miller, Benjamin Franklin 2–3, 164
Miller, Edna 2
Miller, Joseph 50
Miller, Libby 164
Miltimore, George 23
Moffett, Cleveland 34
Moore, Emma 22
Moore, George 128
Moore, Dr. S.P. 22
Morrison, Lulu 165–166
Morton, Chase 73, 82
Morton, Elizabeth F. 72–73, 82–83
Morton, Howard 82
Morton, Jackson "Billy" 72–73
Mulford, Capt. John Elmer 125

Nance, Eaton 98–99, 107
Napoleon, Louis 100–101
National Republican 63
Nebraska Advertiser 23
New York (steamboat) 125, 127–128
New York Herald 92
New York Times 7, 92
New York Tribune 92
Newman, Tommy 158
Norris, William 34
Notre Dame 9, 129–131, 135, 147, 171–173

Oakwood Cemetery 3
Olson (Olsen), Botella "Betsy" 144
On Hazardous Service 7

Paine, Dr. H.E. 3
Pallen, Montrose Anderson 153
Pallen, Moses Montrose 153
Palmyra, Illinois 1
Pavey, Jesse H. 165
Pavey, Napoleon 165
Pavey, Sue 165–167
Perry, Jenny 16
Pierce, Mr. 70–71, 78, 100
Pike's Peak 23, 133
Pilot Temple (horse) 152
Pinkerton, Allan 5–11, 16–21, 24–25, 28, 31–42, 44–47, 49–51, 53–58, 60–71, 76–78, 80–81, 84, 86–88, 90, 93, 95–97, 100, 104–107, 109–111, 114–115, 118, 126, 128–130, 135–141, 142–147, 150, 154, 156, 163, 173–179
Pinkerton, Billy 7–8, 55–56, 65–67, 70, 77–78, 85, 130, 145, 163, 177–179
Pinkerton, Geoff 176–177
Pinkerton, Mary 177

Pinkerton, Robert 130, 145, 177–178
Pinkerton, Robert II 175
Pinkerton, Sarah Eaves 177, 179
The Pinkerton Story 47
Pomeroy, Laura 149
Pope, Capt. John 38
Porter, John C. 75
Potter, Norman 134
Prendergast, Justice 15
Prescott, Kate 145; *see also* Lawton, Carrie

Racine Bank 22
Raleigh Register 99
Randolph, Sec. of War 123
A Rebel War Clerk's Diary 49, 53
Recko, Corey 8
Reed, J.R. 29–32, 39–40, 43–44, 116–118; *see also* Webster, Timothy
Richardson, John (aka John Dailey; aka John Richards) 101
Richmond Daily Whig 91, 125
Richmond Dispatch 48, 79, 91, 93–94, 107, 109, 115, 125–127
Richmond Enquirer 52–53, 70, 76, 91–95, 98–100, 126
Richmond Examiner 66, 87, 90–91, 93–95, 101, 105–107, 109–111, 126
Richmond Times-Dispatch 94
The Road to Wigan Pier 177
Robertson, D. 156
Rock Island Argus 30, 115–116
Rock Island Arsenal: In Peace and in War 27
Rock Island Bridge 26–30
Rock Island Line 26
Rock River Bridge 30
Rogers, Frances (alias Frankie or Frank) 160
Rogers, Maggie (alias Roberta Margaret; also Bertie, Kate, or Kittie) 160
Rogers, Magy *see* Rogers, Maggie
Rowan, Richard Wilmer 8, 142–143
Rucker, Edward A. 18
Rucker, Dr. William 120
Ryan, David D. 113

St. Lawrence University 8, 67–68
St. Louis Chamber of Commerce 26
St. Louis Post-Dispatch 165, 167
St. Louis Star and Times 167
Sandburg, Carl 7
Sanford, E.S. 37
Schultz, William Frederick August 167
Scobell, John 140, 142–143
Scott, Annie 90, 113, 118
Scott, William H. 34, 44, 48, 64, 83, 129
Scully, John 46–47, 64–67, 69–74, 76–78, 80–81, 83–86, 88, 90–91, 93–100, 102, 112, 122, 125, 128–129
Seaford, John 34
Seward, Sec. of State William 44–45, 92, 101
Seybolt, H.B. 178

Seymour, Henry B. 129
Shaffer, Fred 118
Shelton, Wallace 1
Shoen, Harriet 67, 70
Simmons, Sarah 13, 16
Sklar (Sklor), Mary 165
Sklar (Sklor), Sarah 165
Sloan, Sam 50
Smith, Mrs. George 1, 3–4, 10
Smith, George D. (book dealer) 175
Smith, Hattie L. (Mrs. T.J. Smith) 9–11, 130, 154, 156–158, 163–164, 166–167, 171, 173; *see also* Lawton, Hattie
Smith, T.J. 2–3, 151–153, 155, 157–159, 162–164
Smith, William C. 152, 155
Smithers, John A. 151, 157
Snyder, Peter 15
Spencer, W.A. 154
Springer, John G. 173–176
A Spy for the Union 8
The Spy of the Rebellion 6–8, 19, 35, 50, 56, 64–66, 68–70, 77, 81, 93, 105, 109, 111, 113–114, 140, 142–143, 146–147, 175
Stafford, Gentle Annie 16
Stanton, Edwin M. 122–123, 129
Stanton, Mr. 56
Staples, Thomas A. 81
suicide 1–3, 7–8, 44
Swett, Leonard 36
Swiggett, Howard 47

Tabb, Mrs. 120, 124
Talman, Maj. John 55
Tanner, Lt. Alfred 139
Taylor, Ann 79
Taylor, Harriet Beall McKall 79, 87–88, 96, 100
Taylor, Martha 79
Taylor, Mary (alias Rocky Rhodes) 16
Taylor, Walter Hanson Stone 79
Teillard, Dorothy Lamon 175
Thompson, Jared 138
Thompson, Justice J.D.N. 24
Tillinghast, B.F. 27
Timothy Webster: Spy of the Rebellion 30
Tom Sawyer 165
Towler, Belle 146–147, 149, 151, 157; *see also* Warn, Belle
Tracy, John F. 27–28, 31
Twain, Mark 165
Tyler, Nat 98, 100

Underwood, Maria 125–127

Van Lew, Elizabeth 113–114, 124
Villagers of 1840-3 165

Wadsworth, Gen. James S. 121
Wakefield, Alanson Bankson 159

Warn, Alice Andrews 24, 134, 155
Warn, Allen B. 22–24, 133–134
Warn, Belle 9, 147–148
Warn, Edward Thompson "E.T." 24, 131
Warn, Ella 2, 157–158, 164
Warn, Emma 133–134
Warn, Franklin B. 22, 134
Warn, George 9–10, 130–131, 135, 147, 153, 156–157, 164, 171–173
Warn, I.P. 171–172
Warn, Johnny 24, 131–134, 155, 160–162
Warn, Kittie *see* Rogers, Maggie
Warn, Libby 2, 157–158, 161
Warn, Lucy Ann 10, 13, 167
Warn, Mahala Ann "Angie" (aka Kate) 9–10, 13, 16–21, 34, 36–38, 41–42, 129–131, 135–140, 144–146, 163, 174, 176; description 18–19
Warn, Samanda Catherine "Kitty" 9, 21, 146–148, 161–162
Warn Castle 155, 161
Warner, A.C. 164
Warner, Francis 34, 129
Washington, Sam 178
Waters, Minnie (alias Ann Brown) 16
Watts, William B. 178

Waugh, the Rev. Dr. James Walter 154
"We Never Sleep" logo 18
Webster, Charlotte 10, 39, 86
Webster, Mary Ellen 31
Webster, Timothy 4–9, 24–25, 29–32, 34–35, 38–42, 44–49, 51–66, 70–73, 76–80, 83–84, 86–102, 104–120, 122, 126, 128, 140, 142, 144, 173, 176
"Webster the Spy" 94
Weik, Jesse 35, 174, 176
Western Democrat 94
Williams, Charles D.C. 34
Williams, Eliza (alias Eliza Roe) 16
Williams, John G. 98–99, 107
Winder, Brig. Gen. John Henry "Hog" 5, 51–53, 71, 73–75, 78–80, 82–83, 85–89, 95–97, 102, 105–106, 108, 111–112, 114–115, 118–120, 122–123
Winder, Capt. William A. 51, 53–54
Wood, Big Lib 14
Wood, William P. 120–122, 124
Woodbridge, George 111
Wright, James W. 135

A Yankee Spy in Richmond 113

www.ingramcontent.com/pod-product-compliance
Ingram Content Group UK Ltd.
Pitfield, Milton Keynes, MK11 3LW, UK
UKHW041944140426
5217IPUK00014B/643